Kennyo Ismail

ORDER OUT OF CHAOS

Decoding the Scottish Rite

ORDER OUT OF CHAOS: Decoding the Scottish Rite
Kennyo Ismail

Picture Credits

Book cover and Genealogy in appendix:
Felipe Bandeira de Medeiros

Heraldic emblems in book core:
João Guilherme da Cruz Ribeiro

Joubert understood that the word excites, the example teaches. Schweitzer agreed, arguing that example is the only way to influence others. Burke thought the same, as did Seneca, Locke and so many others. For Goethe, the example makes the difficult easy. And the gospel of John brings the lesson of Jesus, who taught by example, by washing the feet of his disciples.

My experience as a professor and as a freemason also tells me the same thing. For this reason, I dedicate this book to my two sons, for whom I must serve as an example, Mateus and Eduardo.

TABLE OF CONTENTS

1. INTRODUCTION

There is no way to reach the Scottish Rite without crossing the bridge of Freemasonry. For this reason, it would be prudent to deal with the Scottish Rite without first guaranteeing a certain level of information on the definition and purpose of Freemasonry, even with the risk of monotony to those well-educated readers. If you are one of them, I hope you understand.

The most common definition in use in the Masonic world states that Freemasonry is "*a beautiful system of morality veiled in allegory and illustrated by symbols*".[1] It is a simplified definition of the concept presented by William Preston, in his classic work, Illustrations of Masonry, which considers Freemasonry "*one regular system of morality, conceived in a strain of interesting allegory, which unfolds its beauties to the candid and industrious inquirer*".[2]

The respected Coil's Masonic Encyclopedia presents this concept of the system of morality in a very didactic way:

> Freemasonry, in its broadest and most comprehensive sense, is a system of morality and social ethics, a primitive religion, and a philosophy of life, all of simple and fundamental character, incorporating a broad humanitarianism and, though treating life as a practical experience, subordinates the material to the spiritual/ it is a religion without a creed, being no sect but finding truth in all, it is moral but not pharisaic, it demands sanity rather than sanctity, it is tolerant but not supine/ it seeks truth but does not define truth, it urges its votaries to think but does not tell them what to think/ it despises ignorance but does not proscribe the ignorant, it fosters education but proposes no curriculum/ it espouses political liberty and the dignity of man but has no platform or propaganda/ it believes in the nobility and usefulness of life/ it is modest and not militant (...).[3]

In these definitions, Freemasonry is seen as a system of teaching morality; and when consulting other renowned authors on the same subject, very similar phrases are replicated. Christopher Hodapp, in his famous work, Freemasonry for Dummies, states that Freemasonry "*is a philosophy and a system of morality and ethics - and a pretty basic one at that*" and even that it "*teaches lessons of social and moral virtues based on the symbolism of the tools and language of the ancient building trade, using the building of a structure as a symbol for the building of character in men*".[4]

As Jay Kinney, in his celebrated work, The Masonic Myth: Unlocking the Truth About the Symbols, the Secret Rites, and the History of Freemasonry, the United Grand Lodge of England declares that Freemasonry is:

> a society of men concerned with moral and spiritual values. Its members are taught its precepts by a series of ritual dramas, which follow ancient forms, and use stonemasons' customs and tools as allegorical guides (UGLE *apud* Kinney, 2009, p.23).[5]

There is also the concept available in the ritual of the Ancient and Accepted Scottish Rite of 1928, also known as the "Behring Ritual", used by most Brazilian blue lodges:

> It is, therefore, a system and a school, not only of Moral as of social and spiritual Philosophy, revealed by allegories and taught by symbols, guiding its followers to the practice and the perfection of the highest duties of the man-citizen, patriot, and soldier.[6]

Thus, according to these concepts and congruent definitions presented, it can be said that Freemasonry is essentially:

1. a system of morality ...
2. that is taught and learned ...
3. through its own teaching method (allegories and symbols).

From this understanding, Freemasonry can be affirmed as a science, in the broadest sense of the word: a systematized body of knowledge. And this understanding of Freemasonry is not something new, having already been included in classic works of the Order, written more than two centuries ago, as in Ahiman Rezon, by Laurence Dermott, when he records that irregular lodges are "*incapable of giving proper instructions to their pupils*".[7] The very term by which Freemasonry is historically called, Royal Art, denotes this nature of science, since the term "Art", originated from the Latin, "Ars", meant something similar to what today is called "Applied Science ".[i]

As a science or system of morality, Masonic rites, among them the Scottish Rite, act as courses, with their curriculum to teach this systematic Masonic knowledge. These courses have different modules or grades (degrees) and textbooks (rituals). One course is not the same as another, although in some cases it has one or the other subject in common or similar. The same occurs in some Masonic rites, which have one degree or another with the same origin.

Further, exploring the allegory of a higher education course, there are, in general, two types of people who enter. For example, a medical course: those who want to save lives and those who want to earn money. Something similar occurs in the Masonic Order. This work is aimed at those who are in Freemasonry to develop morally and chose the Scottish Rite, not for its plaques, diplomas and titles, but for its content, values and principles.

Justifying the importance of studying the degrees of the Scottish Rite, in addition to simple initiation into its degrees and reading their rituals is somewhat simple. This beautiful and, at the same time, complex course (Scottish Rite) is granted by different educational institutions (Supreme Councils) all over the world. The course is the same, with only minor variations in some subjects (degrees) or in the order in which they are taken. Besides, although the pedagogical method (allegories and symbols) is the same, there are different approaches, and these variations have an impact on students' learning.

Rather, it is necessary to conceptualize these two pillars in support of the Masonic pedagogical method. Allegories are the legends of each degree and symbols are signs, images, or objects that represent activities, behaviors, or feelings. Allegories are at the heart of learning moral lessons, while symbols are the anchor of their memory. They are closely linked and together form the whole of Masonic education. They are like the crumb and peel of a fruit or the filling and icing on a cake. Through the allegories the Freemason learns the Masonic lessons, and through the symbols he keeps and remembers them. A symbol present in a degree has a meaning and relevance for the Freemason initiated in it who will not have an uninitiated one, since it will be the trigger of the memory of the allegory of that degree and, consequently, of the moral lessons veiled in it. Thus, in the absence of allegories, the Freemason does not learn moral lessons; and in the absence of symbols, he does not remember them. In practice, the moral result is the same: none.

In this context, there are jurisdictions, such as those in the United States, that prioritize allegory in their rituals; and others, such as the

---

[i] Like the Seven Liberal "Arts", which were Applied Sciences.

descendants of the Supreme Council of France, who prioritize the symbol. It is not uncommon to find an American freemason who marveled at the high-level rehearsals of the Scottish Rite, but as time goes by, he does not remember the moral lessons of many of them. On the other hand, it is not uncommon to witness Brazilian freemasons who leave a ceremony bombarded by symbols, but without understanding its narrative and the moral lessons veiled in it. In the first case, there is a lack of fixation on the legends and its lessons through symbols. In the second, there is a lack of clarity in the transmission of legends, as veiled in some cases as the lessons they should teach, converting the symbols of these degrees into empty formulas. This "calibration" between allegories and symbols is achieved, in the case of the United States, through meetings of complementary instructions, books, and education programs, such as the Scottish Rite Master Craftsman Program (Southern Jurisdiction) and the Hauts Grades Academy (Northern Masonic Jurisdiction). This book is an alternative calibration proposal.

Here, the origin of the Scottish Rite will be revealed; its expansion around the world; the structure and functioning of the rite; and each degree will be deciphered and decoded, exposing the chronology of the narrative, the legend and curiosities of the degree, comments on different versions and relationships with other degrees, the moral lessons veiled in it, the main symbols and its meanings, as well as a biblical passage that illustrates it in most jurisdictions. Then, each group of degrees will be analyzed together and holistically, understanding its role in the rite.

However, it is noteworthy that, although the Northern Masonic Jurisdiction version from the beginning of the 20th century was one of the consulted sources, its current version of the rituals, developed from the 70s, is not addressed in the comments, since, in many degrees, there were breaks with the original allegories, which serve as the basis for this study and its comparisons.

The presentation of each degree also has the respective heraldic emblem (or coat of arms), all developed at the beginning of this century by the Brazilian illustrator and freemason, João Guilherme da Cruz Ribeiro, being the result of extensive and deep research and recovery project at the request of the Supreme Council of 33th Degree of the Ancient and Accepted Scottish Rite of Freemasonry for the Federative Republic of Brazil.[ii] These emblems illustrate the themes of the degrees and their main symbols and were based on those used in the 19th century by the Italian and French Supreme Councils, as well as publications by the Scottish Rite Research Society that addressed the theme.[8]

[ii] My most sincere thanks, both to the artist and to the Brazilian Supreme Council, who kindly authorized the use of the images in this book.

[9] Thus, I hope that, after drawing attention to the importance of balancing allegories and symbols, I have not failed in exactly that.

2. THE AMAZING STORY OF THE SCOTTISH RITE

To discuss the history of the Scottish Rite, one goes back almost two centuries before its actual "birth", and travel for years through countries on different continents, just glimpsing the shape of people whose summaries of their lives could already yield bulky books. Furthermore, this travel in time and space is fabricated with the limitation of the available information, so that, as dimensional travelers at high speed, we know that those few seconds in which an event is observed on your right means the loss of everything that is passing to the left. Thus, choices had to be made, in the hope that they were, at least, satisfactory to talk about this victorious saga.

2.1. Origin and embryonic development of the Scottish Rite

After all, what is the origin of the Ancient and Accepted Scottish Rite? Is it Scottish, French, or American? There are many Freemasons around the world who claim, without batting an eye: "It is French!" But we will see that everything depends on what you consider by "origin".

If you answer that the origin of the Scottish Rite is Scottish, you are not at all wrong. The basis of the Rite has historically been taken by the Stuarts and their court when exiled in France. All were from Scottish families.

James VI was king of Scotland in 1601 when, at the age of 35, he was supposedly initiated into Scottish Freemasonry at the “Perth and Scone” Lodge.[10] [11] He is the first Head of State to have news (or rumor) of the initiation into Freemasonry.[iii] Two years after his initiation, he also assumed the throne of England and Ireland, becoming for these “James I” and thus initiating the “Stuart Period”. King James I was known to have devised and sponsored the translation of the Bible into the English language, which until today is described as a version authorized by King James. It is believed that all men of the family and nobles of his court traditionally entered Freemasonry.

Summarizing history a little, to focus on what matters to Freemasonry, in 1715, the Stuarts were exiled in France, more precisely in Bar le Duc. That

---

[iii] Robert Cooper, a researcher, writer and curator at the Grand Lodge of Scotland museum, believes that this initiation by James VI is unlikely, despite recognizing the strict relationship between Jacobites and Freemasonry.

same year, James Radclyffe, earl and best friend of the pretender to the throne, James III, "The Old Pretender", accompanied by his brother Charles Radclyffe, both faithful to the Stuart cause, returned to Scotland to participate in a rebellion. The rebellion failed and both were arrested, with Count James Radclyffe executed and Charles Radclyffe managed to flee and return to France.

Ten years later, Charles Radclyffe, then secretary to Prince Charles Edward Stuart, known as "The Young Pretender", in France, fulfilling the prince's and his court's wishes, founds the 1st "Scottish" Masonic Lodge in French territory. Through his leadership, the Jacobite Lodges, soon called "Scottish Lodges" in France, quickly proliferated in French territory. In the same intensity as the proliferation of Lodges, there was a proliferation of degrees and rites, thanks to another Jacobite Scotsman: Ramsay.

Andrew Michael Ramsay was a Scottish nobleman well-liked by the French nobility, to the point of winning the desired title of "Chevalier" of France. He became, for a short time, a tutor to Prince Charles Edward Stuart. Ramsay had been initiated into Freemasonry in 1730, through the "Horn" Lodge of Westminster, at the same time as the introduction of Master Mason Degree. As early as 1736, collaborating with the development of "Scottish Lodges" in France, Ramsay was invited to give a speech to a group of initiates during a major initiation, which would take place on December 26 of that year.[12] It is not known whether the speech, better known as "Ramsay's Prayer", was read by Ramsay in Lodge or if it was, in some way, edited and distributed to those present during such initiation. What is known is that it was printed in some way, spreading among the lodges in the region, until it was published in an unholy booklet in 1741, which earned him a lot of attention and attracted candidates.

Here are some interesting excerpts from the speech:

> Our ancestors, the Crusaders, gathered from all parts of Christendom in the Holy Land, wished to bring together in one Fraternity individuals from all nations ...
> Our founders were not simple stone workers or curious geniuses. They were not only qualified architects, engaged in the construction of temples, but also religious and knight princes who planned, built and protected the Temples of the Highest.
> King Solomon wrote in hieroglyphic characters our statutes, our maxims, and our mysteries, and this ancient book is the original Code of our Order. ... After the destruction of the First Temple ... Zerubbabel was appointed as Grand Master of the Jerusalem Lodge and instructed the laying of the bases for the Second Temple, where the mysterious book of

> Solomon was deposited. ... This book was lost...... until the time of the Crusades when a part of it was rediscovered after the surrender of Jerusalem.
> Kings, princes, and lords returned from Palestine to their lands and established several Lodges there ... Our degrees, our Lodges, and our rites have been neglected in most places. ... However, its splendor among the Scots has been preserved, to whom the kings of France have confided for many centuries the safeguarding of their royal family.[13]

It is seen in the speech the intention to untie the image of the Freemason and that of a bricklayer and link it to that of a noble knight, especially by the Scottish Masonic practice in France in contrast to the English ("modern") practice that coexisted in the territory French. Another interesting point is that at no time did Ramsay mention the Order of the Temple, but his speech was the initial flame of the idea that Freemasonry was the direct successor of the Templars, which was reflected in numerous degrees.

But some argue that Ramsay and his countrymen were not restricted only to the valorization of their Scottish Freemasonry, but used it for political (and monetary) purposes. This "use" of Freemasonry for Jacobite (Stuartist) purposes in France was the subject of attention by some writers, such as Clavel and Mackey. Clavel credits the Stuarts with the final format of the legend of the Master Mason degree:

> We saw that the refugees from King James's court and the defenders of his son, Francis Edward Stuart, tried to use Freemasonry for a political purpose. The first way they used it was to give the symbols and allegories of the three degrees a meaning appropriate to their opinions. Thus, they claimed that the Masonic association was not a continuation of the construction workers' brotherhoods, but that it constituted a new aggregation, a real conspiracy to facilitate the restoration of Stuart's house on the throne of England. According to this doctrine, the assassination of Hiram-Abiff alluded to the tragic death of Charles I, and the bad companions represented Cromwell and the other heads of Parliament.[14]

Mackey follows the same reasoning, suggesting the use of anagrams to replace the names of supporters and opponents in the different degrees developed:

> The same method (anagram) was adopted by the adherents of the house of Stuart when they manufactured their system of high degrees as a political engine, and thus, under an anagrammatic form, they made many words to designate their friends or, principally, their enemies of the opposite party. Most of these words it has now become impossible to restore to their original form, but several are readily decipherable. Thus, among the Assassins of the Third Degree, who symbolized, with them, the foes of the monarchy, we recognize Romvel as Cromwell, and Hoben as Bohun, Earl of Essex. It is only thus that we can ever hope to trace the origin of such words in the high degrees as Tercy, Stolkin, Morphey, etc. To look for them in any Hebrew root would be a fruitless task. The derivation of many of them, on account of the obscurity of the persons to whom they refer, is, perhaps, forever lost; but of others the research for their meaning may be more successful.[15]

In another entry, Mackey goes further, deepening his theory:

> The names given to the Assassins of the Third Degree by some of the inventors of the high degrees, are of so singular a form as to have almost irresistibly led to the conclusion that these names were bestowed by the adherents of the house of Stuart upon some of their enemies as marks of infamy. Such, for instance, is Romvel, the name of one of the Assassins in certain Scottish degrees, which is probably a corruption of Cromwell. Jubelum Guibbs, another name of one of these traitors, has much puzzled the Masonic etymologists. I think that I have found its origin in the name of the Ver. Adam Gib, who was an anti-burgher clergyman of Edinburgh. When that city was taken possession of by the Young Pretender, Charles Edward, in 1745, the clergy generally fled. But Gib removed only three miles from the city, where, collecting his loyal congregation, he hurled anathemas for five successive Sundays against the Pretender, and boldly prayed for the downfall of the rebellion. He subsequently joined the loyal army, and at Falkirk took a rebel prisoner. So active was Gib in his opposition to the cause of the house of Stuart, and so obnoxious had he become, that several attempts were made by the rebels to take his life. On Charles Edward's return to France, he erected in 1747 his "Primordial Chapter" at Arras; and in the composition of the high degrees there practiced, it is very probable that he

> bestowed the name of his old enemy Gib on the most atrocious of the Assassins who figure in the legend of Third Degree. The letter u was doubtless inserted to prevent the French, in pronouncing the name, from falling into the soft sound of the G and calling the word Jib. The additional b and s were the natural and customary results of a French attempt to spell a foreign proper name.[16]

Still in his encyclopedia, Mackey makes other mention of the use of Freemasonry and the creation of high degrees by the Jacobites in France, suggesting that the founding of several Masonic organizations had this purpose, as the mentioned Primordial Chapter, the College of Clermont, the Metropolitan Chapter in France, among others. There is controversy as to whether some of these bodies, such as the Primordial Chapter, actually existed. Others existed, as is the case of the College (or Chapter) of Clermont, and many of them created degrees that made direct mention of Prince Charles Edward, James VI, and other real Jacobite characters, as well as had the habit of creating degrees whose titles used the term "Ecossais", which in French means "Scots": Scottish Master, Grand Scotsman, Scottish Grand Master, Scottish Knight, Grand Scottish Architect, Perfect Scottish, are just a few examples of degrees that made up a series of "Scottish" rites.

A supposed heritage of this "Jacobinism" in the Scottish degrees would be preserved in the famous degree of revenge of the Scottish Rite, the 30th degree, of Knight of the White and Black Eagle, which was the penultimate (24th) degree of the Rite of Heredom.[iv] In it, one can find the fruit of Ramsay and the dream of the Jacobites: the Freemasons avenging the death of the last Grand Master of the Templars, Jacques de Molay, betrayed by the State and the Church. It would be an allegory for the desired revenge for the death of King Charles I, killed at the behest of Parliament, and of James II, dethroned for religious intolerance.

However, concerning the legend of the third degree, considering the historical evidence of its emergence, it is more plausible to suppose that the Jacobite ritualists sought to interpret an older history from a party perspective than to suppose that they would have created the third degree.

In any case, in 1745, supporting an unsuccessful attempt by the Stuarts to retake the throne of England, Count Charles Radclyffe is captured and executed in London. However, his Masonic initiative was the embryo of what would become, among several Masonic rites, the Rite of Heredom.

[iv] Rite of Heredom, or Rite of Perfection.

In the 1750s, "Scottish Freemasonry" and its degrees were developing rapidly, dominating the internal policy of Freemasonry in that country. It was then that, in 1756, the “Council of the Knights of the Orient” appeared, directed by middle class (bourgeois) Freemasons, intending to organize the High Degrees of the rite. But the masons of the highest class and the nobility, led by Stephen Morin and not wishing to stay behind the bourgeois, created the “Supreme Council of Emperors of the East and the West” in 1758.[17] Both were fruits of the Chapter of Clermont.[18] Well, a "Supreme Council" sounds bigger than a simple "Council", and "Emperors" are logically superior to simple "Knights". Furthermore, "East and West" is twice as much as just "East"! In this way, this Supreme Council of Emperors of the East and the West managed to prevail over the semantically diminished Council of the Knights of the East, becoming the legitimate “incubator” of the Rite of Heredom, apparently concluded in the format of 25 degrees in the early '60s of that century, and inventing Morin's patent that guaranteed the export of the rite to the new continent.

As an emblem, this Supreme Council of Emperors of the East and the West sought inspiration in the Roman Empire, which, at its peak, ruled the East and the West and adopted a system of two simultaneous rulers. In this phase of the Roman Empire, the double-headed eagle was adopted to symbolize it.[19] The Supreme Council found the double-headed eagle the ideal symbol for "East and West" and added a crown over both heads of the eagle to symbolize royalty, after all, it was a Council of "Emperors".

Starting from the Rite of Heredom, if you answer that the origin of the Scottish Rite is French, this will not be a mistake at all. The 25 degrees of the Rite of Heredom and its spread in the United States gave rise to the Scottish Rite. However, there is a difference of eight degrees between the Rite of Heredom (25 degrees) and the Ancient and Accepted Scottish Rite (33 degrees). Which Freemason never asked himself what those eight degrees would be? To unravel this mystery, I present a comparative table between the 25 degrees that formed the Rite of Heredom and the 33 degrees that form the Scottish Rite:

COMPARATIVE TABLE – RITE OF HEREDOM *vs* SCOTTISH RITE			
RITE OF HEREDOM[20]		**SCOTTISH RITE[21]**	
1°	Apprentice	1°	Apprentice
2°	Fellow Craft	2°	Fellow Craft
3°	Master Mason	3°	Master Mason
4°	Secret Master	4°	Secret Master
5°	Perfect Master	5°	Perfect Master
6°	Intimate Secretary	6°	Intimate Secretary

7°	Intendant of the Building	7°	Provost and Judge*
8°	Provost and Judge	8°	Intendant of the Building*
9°	Elect of Nine	9°	Elected Knight of the Nine
10°	Elect of Fifteen	10°	Illustrious Elect of the Fifteen
11°	Illustrious Elect, Chief of the Twelve Tribes	11°	Sublime Knights Elect of the Twelve
12°	Grand Master Architect	12°	Grand Master Architect
13°	Royal Arch	13°	Knight of the Ninth Arch, or Royal Arch of Solomon
14°	Grand, Elect, Ancient, Perfect Master	14°	Grand Elect, Perfect and Sublime Mason
15°	Knight of the Sword	15°	Knight of the East
16°	Prince of Jerusalem	16°	Prince of Jerusalem
17°	Knight of the East and West	17°	Knight of the East and West
18°	Rose Croix Knight	18°	Prince Rose Croix
19°	Grand Pontiff	19°	Grand Pontiff
20°	Grand Patriarch	20°	Grand Master of Symbolic Lodges*
21°	Grand Master of the Key of Masonry	21°	Noachite, or Prussian Knight*
22°	Prince of Libanus	22°	Knight of the Royal Ax, or Prince of Libanus
		23°	Chief of the Tabernacle
		24°	Prince of the Tabernacle
		25°	Knight of the Brazen Serpent
		26°	Prince of Mercy
		27°	Knight Commander of the Temple
23°	Sovereign Prince Adept Chief of the Grand Consistory	28°	Knight of the Sun, or Prince Adept
		29°	Grand Scottish Knight of Saint Andrew
24°	Illustrious Knight, Commander of the Black and White Eagle	30°	Knight Kadosh
		31°	Inspector Inquisitor Commander
25°	Most Illustrious Sovereign Prince of Masonry, Grand Knight, Sublime Commander of the Royal Secret	32°	Sublime Prince of the Royal Secret

		33°	Sovereign Grand Inspector-General

It is interesting to note that, originally, the degree of "Intendant of the Building" preceded the degree of "Provost and Judge", contrary to what we have today. The same occurred between the "Prussian Knight" degree, which preceded the "Grand Patriarch" (currently "Grand Master of Symbolic Lodges"), and which were also reversed when the Scottish Rite was first organized. The degrees that arose in the United States and were added between the degrees of the Rite of Heredom, forming the system of the Scottish Rite as we know, the degrees today are numbered between the 23rd and 27th, and the 29th, 31st and 33rd degrees.

Pike believed that these added degrees originated from other French rites, the latter two, 31st and 33rd, linked to the *Saint Jean d'Ecosse du Contrat Social: Mère Loge Ecossaise de France*, of which Grasse-Tilly was a member before his military service on the island of Santo Domingo and, later, his stay in Charleston, in the United States.[22]

And since we mention the United States, if you answer that the origin of the Scottish Rite is American, you will not be able to deny it. In 1763, Stephen Morin, carrying his patent that granted him the authority to establish the Rite of Heredom on the American continent, granted another patent to Henry Andrew Francken. Starting in Santo Domingo, Jamaica and probably Louisiana, in 1767 the Rite of Heredom was already being granted in New York and from there it quickly spread across the country, with dozens of Grand Inspectors vying for candidates, without divisions of territories, and granting other French degrees or even inventing new degrees to attract more customers. Real chaos.

It was in the United States, more precisely in the state of South Carolina, that, at the initiative of the so-called eleven gentlemen of Charleston, where the system was defined by 33 degrees, which some years later would be baptized with the name "Ancient and Accepted Scottish Rite", placing "order out of chaos". On that occasion, back in the United States, the 1st Supreme Council of the Scottish Rite in the world was born, in May 1801.[23]

It is worth mentioning the cosmopolitan profile of Charleston at the time, which was also evident in these eleven gentlemen, "parents" of the Scottish Rite: John Mitchell (Irish, US colonel), Frederick Dalcho (Londoner, son of Prussians and pastor), Thomas Bowen (Irish and Past Grand Master of the Grand Lodge of South Carolina), Abraham Alexander (London rabbi), Emmanuel de la Mota (Jewish, from the Danish West Indies), Isaac Auld (Jacobite Scottish), Israel de Lieben (Prague Jew), Count de Grasse-Tilly (French), Jean

Delahogue (French), Moses Levy (Polish Jew), and James Moultrie (the only American).

Therefore, if you consider the origin based on the name and format, the Scottish Rite is American. If you consider the origin based on the place where its practice developed, the Rite is French. But if you consider the origin based on its roots and traditions, the rite is Scottish.

There is no way to say that one origin is more legitimate than the other. We cannot ignore the fact that, all over the world, black people are called Afro-descendants and Jews as Zionists, regardless of the place of birth. The great-grandchildren of Irish born in the USA, for example, still consider themselves Irish. In_ these cases, the origin is not in the place where they were born, but in the place where, in some way, their roots are. It was following this line of reasoning that the Americans called the Rite "Scottish". Already following the formal, legalistic point of view, the rite is undoubtedly American, since it was in the United States that it was organized, defined, named, and where the first institution to administer the Rite was created. However, when observing its practices, there is no way to discard the essence of French "Scottish" Masonry embedded in their rituals.

Finally, we have a rite with Scottish roots, developed in France and concluded in the United States by brothers of different beliefs and origins. A multinational rite_ consistent with the complexity and depth of its degrees, and with its practice in dozens of countries around the world.

2.1.1. The role of King Frederick II of Prussia

Soon after the creation of the Mother Supreme Council of the World, in May 1801, its curious status, dated 1786, and having Frederick II, King of Prussia, as its patron, evolved._

The fictional role of King Frederick II of Prussia, as patron of the Ancient and Accepted Scottish Rite, can be credited to his namesake, the physician and reverend Frederick Dalcho, one of the "eleven gentlemen of Charleston". Dalcho's father had been a loyal officer in the army of King Frederick I, "the Soldier King ", father of Frederick II.

There is Dalcho's "fingerprint" between the lines of degrees like the 21st and the 27th, in which his fatherland, Prussia, is, in some way, allegorically present. And the same can be said about the first statute of the Mother Supreme Council of the World, supposedly from 1786 and, if it were the case, mysteriously written fifteen years before its foundation, which occurred only in 1801.

The choice of the year 1786 for the status of the Scottish Rite would not have been by chance. This was the year of the death of King Frederick II of Prussia. Thus, any date after that would undermine the likelihood of the hoax that the statute had been ratified by the monarch. The first known edition of the statute is from February 1801 and handwritten by Dalcho, having won a print edition the following year.

It is known that Frederick II had been initiated in the three symbolic degrees, in 1738, two years before he became king. It is also known that, as king, he allowed secret societies to function; however, there is no record that it started in degrees beyond the three symbolic ones, just as there is no record about it related to Freemasonry after 1744. Besides, on May 1, 1786, a few months before his death, which occurred on August 17, 1786, it is not only improbable but practically impossible that the monarch, already senile and awaiting death in his bed, created the 33rd degree and ratified the status of a new rite, entrusting it to a group of Freemasons of the then newly created Republic of the United States of America, in the "New World".[24]

Frederick II, the greatest symbol of enlightened absolutism, was a king admired and respected throughout Europe for his love of the arts and sciences, and his wisdom. He was regarded as a kind of King Solomon from the second half of the 18th century. He was a Prussian, which counted a lot for Dalcho, who had probably learned this feeling from his father, having for Frederick II the same admiration and loyalty that his father had for Frederick I. This identification can also be justified by another point in common among the sharks: Dalcho's father was a military man, while Dalcho followed the path of science; as well as Frederick II, who preferred science to the army, much to the chagrin of his father, Frederick William I, not by chance known as "the Soldier King".

The Mother Supreme Council of the World itself recognized, since Albert Pike, the mention in the statute of Frederick II, King of Prussia, as well as the date of 1786, as a kind of homage to the monarch.[25] Since then, historians, scholars, and researchers have considered this first status strictly for its "traditional" and not historical or legal value. Despite this, many masonic books around the world have propagated and still propagate this fiction as a reality.

However, it would not be prudent to judge this ideological falsehood with the rule of current ethics. At that time, it was not uncommon to include this type of fantasy, even in statutes and constitutions. As an example, there is the famous Anderson's Constitutions, which points to Adam as the first Mason and Caesar Augustus as a Grand Master, among other follies. Anderson's constitutions was considered "*a mixture of compilation and fantasy, invention and manipulation, clarity and ambiguity, and of fact and error*",[26] and was soon replaced in England by a more coherent version. But that did not prevent the development of a blind and mistaken belief in many Freemasons that the Anderson's Constitutions has legal value, being the basis of Masonic regularity.

It may be impossible, even in this 21st century, to reverse the effects of this belief in the fallacy of Anderson's Constitutions. But it seems admissible, due to the study profile characteristic of the high degrees of the Scottish Rite, the hypothesis of the triumph over the taboo of the Frederick II Statute.

2.2. The good son returns to France

The term "the good son returns to home" is related to the Christian parable of the prodigal son. In this particular case, it refers to that son (Rite of Heredom), who travels abroad (United States) with his inheritance (Scottish) and after years returns to his home (France). In the parable, two children receive their father's inheritance in advance. One of them decides to travel and enjoy what the world has to offer. After spending all his money on lust, he realizes that the real value is in the family and returns to home, where he is welcomed with open arms by his father.[v] However, in this Masonic case, he does not return poorer than he was, but "enriched" with degrees.

As already explained, the Rite of Heredom, developed in France and with its 25 degrees, was introduced in the United States, from 1767, and it is transformed into the Ancient and Accepted Scottish Rite, of 33 degrees, more precisely in Charleston, South Carolina, culminating in the creation of the Mother Supreme Council of the World, on March 31, 1801.

In Charleston, since 1795, lived Count Alexandre François Auguste de Grasse-Tilly, a French aristocrat and military officer, who had moved to the United States after the black revolt on the island of Santo Domingo, which today is divided between the Dominican Republic and Haiti. He was a member of the famous Parisian Masonic Lodge “Saint John of Scotland of the Social Contract”, then under jurisdiction to the Grand Orient of France.[27]

When mentioning this Lodge, it is necessary to include a small observation: this Lodge called itself, in 1776, the "Scottish Mother Lodge", embracing around itself thirty other "Scottish" lodges, that is, adepts of rites originated from the Lodges formed by Scots from the court of the exiled Stuarts in France. This initiative was due to the position of the Grand Orient of France in adopting the newly created Modern Rite, to the detriment of the other rites. The friction of these Lodges, led by the “Scottish Mother Lodge”, with the Grand Orient of France lasted until 1781 when a truce was reached.[28]

---

[v] Luke, 15:11-32.

Resuming the chronology of the facts, when he was invested in the 33rd degree, in March 1802, becoming Grand Inspector General, the Count of Grasse-Tilly received from the Supreme Council of Charleston a letter that allowed him to create a Supreme Council for the French Antilles. Just two months later, in May 1802, he returned to Santo Domingo and founded his Supreme Council, the Supreme Council of Port-au-Prince, becoming its Sovereign Grand Commander.[29]

However, after two more years of military service in Port-au-Prince, the Count was able to guarantee his return to his native land, disembarking in Bordeaux in June 1804, and going with his family to Paris. And while he awaits his new assignment in the army, he takes the opportunity to grant the "new Scottish degrees", created in the United States, to members of "Scottish" Lodges in the French capital, causing frisson in the local Freemasonry.

The reflection of the Count of Grasse-Tilly's dedication occurs in less than four months after his return to France, with the foundation of the Supreme Council of the 33rd degree of the Ancient and Accepted Scottish Rite of France, on October 20, 1804, with the Count assuming as its Sovereign Grand Commander. Taking advantage of the movement initiated by the count, five "Scottish" Lodges (*La Parfaite Union, La Réunion des Étrangers, Les Élèves de Minerve, Le Cercle Oriental des Philadelphus, Saint-Alexandre d'Écosse*), who were facing difficulties with the Grand Orient of France for not adopting the Modern Rite, just two days after the foundation of the Supreme Council, they meet to found the Grand Lodge of the Ancient and Accepted Scottish Rite of France, choosing Prince Louis Bonaparte as Grand Master and the Count of Grasse- Tilly as his Deputy Grand Master. On the occasion, they justified the initiative because the "*Scottish system is the only one (of the French systems) known abroad and in which Freemasons from all over the universe can unite and fraternize, while the Modern Rite is not allowed in any country.*"[30]

Upon hearing of the event and the personalities involved, the Grand Orient of France is available to sit at the table and begin a process of union. The result of the agreement was consummated on November 27 of that year, 1804, with Joseph Bonaparte taking over as Grand Master of the Grand Orient of France and Louis Bonaparte, who had previously taken on as Grand Master of the Grand Lodge of the Scottish Rite, becoming his Deputy Grand Master. On December 1, Napoleon was crowned Emperor of France, and on December 3, the Grand Orient and the Grand Lodge (already with a dozen lodges) signed an act of union, whereby the Grand Lodge ceased to exist and the Grand Orient began to recognize the government of the high ranks by the Supreme Council.

The Grand Orient of France, still attached to the government of all degrees, decided, on July 21, 1805, to create under its administration a "Grand

College of Rites", causing a revolt in the Scottish Rite freemasons, who understood that the act of union was being violated and decided, for that reason, to reopen the Grand Lodge. The Grand Orient goes back, but not completely: it maintains the newly created "Grand College of Rites", but slightly modifying its scope.[31]

In 1805, the Count of Grasse-Tilly, on account of his military obligations, was sent to Italy. He then asks for a resignation from the post of Sovereign Grand Commander of the Supreme Council of France, being replaced by the future Duke of Parma; however, he again manages to combine his obligations with his Masonic commitment, thus creating the Supreme Council of the Ancient and Accepted Scottish Rite of Italy, with Prince Eugene de Beauharnais, viceroy of Italy, as Sovereign Grand Commander and Grasse-Tilly as an honorary member.[32]

Not satisfied, the Count of Grasse-Tilly continues his Masonic mission of European expansion of the Scottish Rite, collaborating for the foundation, in 1809, of the Supreme Council of the Two Sicilies, in Naples; and, in 1811, for the foundation of the Supreme Council of Spain. In both, the count also receives the title of honorary member. In that same year, 1811, the Grand Orient of France already had 91 Ancient and Accepted Scottish Rite blue Lodges.

Although this period was fertile and productive for the Scottish Rite in the rest of Europe, the problems in the heart of the Grand Orient of France persisted. The last straw seems to have been poured out on August 26, 1815, when, after years of attempts, the Supreme Council of France decides to break with the Grand Orient of France, declaring that it cannot agree with the "*centralization of the Rites proposed by the Great East of France*".

Back in France in 1815, the Count of Grasse-Tilly continued his work of expansion. In 1817, he collaborates with the foundation of the Supreme Council of the Kingdom of the Netherlands, based in Brussels. "No one is a prophet in his own country". In France, the absence of a Grand Lodge to provide candidates for the high degrees granted by the Supreme Council of France led to it falling asleep in 1819.[33]

The sleep of the Supreme Council of France ended on January 1, 1821, with a movement to re-erect and reorganize it. The Count of Valence becomes Sovereign Grand Commander and the Count of Ségur as Lieutenant Commander, and the Supreme Council, in order not to depend exclusively on the Grand Orient of France, now also grants the symbolic degrees of Apprentice, Companion, and Master of the Ancient and Accepted Scottish Rite, thus governing from the 1st to the 33rd degree. In response, the Grand Orient of France turned the membership in Supreme Council into a Masonic infraction.[34]

After twenty years of unsuccessful merger attempts on the part of the Grand Orient of France, in 1841 it decided to lift its members' ban on admission to the Scottish Rite High Degrees and allow visitation with the Supreme Council blue lodges.

On June 10, 1845, the Count of Grasse-Tilly died at the age of 80, responsible for bringing the good son, Heredom, after it was renamed (Ancient and Accepted Scottish Rite) and enriched (with degrees), back to his home, France, and introduced it to all of Europe.

Relations between the Grand Orient of France and the Supreme Council of France remained reasonably fraternal, thanks to the goodwill of their leaders, until at least January 1862, when King Napoleon III declared Marshal Bernard Pierre Magnan, a non-mason, as Grand Master of the Grand Orient of France. Marshal Magnan is then initiated and raised to the 33rd degree of the Scottish Rite in just two days. And one of his first acts was to try to compel the absorption of the Supreme Council by the Grand Orient, but not without resistance from the Supreme Council, especially from his Sovereign Grand Commander, Jeans Pons Guillaume Viennet, who was forced to break up with the Grand Orient to guarantee its autonomy and independence. Here is an excerpt from his response to Marshal Magnan's subpoena:

> Our two Orders are independent of each other (...) Our interests are different. Our relations extend to the extremes of the world, while yours do not cross borders. This merger to which you invite us is prohibited by our bylaws. Only fraternity is required of us, and we practice it more than these men to whom the Great East owes its divisions and who have never abandoned the thought of absorbing us, in an interest that is not at all Masonic. The attempt they make today, through you, does not surprise us, but they know that any merger is impossible.[35]

Only in 1874 did the Grand Orient of France and the Supreme Council of France again reach a truce, which ended soon after, in 1877, when the Grand Orient of France decided to suppress any mention of the Grand Architect of the Universe and to abolish the dogma of immortality of the soul. This was the final stab, which put a definitive end to the relationship of love and hate, which had lasted seventy years between both institutions.

The Supreme Council of France, one of the creators of the Lausanne Congress, which brought together Supreme Councils from around the world in 1875, could not agree with the decision of the Grand Orient of France. Despite not sharing this "evil", the Supreme Council practiced another: it still had Symbolic Lodges under its government. This irregularity only ended in 1880, when the Supreme Council supports the foundation of the Scottish Grand Lodge of France, today called the Grand Lodge of France, initially formed by twelve Supreme Council blue Lodges.[36]

From then until today, there are not many facts to mention about drastic changes in the functioning of the Supreme Council of France and its relations with Symbolic Degrees, except in 1964, when its Sovereign Grand Commander and the majority of the Effective Members, accompanied by hundreds of members, chose to break with the Grand Lodge of France and recognize the French National Grand Lodge - GLNF, the only French Grand Lodge recognized by the main block of the Grand Lodges in the world. The rest of the Effective Members and other members chose to maintain their link with the Grand Lodge of France, thus declaring the continuity of the Supreme Council. Both Supremes claim to be the genuine Supreme Council founded in 1804, however, only the one linked to GLNF has obtained the recognition of the regular Supreme Councils of the world as being the legitimate one.

2.3. The first rituals of the Scottish Rite Symbolic Degrees emerge

As explained, in 1804 the Count of Grasse-Tilly, one of the Eleven Gentlemen of Charleston, founded the Supreme Council of France and a Grand Lodge to work on the symbolic degrees of the Ancient and Accepted Scottish Rite; however, the Mother Supreme Council of the World, which he had helped to create and where his legitimacy for the creation of the Supreme Council of France would have come from, did not (and still does not have) symbolic degrees and rituals. In other words, A&ASR originally did not have symbolic degrees, only recognizing the three symbolic degrees common to all rites; yet, when creating a Grand Lodge of the Scottish Rite in France, he would need to invent them.

Based on the 1801 edition of the rituals of the symbolic degrees of the Modern Rite of the Grand Orient of France (based on the practices of the Grand Lodge of the Moderns) and the book Three Distinct Knocks, originally published in 1760 (based on the practices of the Grand Lodge of the Ancients), Grasse-Tilly develops a simple ritual, dedicated to God and "Saint John of Scotland",[vi] which invokes the Grand Architect of the Universe, and in which

[vi] Robert Cooper understands that he is Saint John the Evangelist, due to the historical connection with the Grand Lodge of Scotland, the Grand Lodge of York and the Grand Lodge of the Ancients, as opposed to Saint John the Baptist, for the Grand Lodge of Moderns.

the candidate makes his will in the Chamber of Reflections. There is the sacred cup (that becomes bitter), the Terrible Brother, and Huzzah's acclaim three times. However, the similarities with the A&ASR rituals currently practiced in symbolic lodges in the Latin world stop there. Due to the influence of the "innovative" practices of the Grand Lodge of Moderns, the sacred word of the Apprentice degree in this first version is "J ..." and the password, "T ... C ...".[37]

The 1806 version does not present many changes compared to the first, from 1804. The difference with the Modern Rite is emphasized, affirming the Scottish Rite as "*the pure essence of Freemasonry*", despite teaching the signs and grips of the Modern Rite to the new apprentices upon initiation.

The 1829 version, on the other hand, is considered the masterpiece of the Supreme Council of France, at the time under the government of Count de Valence. At that time, the Supreme Council, in dispute with the Grand Orient of France, held its symbolic lodges. You can see a little of this version in the current versions of Latin countries. It is here that the temple gains the famous elevated orient with four stair steps. In this version, the Lodge is dedicated to Saint John, but it is not said which of the saints by the name of John. The differences between the Scottish Rite and the Modern Rite are no longer highlighted and the panel of the degree, finally, appears, in the center of the Lodge, inside the mosaic floor. In it, the Apprentice is also seen receiving only one sacred word, "B ...", as in the current versions. Besides, the apprentice, the companion, and the master gain a symbolic age.

An interesting detail of the 1829 version is that, in the Companion degree, the letter G continues to mean only Geometry, as in the oldest rituals. And in this version, the original term "Raising" to the degree of Master Mason was maintained. The innovation in the use of the term "Exalting", originated in the High Degrees, instead of "Raising" in this case had not yet occurred, which occurred in more than half a century when the Supreme Council of France functioned as mixed obedience, governing symbolic degrees and high degrees.

After this version, from 1829, the versions of the rituals of the symbolic degrees of the Ancient and Accepted Scottish Rite lose any possibility of linear logic, appearing multiple versions of the most diverse Grand Lodges from the most different countries for the most different reasons, fair or not.

2.4. The Lausanne Congress: Watershed

The Supreme Council of England and Wales had, in 1857, the idea of bringing together the regular Supreme Councils of the Ancient and Accepted

Scottish Rite of the world in a congress. Albert Pike, when he assumed, in 1859, as Sovereign Grand Commander of the Mother Supreme Council of the World, to whom the Supreme Council of England had submitted the proposal, adopted this dream as if it were his own. Until, after more than fifteen years of negotiations, his dream was effectively realized, between the 6th and the 22nd of September 1875, in Lausanne, Switzerland; but, unfortunately, Pike was not present.[vii]

At this point, it is important to make an addendum: In 1813, Joseph Cerneau founded a Supreme Council in New York by "spontaneous generation" (without charter). It was not enough for his Supreme Council to be within the jurisdiction of the Supreme Council of the Northern Jurisdiction of the USA, he claimed jurisdiction over the entire territory of the United States. This irregular Supreme Council granted, in 1826, a letter to David Jewett to found a body in Brazil. Just a few years after that, the Supreme Council of Belgium provided a similar letter for Montezuma to also found a Brazilian Supreme Council. Montezuma, very diplomatic, founded with his letter (from Belgium), granting the post of Lieutenant Commander (second in command) to David Jewett, holder of the letter from the Supreme Council of Cerneau.

In 1834, the Supreme Council of France, that of Belgium (founded by France), that of Brazil (with a letter from Belgium and Cerneau), and the Supreme Council of Cerneau, signed an treaty of alliance, the first of its kind in the world, but which has for decades been criticized and denounced by the two US Supreme Councils, and especially by Pike, which may have motivated, in part, his desire to hold a world Supreme Councils congress, to place "order out of chaos". Luckily, most members of Cerneau's Supreme Court migrated to the Supreme Council Northern Masonic Jurisdiction in 1867; and the remaining few who decided to buy this fight were expelled from their respective Grand Lodges.

But the damage from Cerneau's Supreme Council did not stop there and may have reflected the absence of Albert Pike at the congress that he, for so long, idealized and promoted. In 1834, the Supreme of Cerneau granted a charter for the founding of a Supreme Council of Louisiana, based in New Orleans. As Louisiana had been a French territory, sold to the United States in 1803, this historic relationship motivated (or served as an excuse for) the Grand

---

vii Regarding the Lausanne Congress of Supreme Councils, I suggest reading the collection of articles by Alain Bernheim, 33°, available in the Pietre-Stones Review of Freemasonry.

Orient of France[viii] to recognize the Supreme Council of Louisiana, in 1868.[ix] It was not enough, with only six months to go to the event, the Supreme Council of France questioned the Mother Supreme Council of the World on the foundation of high bodies in Hawaii (then an independent country), where the Supreme Council of France also maintained bodies.[38] For these reasons, perhaps Pike was not motivated to meet the French delegation face to face. But the event he envisioned would take place even without him.

With the opening of the event on the Sept. 6th and the creation of work commissions on the Sept. 7th, the Sept. 8th brought the fact that, unexpectedly, it would change the entire world Masonic geopolitics. One of the committees began discussing the terms of the Ancient and Accepted Scottish Rite declaration of principles, and, early on, stuck to the proposal to demand belief in a "Creative Principle" instead of "God". The theme led one of the committee members, Lindsay Mackersey,[x] Past Sovereign Grand Commander and representative of the Supreme Council for Scotland, who was already bothered by discussions in French, a language he did not speak, to withdraw from the committee and leave the event. In his view, the adoption of a "Creative Principle" in substitution for God would hurt one of the main landmarks of Freemasonry and, for that reason, it could not even be considered, let alone voted. From the hotel where he was staying, he wrote a letter and had it delivered to his host, Sovereign Grand Commander of the Supreme Council of Switzerland.[39]

During the next days of the congress, another matter presented and approved ensured that the Supreme Council of England had jurisdiction over all overseas territories under Great Britain and the Supreme Council of France had jurisdiction over Hawaii. Unfortunately, Mackersey, Scotland's representative, was no longer present to object and to ensure that the Supreme Councils of Scotland and Ireland would not be harmed. For this reason, some argue that the stir caused by Mackersey on the first day of debates with the question of the declaration of principles was just a pretext to try to discredit the event, to leave, and with that to try to prevent this English proposal from being voted.

[viii] The Grand Orient of France and the Supreme Council of France lived a relationship of love and hate, with much more hate than love, from the day the Supreme Council was founded until at least 1880. This was because the Grand Orient of France was stubborn to maintain a structure called the Grand College of Rites, which governed the High Degrees of the different rites, clashing with the Supreme Council. But in 1874, a year before the Lausanne Congress, they signed a kind of peace agreement.

[ix] Interestingly, shortly after the Supreme Council of Cerneau, which the Grand Orient of France recognized, closed its doors.

[x] Lindsay Mackersey served as Sovereign Grand Commander of the Supreme Council for Scotland from April 12, 1873 to October 12, 1874. He went to the Lausanne Congress representing his successor.

But I find it hard to believe that a Scotsman would flee the opportunity to fight England over territory. I prefer to believe that England took advantage of the absence of Scotland and Ireland to support this proposal of "market reserve".[40]

At the end of the Lausanne Congress, the following documents were approved for publication and submission to the Supreme Councils: a treaty on union and confederation of the Supreme Councils; the review of the constitution of the Scottish Rite; a *Tuileur*[xi] of the rite; and the Declaration of Principles, with the Creator Principle instead of God.

In the following months, the consequences of the event began to emerge:

- The Supreme Council for Scotland formally questioned the decision regarding the Creative Principle in the Declaration of Principles, accompanied by Greece, and regarding the territorial issue involving the Supreme Council for England;
- The Supreme Council of France notifies Pike about the jurisdictional issue involving Hawaii and the congressional decision on it, and the Mother Supreme Council of the World breaks with France for that reason;
- Scotland, Greece, and Ireland decide not to participate in the confederation of the Supreme Councils for the deist-theistic issue, formally communicating the then host, Supreme Council of Switzerland, about this decision;
- Mackersey sends a letter to Pike explaining the position of Scotland, Ireland and Greece, and suggesting to Pike, as the idealizer of the creation of the confederation, to take a position and take action on the issue;
- After reading Scotland's manifesto on the deist-theist issue, Pike is in favor of the Scottish position and against the decision taken at the Lausanne Congress on the issue, which Pike classified as "depravity";
- The Supreme Councils of Scotland, Ireland, Greece, and the Southern Jurisdiction USA create a league in opposition to the confederation created in Lausanne, which meets in Edinburgh, in September 1877;
- In response to this conflict promoted by the Supreme Council for Scotland, in October 1878 the Supreme Council of England

---

[xi] *Tuileur*: French term corresponding to Tyler.

resolves to break off relations with it and to change the name adopted in its jurisdiction, from the Ancient and Accepted Scottish Rite to the Ancient and Accepted Rite, thus deleting the term "Scottish" to make no further reference to Scotland.

Meanwhile, in 1877, the Grand Orient of France (which did not give up the irregularity of granting the High Degrees of the adopted rites, including the Ancient and Accepted Scottish Rite, even granting the 33rd degree, to the detriment of the Supreme Council of France) and the Grand Orient of Belgium decided to take sides in the deist-theistic discussion and remove from their laws the only two Masonic dogmas, that is, the obligation to believe in a Supreme Being and the immortality of the soul.[xii] However, the Supreme Councils of France and Belgium maintained dogmas in its postulates, under the watchful eyes of the Supreme Council for England, which hastened to declare that it had been deceived on the deist-theistic issue, which was being used to initiate atheists in Freemasonry; and to inform of its departure from the confederation created in Lausanne.

Amid all this turmoil, the Lausanne Confederation fell asleep and, consequently, the "Edinburgh League" (Southern Jurisdiction USA, Scotland, Ireland, and Greece) took over. The relationship between the Supreme Councils on a world scale was only resumed in 1907, with a new world congress, this time in Brussels.

The Lausanne Congress should not be remembered only as a stage for events that divided and redesigned world Freemasonry. Except for the controversy surrounding an item of the Declaration of Principles, the other documents produced there, in particular its *Tuileur*, served and still serve, to some extent, as a reference to the Supreme Councils around the world and many publications.

2.5. Albert Pike, Morals and Dogma, and Masonic theaters

Contrary to what some brothers may think, Albert Pike is not the father of the Ancient and Accepted Scottish Rite. Born in 1809, he could not be the father of a rite whose current format was launched in 1801. This does not diminish his relevance to the Scottish Rite, considering that his studies and writings have shaped the philosophy of A&ASR as we know it.

[xii] It did not take long for the Lusitane (Portuguese) Grand Orient to join the Grand Orient of France and of Belgium in such an initiative, which persists today.

A prodigious boy, fluent in more than a dozen languages, including some "dead" languages, and having been accepted at the renowned Harvard University at the age of 16, his Masonic life also followed this rhythm. He was initiated into Freemasonry in 1850. In March 1853, Albert Mackey endeavored to convince Pike, already a celebrated freemason, to travel from Arkansas to Charleston to receive from the 4th to the 32nd degree of the Scottish Rite. Pike, then a Royal Arch Mason and a Templar Knight in the York Rite, already stood out in the Masonic milieu for his intelligence and culture and, in Mackey's view, could help the Supreme Council to consolidate the Scottish Rite in Arkansas and the region.[41] Little did he know that Pike could do much more than that.

Between 1854 and 1855 he transcribed all the rituals of the A&ASR, being appointed to a review committee that lasted five years. His work of revision earned him the investiture to the 33rd degree, in 1857; the election as an Effective Member, in 1858; and, finally, the election for Sovereign Grand Commander, in 1859. And as no other member of the 1855 committee presented any results, Pike alone presented his full version of the rituals in 1861. Although he was not officially adopted by his Supreme Council, it served as the basis for editions of the Supreme Councils' rituals around the world.[42]

The American civil war interrupted the evolution of his work, as well as the move of the Supreme Council to Washington, DC, accomplished a few years after the end of the war, in 1870. The following year, in 1871, Albert Pike published his book “Morals and Dogma”, with his lectures, resulting from his studies on each degree of the Ancient and Accepted Scottish Rite. He died in 1891, still in the position of Sovereign Grand Commander.

Morals and Dogma is undoubtedly the most well-known Masonic book by Freemasons and anti-Masons. Covering the author's personal understanding (and not the Supreme Council's official position) of the moral and spiritual teachings of the Ancient and Accepted Scottish Rite degrees, Albert Pike's vast knowledge of history, theology, and languages are observed in this work; however, Morals and Dogma also served as fertile ground for the accusations of religious fanatics. Invented quotes, quotes from other authors, and modified quotes, all taken out of context and misinterpreted are credited to Pike and his Morals and Dogma and are multiplied and perpetuated in books and websites that attack Freemasonry, accusing it of Satanism, polytheism and any other things deemed bad by the accusers.

During his tenure at the head of the Supreme Council, Pike faced a major challenge. His leadership and renown, as well as the move of the Supreme Council to the capital of the country, had contributed to the growth of the Ancient and Accepted Scottish Rite, but still showing a timid growth, far from the dimension of symbolic Freemasonry. Consultations were made to the base and the answer came at a gallop: the rituals were considered too complex and the practitioners ended up too caught up in the ritual, to the detriment of the allegorical content and their moral teachings. Pike's reaction was tailor-made: the transformation of the rituals, published in 1884, into real "plays", giving up much of the ritual in favor of the dramatic presentation of its allegorical contents. Lodge rooms were replaced by theaters and auditoriums and the officers became amateur actors.[43]

Initially, there were many criticisms, with many "scholars" claiming the abandonment of Masonic customs, the desecration of content, the empty commercialization of degrees, and the exchange of meritocracy for simple attendance; however, a crowd of freemasons soon appeared interested in the new "Masonic entertainment", as it was sarcastically called by critics. If, in 1850, just before the entrance of Albert Pike, the Supreme Council had just over 1,000 adherents, and in 1890, a year after the publication of the rituals reviewed by Albert Pike, that number surpassed the mark of 10,000, in 1930 that number was already over 500,000 members.[44]

Pike died without being able to see the real success that became the theatrical staging of the Scottish Rite. While the climb from 29 degrees, from 4th to 32nd, used to take a few years for groups of a few dozen members, it started to be done in 3 to 4 days for groups of several hundred brothers. Sometimes the classes were over a thousand members.[45]

The dizzying increase in the number of members was reflected proportionally in the monetary collection. So much money needed to be used in some way, and the "Valleys" tried to invest for the benefit of their members, constructing buildings with ballrooms, libraries, game rooms, and increasingly sumptuous theaters.[46] In the first half of the 20th century, the Valleys of the Supreme Council, Southern Jurisdiction, USA tried to build and equip theaters that stood out, and some still stand out among the best in the country.

All this development did not drown out the criticism that the initiates, before protagonists who actively participated in the rituals, became simple spectators, passive in the face of the dramatic process and, in a way, pruned from the initiation process. This aspect explains why the Scottish Rite, in the Southern Jurisdiction of the USA, was called by critics "Masonic entertainment", and its theatrical format was initially accused of being a menace to Masonic morals and philosophy.[47] [48]

On the other hand, there was no shortage of supporters of the Masonic staging model in the Scottish Rite, arguing that the dramatization, when done well, contributes to a better understanding and emotional relationship with the lessons taught.[49] Besides, it should be noted that, despite the ease and speed with which the North American brethren reach the 32nd degree, the high bodies of the rite meet periodically to give instructions and lectures and hold debates on the preceding degrees.

And so, this successful case of the model of the Scottish Rite, Southern Jurisdiction, USA, which, with its more than one hundred years, has generated a level of semi professionalism and a whole culture around it, has been the object of study by researchers, Freemasons and others.[50] Its reduction in the degrees' interstice ended up influencing the North American Grand Lodges, which also started to grant the three blue lodge degrees in periods of a few days. Without entering into the discussion of merit, the fact is that this format contributed to the concentration of almost 2/3 of the world's Freemasons on United States territory.

It is worth mentioning that Pike's version of the rituals from 4th to 32nd degrees remained practically intact, only suffering minor corrections of editing errors or addition of observations, until 1985. That year, Clausen's version appeared, who served as Sovereign Grand Commander of the Mother Supreme Council of the World. It is intended to modernize the language, reduce repetition and facilitate memorization; however, its version was not well accepted by the adept members, which led to the emergence of the so-called revised "Standard" version of Pike, demanded by the Supreme Council in 1995 and published in 2000, which is still in force today.[51]

One of the advantages pointed out in this Pike's standard version is that most initiation degrees can be granted in less than an hour, which encouraged the practice of Scottish Rite weekend festivals in the USA, where brothers climb to the 32nd degree in one or two weekends. Besides, the virtual version offers slides, music, costume instructions and theatrical performance, taking advantage of 21st century technology to improve the Masonic experience in a ritual that dates back more than 150 years.

3. SCOTTISH RITE IN THE WORLD

Like a patchwork of degrees so well stitched by the eleven Gentlemen of Charleston, this polynationalist rite, the Ancient and Accepted Scottish Rite, quickly spread throughout the world through the foundation of the Supreme Councils.

This initial phase of expansion and the pioneering process of the international organization will be exposed in this chapter and indicate why the global phenomenon of the Scottish Rite was unique and unreplicable among all Masonic rites.

3.1. The foundation of the Supreme Councils

There is a certain consensus that there are few Supreme Councils that have not suffered any kind of interruption or split in the course of its history, so as not to leave room for questioning their antiquity.[xiii]

It is possible to determine a period for the creation of a Supreme Council, without going into the merit of the legitimacy of one or another current Supreme Council as continuity or succession of that one. And this data is important to understand how the process of internationalization of the Scottish Rite took place.

For this reason, we have to follow the list of Supreme Councils in order of seniority, from the creation of the "Mother Supreme Council of the World" (1801) to the holding of the Lausanne Congress of Supreme Councils (1875). Not all of them exist or are recognized as regulars by the International Conference today:

1. **The Supreme Council, Scottish Rite of Freemasonry, Southern Jurisdiction, USA**, whose full name is The Supreme Council (Mother Council of the World) of the Inspectors General Knights Commander of the House of the Temple of Solomon of the Thirty-third Degree of the Ancient and Accepted Scottish Rite of Freemasonry of the Southern Jurisdiction of the United States of America. It was founded on May 31, 1801, by the

[xiii] Statement by the Committee of History in the XIX International Conference of Supreme Councils.

eleven Gentlemen of Charleston, in Charleston, South Carolina, in the United States of America.

2. **Supreme Council of the French Islands of America.** [xiv] Founded by Count de Grasse-Tilly, one of the eleven Gentlemen of Charleston, in Port-au-Prince, in May 1802. Port-au-Prince had been Grasse-Tilly's place of residence as a military officer on duty, before going into exile with his family in Charleston, on account of the Haitian Revolution. While living on the island, Grasse-Tilly had purchased a rural property and, in 1802, returned to Santo Domingo intending to recover his property, resuming his military career, and founding the Supreme Council; however, his activities ceased with yet another battle on the island lost by the French, which led to the return of Grasse-Tilly to Charleston and soon afterward to France. Grasse-Tilly raised this Supreme Council with the status of "in exile", as soon as he founded the Supreme Council of France. But, on May 7, 1821, the members of that Supreme Council in exile abandoned him to rebuild the Supreme Council of France.[52]

3. **Supreme Council of the 33rd degree of France**. Founded by Grasse-Tilly in Paris, on October 20, 1804, just four months after his landing in his homeland, having himself as his first Sovereign Grand Commander. Two days after the founding of the Supreme Council of France, some Parisian lodges come together and found the Grand Lodge of the Ancient and Accepted Scottish Rite of France, with Prince Louis Bonaparte as Grand Master and Grasse-Tilly as his Deputy leads to the creation of the Scottish Rite rituals for the first three degrees. In less than two months (December 5, 1804), this Grand Lodge is incorporated into the Grand Orient of France, which started to allow Scottish Rite blue Lodges.

4. **Supreme Council of the 33rd degree of the Kingdom of Italy**. Founded by Grasse-Tilly in Milan on March 16, 1805, it was later known only as the Supreme Council of Milan. Napoleon Bonaparte's stepson and Viceroy of Italy, Eugênio de Beauharnais, takes over as Sovereign Grand Commander. On June 20 of the same year, the Supreme Council founds the Grand Orient of Italy.

[xiv] Also called the Supreme Council of the French West Indies, or the Supreme Council of Port-au-Prince. These variations are used by different authors.

5. **Supreme Council of the 33rd degree of the Kingdom of the Two Sicilies**. Founded by Grasse-Tilly, in Naples, on June 11, 1809, with the support of the Supreme Council of Italy. Napoleon Bonaparte's brother-in-law and newly crowned King of Naples, Joaquim Murat, was its Sovereign Grand Commander.[53]

6. **Supreme Council of 33rd Degree of Spain**. Founded by Grasse-Tilly, on July 4, 1811, in Madrid. He had Miguel José de Azanza as his first Sovereign Grand Commander.[54] This Spaniard had been a diplomat and Viceroy of New Spain, before embracing the Napoleonic cause, earning from Joseph Bonaparte the title of Duke of Santa Fé. Joseph Bonaparte was Napoleon's older brother and was King of Spain between 1808 and 1813 This, which was one of the first Supreme Councils in the world, was pursued by the Franco's Dictatorship, surviving in exile in Mexico for almost forty years.

7. **The Supreme Council, Scottish Rite, Northern Jurisdiction, USA**, whose full name is The Supreme Council of Sovereign Grand Inspectors General of the Thirty-third and Last Degree of the Ancient Accepted Scottish Rite of Freemasonry for the Northern Masonic Jurisdiction of the United States of America. While the Mother Supreme Council of the World was still being structured, two freemasons led separate groups that independently granted Scottish Rite degrees in New York and the region: Joseph Corneau, who had received the degrees in Cuba through Antoine Matthieu Du Potet, member of the Supreme Council of the French Islands of America; and Antoine Bideaud, who also came from the Supreme Council of the French Islands of America. This situation was analyzed in loco by Emanuel de la Motta, one of the eleven gentlemen of Charleston and Grand Treasurer of the Mother Supreme Council of the World, who concluded that the group of Cerneau was irregular whereas the group of Bideaud if it fulfilled some requests, would be worthy of recognition. Thus, on August 5, 1813, after meeting the requirements and under the authority of his Supreme Council, Emanuel de la Motta founds the Supreme Council of Northern Jurisdiction in New York. Daniel Tompkins, then Governor of the State of New York, was his first Sovereign Grand Commander.[55]

8. **Supreme Council of Cerneau**. Joseph Cerneau received the degrees by Antoine Matthieu Du Potet in Havana, Cuba, before

moving to New York in 1807. In New York, he created a Grand Consistory to grant the high degrees. When the Supreme Council of Charleston, through Emanuel de la Motta, declared his body irregular and collaborated in the foundation of the Supreme Council of the Northern Jurisdiction of the USA, Cerneau transformed his body into a Supreme Council, initially of the "Scottish Rite of Heredom", and later of the Ancient and Accepted Scottish Rite, declaring all the USA as its territory. This irregular competition lasted until 1867, when the Supreme Council of Cerneau was incorporated by the Supreme Council for the Northern Masonic Jurisdiction of the USA.[56]

9. **Supreme Council of Jamaica**. Little is known about this Supreme Council, only that it appeared in 1815, with John Joseph Itter[xv] as Sovereign Grand Commander and Solomon Morales[xvi] as Grand Secretary. There are no known documents to support any connection between this Supreme Council and the Grand Council of Jamaica, created by Estienne Morin in 1770, to grant the degrees of the Rite of Heredom. This Supreme Council probably fell asleep after the Baptist War.
10. **Supreme Council of Belgium**. Founded by Grasse-Tilly as Sovereign Grand Commander of the Supreme Council of France, on March 11, 1817, in Brussels. Its original name was the Supreme Council of the United Kingdom of the Netherlands, because, in 1815, the Congress of Vienna[xvii] had established the United Kingdom of the Netherlands, which included Belgium. After the Belgian Revolution in 1830, the Kingdom of Belgium gained its independence and the Supreme Council in Brussels became only of Belgium.[57]
11. **Supreme Council for Ireland**. Founded on August 13, 1824, with a letter issued by the Supreme Council, Southern Jurisdiction, USA, it had Augustus Frederick FitzGerald, Duke of Leinster and Grand Master of the Grand Lodge of Ireland, as its Sovereign Grand Commander. This Supreme Council followed the decision of his younger brother, the Supreme Council for

---

[xv] J. J. Itter was editor of the Jamaican newspaper "Diary and Kingston Daily Advertiser", as well as a public servant, as a Foreign Language Interpreter and Translator for Courts.

[xvi] Solomon Morales was a Past Master of "The Friendly Lodge", affiliated with the Grand Lodge of the Ancients, who owned a Provincial Grand Lodge in Jamaica, of which he was also Grand Secretary.

[xvii] Diplomatic event concluded in June 1815, whose aim was to geopolitically redesign Europe after the Napoleonic wars.

England and Wales, which in 1878 omitted the term "Scottish" from the name of the rite and began to name it only as "Ancient and Accepted Rite".

12. **Supreme Council of Degree 33 for Brazil**, whose full name is Supreme Council of Degree 33 of the Ancient and Accepted Scottish Rite of Freemasonry for the Federative Republic of Brazil. Founded on March 22, 1829, with a letter issued by the Supreme Council of Belgium (at the time, from the Netherlands), granted to Montezuma, who lived in exile in Europe after the Brazilian "Night of Agony", on November 12, 1823, when Emperor Dom Pedro I ordered the dissolution of parliament and the expatriation of its leaders. With the abdication of Dom Pedro I, on April 7, 1831, Montezuma was able to return to Brazil and install the Supreme Council, on November 12, 1832. It is worth noting that there was an attempt to compete on the part of the American mercenary David Jewett, in Rio de Janeiro at the service of the Brazilian Navy. Jewett had a patent from Cerneau, from November 3, 1826, to found a Supreme Council in Brazil. Montezuma circumvented the problem by inviting Jewett to be his Lieutenant, which he readily accepted.
13. **Supreme Council of Peru**, whose full name is Supreme Council of Sovereign Grand Inspectors General, Knights Commanders of the House of the Temple of Solomon of Degree 33 of the A&ASR of Freemasonry for the Jurisdiction of the Republic of Peru. Founded on November 2, 1830, by nine brothers invested in the 33rd degree, who elected General Domingo Tristan as their first Sovereign Grand Commander. From this Supreme Council, in the following year, the first Grand Lodge of Peru arises. There are two theories as to the origin of these nine founders. The first was that they received the degrees for a high body founded in Lima by the Supreme Council of Cerneau, which would justify the recognition of the Supreme Council for the Northern Jurisdiction of the USA at the end of the 19th century, after having incorporated the Supreme Council of Cerneau.[xviii] The second theory is that these brothers were members of A&ASR bodies linked to Grand Colombia, with a Spanish

---

[xviii] In fact, Cerneau's Supreme Council collected leaders from Latin America and the Caribbean as members, including politicians and military officers. Source: Planas, J. A. 2016. *Masones en la nobleza de España: Una hermandad de iluminados*. Madrid: La Esfera de los Libros.

letter and, upon hearing of the end of Grand Colombia, in 1830, they felt the need to found a Supreme Council of Peru.

14. **Supreme Council of New Granada**. Founded on April 19, 1833, with headquarters in Cartagena (Colombia), it was recognized by the Grand Orient of France, which rivaled the Supreme Council of France through its Grand College of Rites.

15. **Supreme Council of the 33rd Degree of Haiti**. Founded on January 25, 1836, on the initiative of Jean Baptiste Charles Stiguy, with a letter issued by the Grand College of Rites of the Grand Orient of France, rival to the Supreme Council of France.

16. **Supreme Council of Degree 33 for the Republic of Venezuela**. Founded on May 4, 1840, with José Antonio Páez Herrera, President of the Republic, as Sovereign Grand Commander.[58] In 1824, Joseph Cerneau himself traveled to Caracas and granted degrees to several freemasons who had either served in the country's independence or stood out locally, in a total of 77 brothers invested in the 33rd degree, 11 in the 32nd degree, and eight in the 30th.[59] As Cerneau had lived in Santo Domingo and Cuba before New York, it is believed that, in addition to French (his native language) and English, he was also fluent in Spanish. The remnants of that group were started by Cerneau, founded the Venezuelan Supreme Council. Despite its origin via the Supreme Council of Cerneau, at the end of the 19th century, when it no longer existed, similarly to what happened in Peru, the Supreme Council of Venezuela was recognized by that of the North Masonic Jurisdiction of the USA and others.

17. **Supreme Council for England and Wales**. Founded on October 26, 1845, with a charter from the Supreme Council for the Northern Masonic Jurisdiction of the USA issued to Dr. Robert Thomas Crucefix, a close friend of Dr. Oliver, and declared opposition to the Duke of Sussex.[60] This Supreme Council was involved in the commotion of the 1875 Lausanne Congress, which led, in 1878, to a change in the name of the rite in its jurisdiction, omitting the term "Scottish" and being called only "Ancient and Accepted Rite".

18. **Supreme Council of Scotland**. Founded on August 4, 1846, by Dr. Charles Morison of Greenfield, physician of the British army, with a charter issued by the Supreme Council of France.

19. **Supreme Council of Uruguay**. His charter was issued by the Supreme Council of Brazil, on October 7, 1854, in favor of Gabriel Pérez Cabral, who installed it on June 24, 1855. Pérez was a diplomat and served as Consul General of Uruguay in Brazil; however, another group founded a Supreme Council and Grand Orient of Uruguay, on November 21, 1854. The unification of these two Uruguayan Supreme Councils, with the recognition of the Brazilian Supreme Council, occurs on July 17, 1856.
20. **Supreme Council of Argentina**. With a charter issued by the Supreme Council of Brazil, on June 12, 1857, the Supreme Council of Degree 33 and the Grand Orient of the Argentine was founded, with Miguel Valencia as its first Sovereign Grand Commander, which was installed on the 23rd of that same month. Valencia had lived in exile in Brazil for many years; however, on April 1, 1858, another Supreme Council was founded, with the name of Supreme Council of Degree 33 for the Argentine Republic, with José Roque Pérez installed as Sovereign Grand Commander. Pérez was the founder and Grand Master of the Grand Lodge of Argentina, founded on December 11, 1857. His charter was subsequently issued by the Supreme Council of Uruguay, on September 13, 1858. Both Supreme Councils coexisted until 1862, when the first fell asleep and its remaining members migrated to the second, with the Uruguayan charter.
21. **Supreme Council of degree 33 of the A&ASR for the Republic of Cuba**. In the 50s of the 19th century, Cuban Freemasons gathered in the "Fraternidade # 01" and "Prudência # 02" Lodges, sought out one of the most well-known Masonic personalities from all over the world to instruct them on the foundation of a Grand Lodge: Albert Pike, Sovereign Grand Commander of the Supreme Council, Southern Jurisdiction, USA. On November 18, 1859, they founded the third Lodge, "San Andrés # 03", which allowed the founding of the Grand Lodge of Colón, on December 5, 1859. In parallel, Pike granted a charter to the Cuban, André Cassard, who lived in the United States, to found a Supreme Council in Cuba, which was done on December 27, 1859. His first Sovereign Grand Commander was Antonio Vinent y Gola since Cassard was condemned to death by Spanish authorities and could not remain in Cuba.[61]
22. **Supreme Council of Palermo**. Founded in 1860, concomitant with the founding of the Grand Orient of Italy, based in

Palermo, by Giuseppe Garibaldi, a popular leader of the Second Italian War of Independence. In 1860, Garibaldi had led the battles that brought dominion over Sicily and resulted in the Kingdom of Italy, proclaimed on March 17, 1861. Garibaldi declared the headquarters in Palermo temporary until Rome was conquered.[62]

23. **Supreme Council of the United Mexican States**. Founded on December 21, 1860, in the city of Vera Cruz, with the Frenchman Charles Laffon de Ladebat as its first Sovereign Grand Commander. The charter was issued by Albert Pike, while Sovereign Grand Commander of the Supreme Council, Southern Jurisdiction, USA. There is also the record of another Supreme Council in Mexico, founded in 1865, with James C. Lohse as Sovereign Grand Commander. These two Supreme Councils merged into one, on April 28, 1868, in a joint assembly that elected Lohse as Sovereign Grand Commander.

24. **Supreme Council of the Dominican Republic**. Founded on February 16, 1861, through André Cassard, appointed by the Supreme Council, Southern Jurisdiction, USA to promote the expansion of the Scottish Rite in the Spanish-speaking Caribbean. Its first Sovereign Grand Commander was Pedro Santana, then President of the Dominican Republic at the end of his government term.[63]

25. **Supreme Council of Egypt and Turkey**. Founded in 1861, by the English Hyde Clarke, who claimed to have authorization from the Supreme Council of France. Its first Sovereign Grand Commander was Prince Abdülhalim Pasha. This Supreme Council was regularized when recognized by the Supreme Council, Southern Jurisdiction, USA, in 1869. In the previous year, Robert Morris[xix] had praised Clarke and, on recognition, it was the turn of Albert Pike, then Sovereign Grand Commander.[64]

26. **Supreme Council of Turin**. Founded on December 16, 1862, by Ferdinando Ghersi, Frederico Piret, and Gabriele Murin, who were members of the Supreme Council of Palermo. Ferdinando Ghersi was his first Sovereign Grand Commander. Its foundation was driven by the emergence, in the previous year,

---

[xix] Robert Morris was the creator and founder of the Order of the Eastern Star and was Grand Master of the Grand Lodge of Kentucky. He had contact with Clarke during his trip to the Middle East to conduct research.

of the Italian Grand Orient, in Turin, the successor to the Italian Grand Orient of 1805, which had been founded by the Supreme Council of Milan.[xx] As a result, the Supreme Council of Turin declared itself the successor of the Supreme Council of 1805.

27. **Supreme Council Central Colombian**. Founded in 1864, in Bogotá, by Tomás Cipriano de Mosquera, then President of Colombia, who took over as Sovereign Grand Commander[65] and supposedly granted himself a curious 34th degree. It merges with the Supreme Council of Nova Granada, on August 12, 1938, thus creating the Supreme Council of the Degree 33 for the Republic of Colombia, which came to host the 1970 international conference in Barranquilla and remained active until 1983, when it then lost its recognitions.
28. **Supreme Council of Florence/Rome**. Founded in 1869 in Florence, then the capital of Italy, this Supreme Council was transferred in 1872 to Rome, which had become the new Italian capital on January 27, 1871. Its creation was part of the project of Garibaldi and Masonic leaders who followed him, an Italian Masonic unification that reflected and strengthened the idea of a single Italy.
29. **Supreme Council of Chile**. Founded on May 11, 1870, and installed on July 23, 1871, in the historic port city of Valparaíso, with Juan de Dios Merino Benavente as its first Sovereign Grand Commander. His charter was granted by the Supreme Council for England and Wales. The founders' intention was for the Supreme Council to exercise authority over the Grand Lodge of Chile, thus forming the National Grand Orient of Chile, as was the case in other Latin American countries with its Grand Orients, which followed the model of the Grand Orient of France. With the refusal of the Grand Lodge of Chile, most emphatically in its declaration of July 31, 1873, the Supreme Council simply stopped meeting.[66]
30. **Supreme Council of Central America**. Founded on January 9, 1871, in the city of San José, Costa Rica, with a charter issued by the Supreme Council of Nova Granada. Francisco Calvo, a Catholic priest, served as his first Sovereign Grand Commander. Its Masonic jurisdiction covered Costa Rica, El

[xx] This Italian Grand Orient in Turin awarded to Garibaldi, who served as Grand Master of the Grand Orient of Italy in Palermo, the title of Honorary Grand Master Ad Vitam and of "First Freemason of Italy".

Salvador, Nicaragua, Honduras and Guatemala. The headquarters was moved from Costa Rica to Guatemala in 1887.[67]

31. **Supreme Council of Degree 33 of the A&ASR for the Republic of Paraguay**. Founded on June 1, 1871, concurrent with the founding of the Grand Orient of Paraguay. It counted on Dr. Juan Adrián Chaves as his first Sovereign Grand Commander. He was chief of the medical corps of the Marines of Brazil on duty in Paraguay. His Lieutenant was the Brazilian Hermes Ernesto da Fonseca, Colonel of the Brazilian army. At that time, Asunción, the capital of Paraguay, was under the occupation of the Armed Forces of Brazil, which lasted from 1869 to 1876. With the withdrawal of Brazilian troops, the Supreme Council stopped functioning, being re-established only on January 3, 1896, this time with a charter from the Supreme Council of Uruguay.[68]
32. **Supreme Council of Greece**. Founded on July 24, 1872, with a letter issued by the Supreme Council for Scotland. His first Sovereign Grand Commander was Demetrius Rhodocanakis, who had been elected Grand Master just two days earlier.[69] Rhodocanakis was invited by leaders of Greek Freemasonry to become Grand Master for his status as a prince, which, it seems, was false.[xxi]
33. **Supreme Council of the 33rd and Last Degree of Switzerland**. Founded on March 30, 1873, with charter from the Supreme Council of France. Its first Sovereign Grand Commander was Jules Besançon, who, just two years later, was responsible for hosting the memorable 1875 Lausanne Congress.
34. **Supreme Council of Canada**. Installed on October 16, 1874, by the hands of Albert Pike, as Sovereign Grand Commander of the Supreme Council, Southern Jurisdiction, USA. He counted on Thomas Douglas Harington as his first Sovereign Grand Commander. He had been Grand Master of four Provincial Grand Lodges and the Grand Lodge of Canada in Ontario, First Grand Principal of the Grand Chapter of Royal Arch Masons of Canada, and Grand Master of the Grand Council of Cryptic Masons of Ontario.[70]

[xxi] It was a European Masonic custom, observed during the 18th and 19th centuries, to have a member of the Royal Family as Grand Master. In fact, this custom is still maintained in England.

35. **Supreme Council of the 33rd and Last Degree of the A&ASR for Italian Masonic Jurisdiction**. It appears on August 28, 1875, based in Rome, just a month before the Lausanne Congress, with the merger of the Supreme Councils of Rome, Turin, Palermo, and Naples. This was possible thanks to the influence of the "Hero of Two Worlds", Giuseppe Garibaldi, one of the main responsible for the unification of Italy.

Grasse-Tilly's role in the first decade of internationalization of the Ancient and Accepted Scottish Rite is undeniable. However, it is necessary to note that this initial expansion was only possible and occurred thanks to the Napoleonic Wars and the prominent position that Grasse-Tilly held as an adviser to Marshal Kellermann.

Thus, it is observed that France, in the Napoleonic period, adopted a strategy similar to that of the British Empire, which also had Freemasonry an institution present and active in the socio-political consolidation of its expansion.[71] Through Masonic organizations, it was possible to integrate the native elite with the colonizing elite.[72] This integration, regulated by Masonic hierarchy, discipline, and morality, provided a native elite consistent with what Foucault called "docile bodies",[73] as well as social and power networks useful in diplomatic initiatives.[74] This theory is reinforced by the French maintenance of the "Masonic tradition" of choosing a local representative of its empire as the ruler of the then-created supreme council. The observed difference is that, in the British cases, the Masonic organizations were created with subordinate status (Provincial Grand Lodges), while the Supreme Councils were already born independent.

Another phenomenon observed is the standard behavior of those excluded from the mainstream. Both the Supreme Council of Cerneau and the Grand College of Rites of the Grand Orient of France, both in an unfavorable situation in the face of internal competition in its own countries and rejected by the main Supreme Councils in the world, sought to export their models to the Latin American countries that had just achieved independence and were still, in a way, neglected by the mainstream. Still, it is assumed that the fact that they are from the USA and France, the two revolutionary references of the time, was something that collaborated with the process of empathy of the local leaders.

Cerneau's case was solved in 1867. The Grand Orient of France, on the other hand, when it reformed after the Lausanne Congress, in 1877, suffered not only the isolation of the Grand Lodges but also the abandonment of most of his sons, Grand Orients and Supreme Councils.

It is interesting to note that the Scottish Rite, which was born in 1801, initially so timid and respectful in USA because of the blue lodge degrees and its Grand Lodges, would become the driving force behind Freemasonry in the rest of the world throughout that 19th century, creating a new reproduction Masonic process with its Supreme Councils being founded concurrently with the Grand Lodges or Grand Orient of the countries and, in some cases, even before these.

From then on, the Scottish Rite became not only predominant throughout the Latin and Latin American Masonic world, but, as a rule, the cornerstone of it, having been the protagonist or participant in the main changes, be it creation, split, merger, rupture, alliance or tradition, that have occurred in these Masonic jurisdictions in the past two centuries.

3.2. International Conferences

Thirty-two years after the trauma of the Lausanne Congress, the Supreme Council meetings were finally resumed, with the name "International Conference of Supreme Councils", and gained volume and relevance.

It is interesting to note that, of all Freemasonry, its different rites and segments, the Scottish Rite was the first to make efforts, still in the 19th century, to gather its Supreme Councils around the world, all autonomous, independent, and sovereign, in search for a common good. In comparison, its correspondents in the Symbolic Degrees, the regular Grand Lodges around the world, only achieved a similar feat in the 20st century, with the appearance of the World Conference on Regular Grand Lodges.

By observing that the first international organizations emerged in the second half of the 19th century, such as the International Relief Committee for Injured Combatants (1863), the International Telegraph Union (1865), the International Arbitral Tribunal (1871), and the Universal Postal Union (1874), we can understand and envision how much the Lausanne Congress (1875) had been a pioneer, not only in the Masonic milieu but also in the non-Masonic milieu. And the resumption of Supreme Council meetings, already in 1907, further accentuates this pioneer movement of the Scottish Rite, since the world only moved towards a League of Nations in 1919, after experiencing the bitterness of World War I.

The following is the year and place of the international conferences, as well as a summary of what happened in each edition.:

I. **1907, in Brussels - Belgium**: 20 Supreme Councils represented in addition to the host, thanks to the efforts of the then

Sovereign Grand Commander of the Supreme Council of Belgium, Eugène Goblet d'Alviella. They were: Southern Jurisdiction of the USA, Northern Masonic Jurisdiction of the USA, Canada, Switzerland, Italy, Cuba, Guatemala, Mexico, Brazil, Argentina, Paraguay, Venezuela, Dominican Republic, Portugal, Spain, Egypt, Greece, France, Chile, and Peru. However, there is an absence of the Supreme Councils of England, Ireland, and Scotland, which opted to hold an almost parallel event in London, just a few days before this 1st international conference. In Brussels, it was discussed how to recognize each degree, how to defend against irregular Masonic organizations, and decided on the five-year periodicity for the event, the second edition is set for 1912, under the responsibility of the Mother Supreme Council of the World (Southern Jurisdiction, USA).

II. **1912, in Washington, DC - USA**: 17 Supreme Councils present. England, Ireland, and Scotland once again declined the invitation without giving further explanation, which will prove to be a long-term institutional stance. It was discussed (in vain) as to the possibility of standardizing the rite, with regard not only to the modes of recognition but also to the content and order of degrees.[75]

III. **1922, in Lausanne - Switzerland**: The conference, previously scheduled for 1917, had to be postponed due to World War I, which lasted from 1914 until the end of 1918. Although Switzerland maintained its neutrality in the conflict, its geographical position was central position among the main European countries involved in the war: German Empire, Austro-Hungarian Empire, Italy, and France. The Grand College of Rites of the Grand Orient of France, for not meeting the criteria of regularity adopted since 1907, was not accepted by the conference. It was decided that the next conference would be held in Buenos Aires, Argentina, in 1927, which did not happen for problems between the Supreme Council of Argentina and the local Grand Lodge.[xxii]

IV. **1929, in Paris - France**: With 27 Supreme Councils represented, this conference consolidated the rules of regularity and recognition between Supreme Councils, which had been

---

[xxii] The conflicts between the Supreme Council and the Grand Lodge of Argentina only came to an end in 1930.

discussed at the previous conference, and the rules of operation of the international conference itself.[76] During the conference, the Supreme Council of Brazil exposed its conflict and consequent breach with the Grand Orient of Brazil, to maintain its regularity. The recall of total independence between symbolic and high degrees was unanimously approved. Besides, the conference authorized the Supreme Council of France to host in its jurisdiction the Supreme Council of Russia in exile.[xxiii] Havana was defined as the venue for the next conference, which was to take place in 1934.

V. **1935, in Brussels - Belgium**: Due to the political instability and the beginning of the puppet government of Fulgencio Batista in Cuba, the Havana Conference could not be held in 1934. Thus, Brussels, the pioneer of International Conferences, assumed responsibility for itself to host the 5th Conference. While England, Scotland, and Ireland maintained the absence stance, a new Declaration of Principles was passed.

VI. **1939, in Boston - United States**: The Supreme Council of the Northern Masonic Jurisdiction of the USA still had its headquarters in Boston.[xxiv] The international conference was scheduled for September and, due to the declaration of war, already on the first day of September of that year, beginning the Second World War, there was a low number of delegations at the event.[77]

VII. **1956, in Havana - Cuba**: The Supreme Council of Cuba had the opportunity to compensate for the cancellation of the 1934 edition, by holding the 1956 edition. It was the first international conference of Supreme Councils with simultaneous translation.[78]

VIII. **1961, in Washington, DC - United States**: This was a tense year for the whole world and this was reflected in the conference. The Cold War was beginning to heat up, with the US diplomatic rupture with Cuba, the failure of the Bay of Pigs Invasion, and the construction of the Berlin Wall. During the conference break, the Sovereign Grand Commanders and their wives had the opportunity to make a full visit to the White House and were welcomed by John F. Kennedy at the Rose

---

[xxiii] The Komintern, a kind of International Communist Committee, had elected Freemasonry as an enemy since its 1920 congress.

[xxiv] The Supreme Council NMJ moved to Lexington MA in the 1970s.

Garden. Paris was decided to host the IX Conference, to be held in 1966.

IX. **1967, in Brussels - Belgium**: In 1964, due to a treaty between the Grand Lodge of France (which served as the basis for the Supreme Council of France) and the Grand Orient of France, the Sovereign Grand Commander of the Supreme Council of France, Charles Riandey, accompanied by hundreds of brothers, leaves the Grand Lodge of France and joins the French National Grand Lodge - GLNF. With this, some Supreme Councils, among them the "Mother of the World", declare France as an "unoccupied territory" of the Ancient and Accepted Scottish Rite. A group from the Grand Lodge of France tries to rebuild the Supreme Council, while the group that joined the GLNF founds a new Supreme Council with its support. Amid this cloudiness, the 1966 conference in Paris is canceled. The Supreme Council of Belgium takes the event once more to Brussels, but the French Masonic crisis, which led to the situation of these two coexisting Supreme Councils in Paris, generated discussions right at the beginning of the conference, resulting in the withdrawal of delegations from seven Supreme Councils, which greatly weakened this edition of the conference.[79]

X. **1970, in Barranquilla - Colombia**: With 26 Supreme Councils present, the first conference in South America was successful.[80] The controversy between which of the French Supreme Councils would have a seat at the conference, which had condemned the previous conference, is closed in favor of the Supreme Council linked to the GLNF. The thesis that the legitimacy of the Supreme Council follows the line of Sovereign Grand Commanders, as well as that the regularity of a Supreme Council is hostage to the regularity of the Grand Lodge or Grand Orient from which its members originate, emerged once again victorious, consolidating itself as a rule.

XI. **1975, in Indianapolis - USA**: It had the Supreme Council of the Northern Masonic Jurisdiction of the USA as host. Riandey's Supreme Council for France and linked to the GLNF, is recognized by the History Committee as a legitimate successor to the French Supreme Council founded in 1804. Rome is chosen to host the next conference.

XII. **1980, in Paris - France**: For reasons of "force majeure", with justification for the insecurity arising from political terrorism involving parties and the mafia,[xxv] Rome was replaced by Paris, which gave the Supreme Council for France the opportunity to consolidate its recognition with the other Supreme Councils.

XIII. **1985, in Washington, DC - USA**: With more than thirty supreme councils, the Supreme Council, Southern Jurisdiction, USA showed all its political influence by providing delegates of the delegations with an official visit to the White House, with reception and photos with President Reagan and his wife.[81] Three years later, in February 1988, the Sovereign Grand Commanders of the two US Supreme Councils would give Reagan the title of Honorary Member of the Scottish Rite.[82]

XIV. **1990, in Mexico City - Mexico**: In this conference, the 10 principles of the regularity of a Supreme Council were established, which serve as a basis for it to be recognized by others and accepted in international conferences. Many of these rules had already been approved at previous conferences, but from that conference on, it composes a compendium. Among them, the sovereignty of the Grand Lodges over the three first degrees, regularity of a Grand Lodge as having an impact on regularity in the High Degrees, and the need to prove the descent of a Supreme Council up to the Mother Supreme Council of the World.

XV. **1995, in Lausanne - Switzerland**: Held between May 29th and 31st, 1995, it was attended by delegations from 40 Supreme Councils, five of which were observers. The Credentials Committee needed to assess the situation of the two Supreme Councils in Colombia, suggesting that they should unify and elaborating a protocol of intentions for their Sovereign Grand Commanders. The Proposal Committee, chaired by the Sovereign Grand Commander of France, presented a proposal that prohibits a foreign Supreme Council from granting degrees to residents in another country without prior authorization from the Supreme Council of the country of residence, as well as from creating a new Supreme Council in an already occupied territory. This proposal faced opposition from the Supreme Council of the Southern Jurisdiction of the USA, as it understands that it violates the principle of sovereignty of the Supreme Councils, dividing opinions among the other Supreme Councils.

[xxv] Most intense period of the so-called "Lead Years" in Italy.

XVI. **2000, in Rio de Janeiro - Brazil**: It was the turn of the Wonderful City, where the headquarters of the third-largest Supreme Council in the world in terms of number of members[xxvi] is located, to receive an edition of the international conference, which had as its theme "Permanent fight against all forms of prejudice, to guarantee the establishment of universal peace in the third millennium ", and counted on delegations from 32 Supreme Councils.[83]

XVII. **2005, in Sydney - Australia**: In this first conference in Oceania, held from May 22 to 27, 2005, thirty Supreme Councils participated through their official delegations: Southern and Northern jurisdictions of the USA, Brazil, Canada, Mexico, France, Belgium, England, Portugal, Spain, Italy, Bulgaria, Romania, Germany, Netherlands, Austria, Greece, Turkey, Russia, Finland, Serbia and Montenegro (Observer), Israel, Argentina, Colombia, Paraguay, New Zealand, Iran (in exile), South Africa, Togo, and Australia. The theme of this conference was "Ancient and Accepted Scottish Rite: a vision for the future". The plenary approved the reaffirmation of the principle of regularity that, except for the USA and its two Supreme Councils, there can be only one Supreme Council considered regular by country.[84]

XVIII. **2010, in Toronto - Canada**: Held between May 22 and 26, 2010, it was attended by delegates from 31 Supreme Councils. The theme of the conference was "Whence and Whither, the Scottish Rite in your Jurisdiction". The Supreme Council of the Northern Masonic Jurisdiction of the USA presented a proposal to reaffirm the total independence and sovereignty of a Supreme Council as a principle of regularity, which was approved. The Supreme Council of England and Wales, on the other hand, presented two proposals that generated discussion and ended up being withdrawn: that every Supreme Council present at the conference has full participation rights (which would end the existing status of Observers); and recognition of Scandinavian Orders (like Swedish Rite) as part of the Ancient and Accepted Scottish Rite family.[85]

XIX. **2015, in Lisbon - Portugal**: More than 40 Supreme Councils present, with the central theme of "New Ways to a More

---

[xxvi] Behind only the Supreme Councils of the Southern Jurisdiction (1st) and the Northern Jurisdiction (2nd) of the USA.

Humane Future". Among the proposals, that of the Supreme Council of Russia, which requested that a Supreme Council in conflict with your country's regular Grand Lodge can maintain its position at the international conference if it counts with the recognition of a minimum of 20 other Supreme Councils, divided opinions. Based on the principle that the decisions of the conference have no binding effect, the proposal was voted and disapproved.[86]

XX. **2020, in Asunción - Paraguay**. The COVID-19 pandemic postponed its realization.

The structure of the international Conference of Supreme Councils was developed during its editions and works through committees formed by representatives of the different Supreme Councils that make up the conference:

- **Commission of Places and Dates**: evaluates the proposals for venues for the next editions.
- **Credentials Committee (for Recognition)**: examines the credentials of the registered delegations, whether or not they authorize participation in the plenary sessions.
- **History Committee**: coordinates the work of confirming the date of the constitution of the Supreme Councils. This is important because the disposition of the delegations and their pronouncements follow the order of seniority of its Supreme Councils.
- **Proposals Committee**: filters the proposals presented by the Supreme Councils, defining which ones will be voted in the plenary.

Still, it adopted a custom of the Sovereign Grand Commander of the Supreme Council that hosts the event to be elected President of the International Conference when it opens, maintaining this status until the occasion of the next conference, when a new president takes over.

Currently, each conference adopts a central theme, and adherents of the rite can, through their Supreme Councils, submit articles related to the theme. An official delegation of a Supreme Council can present a proposal related or not to the topic, which is previously evaluated by the respective committee to be voted or not in plenary.

As can be seen, some Supreme Councils stand out as protagonists in international conferences. The Supreme Council of Belgium, for example, was the first choice of the two oldest Supreme Councils, the "Mother Supreme Council of the World" (Southern Jurisdiction, USA) and that of France, to host the 1875 Congress. However, due to conflicts with Grand Lodge at the time, the Belgian Supreme Council declined the invitation, and the responsibility for realization fell to the Supreme Council of Switzerland, in Lausanne. And, after more than three decades of the trauma left by the Lausanne event, the Supreme Council of Belgium embraced the cause of rekindling the flame of the congregation of the Supreme Councils of the world, holding, in 1907, the 1st International Conference of Supreme Councils, in Brussels. After that, Brussels would help the conference in 1935, due to the political instability that prevented the edition of the event in Havana the previous year. And later it hosted the ninth conference, in 1967, this time having its 1966 edition in Paris canceled by the incident involving the Grand Lodge of France and the Supreme Council.

Then Lausanne, the French-speaking city of Switzerland, where the seat of the Supreme Council of Switzerland is located, in addition to being the seat of the watershed congress of 1875; hosted the third conference in 1922; and the 15th, in 1995.

This predominance of Belgium and Switzerland in the editions of the international conferences of the Supreme Councils may be related to the view of neutrality and internationality that the world has of these two countries. Brussels is the headquarters of the North Atlantic Treaty Organization - NATO and is considered the capital of the European Union, where many of its bodies are based. Switzerland, on the other hand, has the "global city" of Geneva, home to United Nations Educational, Scientific and Cultural Organization - UNESCO, the Red Cross, and several UN bodies. Geneva and Lausanne are in the French-speaking region of Switzerland, and only 40 miles away from each other.

The city of Washington, District of Columbia, in the United States, is another one that also hosted three editions of the International Supreme Council conferences: 1912, 1961, and 1985. As the home of the one who was the creator of the international conferences and the most well-known name of the Ancient and Accepted Scottish Rite, Albert Pike; and the definitive seat of the Mother Supreme Council of the World; its prestige is easy to understand.

Then there is the Supreme Council of France, which held two international conferences in Paris: 1929 and 1980; and the Supreme Council of the Northern Masonic Jurisdiction of the USA, which held an edition in Boston, in 1939, and another in Indianapolis, in 1975.

It is interesting to note that protagonism as the venue for the international conference editions is prevalent among some of the oldest Supreme Councils in the world: the two Supreme Councils of the USA, France, and Belgium. The four are among the five oldest still in operation, with only the Supreme Council of Spain, founded in 1811 and the third oldest, never hosting an international conference.[xxvii] This may explain why the order of seniority has become such a strategic variable, to the point that there is a committee that investigates the dates of the constitution of the supreme councils.

In the last decades, an attempt was made to rotate, initially between the American and European continents, and later covering Supreme Councils from other regions that applied, as was the case in Australia, in 2005. But this is not a rule. and the lobby of the interested supreme council is still what counts. This seems to be the case with the Supreme Council of Paraguay, which a few years ago was the center of a schism in the Symbolic Grand Lodge of Paraguay. It sewed support to place Asunción as host of the 2020 conference, to the detriment of other older South American Supreme Councils that also never hosted an edition of the international conference, such as Peru, Venezuela, and Argentina.

There is historical support for this reasoning. The Supreme Council for France, hosting the 1980 Conference, a few years after its creation, consolidated its foreign relations vis-à-vis its local competitor. The Brazilian Supreme Council, which had a local competitor in friendship with one of its neighbors, the Supreme Council of Paraguay, reversed this situation when it hosted the 2000 conference, from which the Paraguayan Supreme Council did not want to be left out, but had to break relations with the irregular Brazilian Supreme Council to be invited.

Finally, two points draw more attention, when analyzing almost twenty editions of the International Conference of Supreme Councils, in more than 100 years:

The first is the feeling of gradual abandonment of the debate on the themes inherent in the Scottish Rite. The preservation of its history, rituals, and symbols; better understanding of his teachings; the development of Masonic education in its different forms, in the face of new technologies; the international exchange of information and knowledge regarding successful programs and projects; the search for universal modes of recognition; all relevant topics, some of which boosted the holding of the first conferences, have been avoided. It has been replaced by external, generic, and conciliatory themes, such as

[xxvii] Which is justified by the period of almost forty years that the Supreme Council of Spain remained in exile in Mexico.

universal peace and humanitarianism, which can be discussed by any group of people and which do not offer practical results.

The second point is the observation that, in this 21st century, even after more than one hundred years of conferences, the issue of regularity and recognition has not been exhausted and is still an issue for proposals and debates. Discussing rules of entry and exit, in a system that for over two hundred years has had a clear and indisputable rule that there can only be one Supreme Council per country, except for the USA, reveals a rear Masonic position in Masonic inter-organizational relations by a system that was once its pioneer. In comparison, the Grand Lodges, in a more complex scenario of origin, practice, and jurisdiction, have more recent confederations and conferences and with the issue of regularity and recognition is better established and regulated.

Thus, the conferences have proved to be staged for international relations between the Supreme Councils, providing opportunities that result in new recognition treaties; however, they have great potential to initiate Masonic transformations on a world scale.

4. UNVEILING THE DEGREES OF SCOTTISH RITE

In this chapter, the degrees of the Scottish Rite, from the first to the thirty-third, will be explored, one by one, sequentially, to identify the chronological position of the legend presented, summarizing its plot, revealing its main symbols and understanding the moral exposed or veiled in it.

It is important to clarify that, as previously informed, the Scottish Rite did not originally have symbolic degrees. Furthermore, the differences between the first version of these rituals, of 1804, and that of 1829, for example, are already striking. A process of differentiation was even more intensified from there. Thus, the different approaches that, for example, the legend of the third degree can present in the countless versions of Scottish Rite Master's degree rituals throughout the world and over time, are significant.

In this sense, it was decided to adopt as a parameter the legendary structure present in the so-called Behring Ritual, of 1928. Three reasons justify this choice. The first is that similar to what happened in 1804, when the Supreme Council of France, through its Sovereign Grand Commander, Count de Grasse-Tilly, provided the ritual to the Grand Lodge that it had helped to create; the 1928 ritual was provided by the Supreme Council of Brazil, through its Sovereign Grand Commander, Mario Behring, to the Grand Lodges that he had helped to create. The second reason is that this is undoubtedly the most used A&ASR symbolic degree rituals in the world, practiced by more than one hundred thousand Freemasons. And the third reason is that this legendary structure is common to other rituals of the symbolic degrees of the A&ASR analyzed, with no considerable distinction in terms of legendary content.

For from 4th to 33rd degrees, the legends will be presented according to the revised Pike's ritual, currently used by the Supreme Council, Southern Jurisdiction, USA, having originally served as the basis for most versions adopted in the world, and which has as a characteristic a greater focus on allegories (legends) and less on ritualistic, which is consistent with the proposal of this work, codifying Masonic morals taught in the degrees of the Scottish Rite.

For direct biblical quotations, the King James Bible - 1611 was adopted. This is the faithful translation of the first bible translated from the Vulgate, by order of King James VI and I (VI of Scotland and I of England), originally published in the year 1611. The choice of this edition among the dozens available is because it is the oldest popular edition, the most used worldwide, and, mainly, due to the historical relationship of the Stuart Dynasty with the development of the Scottish Rite.

In time, as for symbology, it is not intended here to address all the symbols of each degree, given the countless number of symbols present in each one, some alien to the content of the degree. A Masonic dictionary of symbols is not part of the scope of this work. Besides, there are divergences between symbols in the different versions, as well as in its presentations, which would make this extra mission useless, if not impossible. For this reason, the targets will be the key symbols of each degree, which have survived the innovations of ritualists over the decades for being part of the context of the degree and its teachings.

4.1. The Blue Lodge and the Symbolic Degrees

Introduction to Symbolic Degrees

Symbolic degrees are a brother's first three Masonic steps. Symbolically, it represents the early years of the trajectory of a young man who was chosen to serve as an apprentice to the ancient craft of construction, during the construction of King Solomon's Temple; until the day when he, already a fellow worker and close to becoming a Master Mason, received news of the death of his Grand Master, Hiram Abiff.

The construction of the Temple was a pharaonic work, practically binational (Israel and Phoenicia), with a project that was then totally innovative, not only in its concept but also in its execution. Workers needed to respect strict rules, due to the nature of the work, while developing skills and techniques with different materials and an intense exchange of knowledge and professional experience, which would guarantee them a competitive advantage after becoming masters.

To be accepted as an apprentice in the craft of building was an honor and the hope of a future for many illiterate young people of humble origin. However, the initial feeling of joining the construction of the Temple as a way of guaranteeing a livelihood is transformed as the brother continues to work, listening to the wise masters, saying his prayers, and learning the first mysteries of the Royal Art. Over time, it becomes a feeling of deep respect and gratitude for the opportunity to collaborate with such an important work. The inputs received as payment for labor become secondary in comparison to the gift of knowledge, a non-perishable, inalienable, and immeasurable asset; and the satisfaction of serving God and others, which is the best job a man can do.

The symbolic degrees illustrate these early years of transformation, from a young man to a man; from an illiterate to a literate and knowledgeable about Sacred Geometry; from an apprentice to a master in a position to develop his projects and teach his craft to others.

1°: Apprentice

Though Masonry neither usurps the place of, nor rapes religion, prayer is an essential part of our ceremonies. It is the aspiration of the soul toward the Absolute and Infinite Intelligence, which is the One Supreme Deity, most feebly misunderstood and characterized as an "Architect". Certain faculties of man are directed toward the Unknown – thought, meditation, prayer. The unknown is an ocean, of which conscience is the compass. Thought, meditation, prayer, are the great mysterious positioning of the needle. It is a spiritual magnetism that thus connects the human soul with the Deity. These majestic irradiations of the soul pierce through the shadow toward the light.[87]

ALLEGORIC CHRONOLOGY:

The fourth year of Solomon's reign and the first year of construction of the Temple: approximately 962 BC.

LEGEND AND COMMENTS:

The legendary content of the degree basically remains the same as other rites: the candidate becomes an Apprentice in masonry during the construction of the King Solomon's Temple, in which he begins to abandon ignorance and learn to smooth out the rough stone, giving it cubic aspects. This learning takes years of dedication, in which he also learns to manage his time, between work and rest.

He does not receive a password because he does not have access to the Temple rooms, as he initially works in the quarries, learning how to cut the rough stones (with the mallet and the chisel and not with the common gavel) in the appropriate size for use in the Temple (with the 24-inch gauge).

A curiosity in this version, which has survived many versions, is the statement that "Freemasonry had its origin in the ancient Initiative Fraternities of Egypt".[88]

MORAL:

The belief in a Supreme Being: the second instruction of the Behring Ritual brings an interesting dialogue, which suggests that Freemasons are linked by the belief in a Supreme Being, the Great Architect of the Universe, who gave man the intelligence to discern right from wrong, just by following a moral, like that taught in Freemasonry. It is an enlightened vision. In a final section of the initiation, the newly initiated is called "investigator of the truth",[89] which is also in line with this Enlightenment inspiration.

It is also said in the ritual that the duties of a Freemason are "to honor and venerate the Gr.'. Arch.'. of the Worlds"[90] and that the Freemason has the attributes of Faith, Perseverance, and Devotion. Thus, the moral transformation of the symbolic illiterate and materialistic young man begins with the reinforcement of that which is the first and main dogma adopted by Freemasonry: the belief in a Supreme Being.

SYMBOLOGY:

The 24-inch gauge, the mallet, and the chisel. The 24-inch gauge alludes to the 24 hours of the day, teaching the apprentice to know how to accurately measure the time for work and physical and spiritual rest. The mallet would be a symbol of work with the use of skill and reason, while the chisel would be the precision achieved with education and perseverance. The union of instruments and its meanings, that is, time management to properly carry out work with education and perseverance, results in knowledge. And the Behring Ritual further states that knowledge overcomes any difficulty and extinguishes the darkness of ignorance.[91]

BIBLICAL PASSAGE:

Behold, how good and how pleasant it is for brethren to dwell together in unity!

It is like the precious ointment upon the head, that ran down upon the beard, even Aaron's beard: that went down to the skirts of his garments;

As the dew of Hermon, and as the dew that descended upon the mountains of Zion: for there the Lord commanded the blessing, even life for evermore.

Psalm, 133:1-3.

2°: Fellow craft

Do not lose sight, then, of the true object of your studies in Masonry. It is to add to your estate of wisdom, and not merely to your knowledge. A man may spend a lifetime in studying a single specialty of knowledge, - botany, conchology, or entomology, for instance, - in committing to memory names derived from the Greek, and classifying and reclassifying; and yet be no wiser than when he began. It is the great truths as to all that most concerns a man, as to his rights, interests, and duties, that Masonry seeks to teach her Initiates.[92]

ALLEGORIC CHRONOLOGY:

Five years after the previous degree, that is, after the construction of the Temple began.

LEGEND AND COMMENTS:

That poor and ignorant candidate who became an Apprentice, in such a short time already shows signs of evolution, because of his work, acquiring knowledge, and demonstrations of morals and virtue. He has already gone halfway, standing between the darkness he was in and the light of the Master's degree, between the profane ignorance and the wisdom of Solomon, between the life of errors he experienced and the virtues he tried to practice, between the rough stone that he worked as an Apprentice and the possibility of developing his construction project as a Master Mason; and this environment in which he finds himself is like the midday of his life, in which, for a certain moment, it is not known whether he is in the morning or the afternoon. It is a brief phase of indecision, in one eye he sees the future, while the other one is still trapped in the past.

While the candidate, at the time of his initiation in the first degree of the A&ASR blue lodge, faced physical tests, to prove he was fit to work as an Apprentice; the Apprentice must prove his knowledge (science) and his morals to become a Fellow craft. Thus, the knowledge of Royal Art, related to the proper use of work tools, is related to the moral teaching symbolized through each of these:

- 1st. Travel: the mallet and the chisels are the wills and the moral;
- 2nd. Travel: the compass and the 24-inch gauge are wisdom and righteousness;
- 3rd. Travel: the lever is the courage of the right man and his power when used intelligently;
- 4th. Travel: the square is the faultless conduct and the equity given to all;

- 5th. Travel: the sword in the heart is the search for Truth, the doubtful situation that the Fellow craft finds himself between the material (Apprentice) and the spiritual (Master).

Besides, the Fellow craft learns about the symbolism of the number five and begins to receive it as a symbolic salary. The flap of his apron is lowered, informing him that, as a fellow craft, he will use his apron like this to symbolize a bag, where he will take the necessary tools for the work (related to the virtues he must take with him). In the end, he is told that when he goes up the spiral staircase, he will see the Blazing Star.

Finally, in the instructions, the Fellow has access to the precious content of his degree. At first, he learns about the legend of his password and the degree panel. In the second, on the letter G and the Blazing Star, and in the third, about Numerical Symbology.

MORAL:

Persistence. This is the main teaching of this degree. One should not give up or retreat. The work of thinning the character, of moral and social construction, needs to continue. The fellow craft needs, as the ritual rightly states, "*to establish a moral code for the improvement of your soul, so that your actions in life are devoted to the maintenance of social order and the happiness of your fellow men*". And for that, the Fellow craft must have the willpower and follow straight (gauge), even if the paths are winding (spiral staircase).

SYMBOLOGY:

The Blazing Star. One of the most well-known Masonic triads is that of the attributes necessary for all work: Strength, Will, and Intelligence. Without these three attributes together, it is not possible to do any work; and each A&ASR blue lodge degree, in a certain way, collaborates symbolically for the best development of one of these attributes: Strength (Apprentice), Will (Fellow craft), and Intelligence (Master).

The Blazing Star, as the ritual refers, is a symbol of the Will, because it speaks of the importance of having a "burning focus", a "devotion without reservations". In this sense, the ritual justifies the choice of the Blazing Star, which shines not only at night, but also during the day, which would be related to the need to apply the Will both on Science and on Morality.

BIBLICAL PASSAGE:

Thus he shewed me: and, behold, the Lord stood upon a wall made by a plumbline, with a plumbline in his hand.

And the Lord said unto me, Amos, what seest thou? And I said, A plumbline. Then said the Lord, behold, I will set a plumbline in the midst of my people Israel: I will not again pass by them any more.

Amos, 7:7-8.

3°: Master

Morality is a force. It is the magnetic attraction of the heart toward Truth and Virtue. The needle, imbued with this mystic property, and pointing unerringly to the north, carries the mariner safely over the trackless ocean, through storm and darkness, until his glad eyes behold the beneficence beacons that welcome him to safe and hospitable harbor. Then the hearts of those who love him are gladdened, and his home made happy; and this gladness and happiness are due to the silence, unostentatious, unerring monitor that was the sailor's guide over the weltering waters.[93]

ALLEGORIC CHRONOLOGY:

Almost seven years after the construction of the Temple began.

LEGEND AND COMMENTS:

In Behring's version, raising of Master Mason is explicitly declared as a retelling of the legend of Osiris, which keeps the mysteries of the afterlife. Three fellows craft who were brothers in blood ambushed the Grand Master of the construction of the Temple, Hiram Abiff, to learn the word of the Master, to go to other nations and be received as such, gaining better salaries. In the face of Hiram's unwavering resistance, they ended up murdering him, burying his body in a shallow grave, marked by an acacia branch.

The following day, the absence of Hiram Abiff creates turmoil among the workers. King Solomon then orders a call for workers to be made to identify whether there were more missing. The three brothers, J...a, J...o and J...um, who already had a bad reputation, are not present.

With a bad feeling, King Solomon orders his guards (not identified as characters) to lead search teams. Upon returning from Joppa, the Senior Warden gives his testimony to King Solomon, narrating how his detachment heard the lamentations of those three murderous fellows in a cave near the port, surrendering and presenting them for trial.

King Solomon condemns the three to death, ordering them to be executed outside the city walls. Then he leaves with the other fellows and guards in search of Hiram Abiff's grave, intending to recover his body and give him a grave befitting his honor and position.

When King Solomon found the grave, marked by a branch of green acacia stuck in the scrambled earth, and when he dug up the body, it was found that it was already in a state of putrefaction, being necessary to use the five points of perfection to raise the body.

As can be seen in the study of the following degrees, this version of the raising to Master Mason adopted in many editions of the A&ASR blue lodge degrees, perhaps influenced by other rites and rituals such as those originated in the United Kingdom, which ends up invading elements proper to the plot of subsequent degrees, in especially those among from the 4th to the 10th degree, when narrating, even inconsistently with the next degrees, the order of the facts involving the search, capture, trial, and conviction of the three murderers. This version, in one of the instructions, goes so far as to discreetly reveal the important secret revealed only in the 13th degree.

MORAL:

Balance. This is the great lesson of the raising to Master Mason. The search for a balance between the material and the spiritual, between reason and heart, between strength and beauty, between virtue and wisdom. Like a portico supported by two columns, it is impossible to give up one or strengthen one at the expense of the other. A Master knows this very well.

Besides, there is a commitment to Masonic relief, born from the raising of the body, also symbolizing that the brethren must be willing to help a brother who suffers a fall. In this sense, the degree materializes this commitment with the granting of a sign for help.

SYMBOLOGY:

The green branch of acacia, a symbol of survival after death, refers to the dogma of the Immortality of the Soul.

BIBLICAL PASSAGE:

Remember now thy Creator in the days of thy youth, while the evil days come not, nor the years draw nigh, when thou shalt say, I have no pleasure in them;

Then shall the dust return to the Earth as it was: and the spirit shall return unto God who gave it.

Ecclesiastes, 12:1/7.

Symbolic Degrees Considerations

At first glance, symbolic degrees may appear to convey basic, primary, or even shallow moral teachings. In a way, this superficial reading may be a consequence of the fragility in which the allegory of operative construction work appears in some versions; however, it does not correspond with the truth.

In the symbolic (blue lodge) degrees of the A&ASR, there is the core of Masonic morality, whose adopted dogmas are those advocated in Rousseau's concept of civil religion, originally published in his collection known as The Social Contract in 1762. Rousseau believed that the minimum creed of a good citizen was the belief in a Supreme Being and the Immortality of the Soul, and there is also the need for belief in some mechanism of final judgment that would guarantee the punishment of errors.[94]

While the Apprentice degree is dedicated to the first and main dogma, that of belief in a Supreme Being, in Freemasonry called the Great Architect of the Universe, which is why Freemasons can consider themselves as brothers; the second dogma adopted by Freemasonry, the Immortality of the Soul, is a lesson veiled in the legend of the third degree. In the High Degrees, it will be observed that this mechanism for judging the concept of civil religion is well explored, either in the form of what Pike called the "Law of Retribution" (law of cause and effect) or in the form of final judgment.

In this way, all Masonic morality is limited to these two pillars of Masonic dogmas, the belief in a Supreme Being and the Immortality of the Soul. Thus, in Masonic morality, there is an eminently theistic morality, the most elementary principles of which are immutable. That is why Freemasonry must preserve its formulas, to teach and remind men of such principles, regardless of the changes that the world accepts.

The first degree calls on the apprentice to dedicate himself persistently to his moral and intellectual development while remembering that he must know how to manage his time and seek a balance between rest and work. In the second degree, the fellow craft is invited to treat everyone with equity (level), to act according to his moral law (plumb), and to follow a straight path (gauge), even if the path is winding (spiral staircase). Persistence is charged once more, this time in the form of Will. In the Master's degree, faith and hope for future life are inculcated through the allegory of Hiram's martyrdom.

The brothers who make the happy decision to continue their studies beyond the third degree quickly understand that there is no need to talk about Masonic fullness, or to arrive at the end of the journey with it. This is because the third degree, even though it is the highest granted in a blue lodge, the base cell of Freemasonry, allegorically ends its work with the Lost Word, the dead Grand Master, and the unfinished Temple.

Grief cannot be eternal. The Grand Master needs to be replaced, the word found and the Temple completed (more than once, as is known). Symbolically, the moral construction of the Freemason is unfinished, and, being in a School of Morals, this construction needs to be completed. So, he still needs to find his Truth (True Word), be the Grand Master of his own life, and help guide those who are in darkness towards the path of light.

4.2. The Lodge of Perfection and the Ineffable Degrees

Introduction to Ineffable Degrees

In Lodge of Perfection, the first Masonic body of the so-called High Degrees, are granted from the 4th to the 14th degrees, which are known as Ineffable Degrees. The name of the body and the degrees, Perfection and Ineffable, although it refers to all degrees of this group, is related especially to the content of the last one that composes it, the 14th, also called Degree of Perfection and its members of Perfect Elu (Chosen).

The allegory of the 14th degree, the main one among the Ineffable Degrees and that therefore names them, is related to the Ineffable Name of God, which justifies the adoption of the name. The word ineffable means that something is inexpressible, unspeakable, that is, unable to be pronounced.

In the case of God, His ineffable name means the confirmation of some of His main attributes: omnipotence, omnipresence, and omniscience. This is because being the only God, He does not need to be named, and; being present everywhere and knowing about everything that goes on, He does not need to be called.

With an unpronounceable name, the Jews referred to Him by titles, such as Elohim (The Authority), El Shaddai (The Almighty), and the most common among them, Adonai (Lord). Only a chosen few knew the correct pronunciation of the name of God, like Enoch and Moses. In the case of Moses, he passed it on to his High Priest, so that he could pass it on to his successors and the kings of Israel.

The writing of the name, however, was known to every literate Jew, who just did not know how to pronounce it. This is because the original Hebrew was a language written only with consonants, by which the reader needs to know the word orally to pronounce it.[xxviii] Paralleling our current situation, we also do a little bit of this in our texts through conversation apps: BTW = by the way, BRB = be right back, TBT = throwback thursday, etc.

Supposedly, the name is written with four Hebrew letters (tetragrammaton), from right to left, corresponding, from left to right, with the letters YHVH in our alphabet, which makes dozens of possible combinations with the existing vowels.

The legends that make up the ineffable degrees present an interesting version of the events after the death of Grand Master Hiram Abiff until the discovery of the Lost Word, and the completion of the construction of the Temple. Thus, the ineffable degrees can be considered as Hiramic degrees, by the direct relationship of its legends with the legend of the Third Degree, whose plot is concluded in the 14th degree that, in a way, completes it perfectly, symbolized by the perfect circle of the ring of the degree, stamping the word that had been lost and everything that it represents.

[xxviii] Currently, there are so-called massoretic points that indicate vowels.

4°: Secret Master

If you will advance, gird up your loins for the struggle! For the way is long and toilsome. Pleasure, all smiles, will beckon you on the one hand, and Indolence will invite you to sleep among the flowers, upon the other. Prepare, by secrecy, obedience, and fidelity, to resist the allurements of both![95]

ALLEGORIC CHRONOLOGY:

In sequence to the previous degree, the day after the finding of the body of Hiram Abiff, at 07:00 AM in the morning.

LEGEND AND COMMENTS:

King Solomon chooses seven men to guard the mysteries of the Holy of Holies, which only priests and Levites were allowed to approach. As is known, Hiram Abiff died in an ambush for not revealing a secret (the word, then lost), and now King Solomon takes this strange initiative, as a way of protecting the secrets veiled in the Holy of Holies; therefore, it can be assumed that the secret kept by Hiram Abiff may, in some way, be kept in the Holy of Holies. This is reinforced by the degree lecture in some versions, which mentions that the Master's Word was lost with the death of Hiram, but that one day it can be recovered. King Solomon also orders Adoniram to arrange for the construction of a black and white mausoleum in honor of Hiram Abiff.

These seven are entrusted with guarding the Holy of Holies but are not allowed to enter. That is, they must keep something that they do not know what it is.

MORAL:

Secrecy and Loyalty. It is mainly about loyalty to duty, even with the risk of death, as happened with Hiram Abiff. One can understand this loyalty to duty as to serve, both to the neighbor and the country. To serve, it is not necessary to know everything, because there is the so-called "benefit of the doubt", whereby you believe that that order received has worthy reasons, even if, perhaps, unknown to you.

Imagine a soldier called up for war. He may not know what motivated his president to decide for the war, but he gives his leaders the benefit of the doubt, believing that such a decision, to put his life on the line, had been made for the right reasons. The attitude of enlisting, attending military service and serving, is a reflection of the love for the country. This love is extended by the Scottish Rite to others, just as the benefit of the doubt is a consequence of it. When someone asks you for something, what is your reaction? To judge? Delay? Or serve?

While, until that period, the Levites were the ones who could render services in that sacred place, the death of Hiram Abiff caused King Solomon to change that rule. Heredity (born in the Levi tribe), that is, the caste system, gave way to meritocracy, with zeal, loyalty, and constancy as criteria. From the seven men chosen to keep the secrets, that "love for the cause" was sought, without waiting for an advantage or reward.

SYMBOLOGY:

The main symbol of the fourth degree is the ivory key, considered the jewel of the degree. The ivory key is a symbol of the "key to the mysteries" and symbolizes that the Secret Master is given the key to the mysteries veiled in the high degrees of the Scottish Rite. It also dates back to the symbolic role of the Secret Master, guardian of the Holy of Holies. Nowadays, in a way, it is as if the Lodge of Perfection, upon receiving the brother for the first time at his entrance door (4th degree), said to him: "Welcome! Here is a copy of the key. Feel at home!".

BIBLICAL PASSAGE:

Then Solomon assembled the elders of Israel, and all the heads of the tribes, the chief of the fathers of the children of Israel, unto King Solomon in Jerusalem, that they might bring up the ark of the covenant of the Lord out of the city of David which is Zion.

And all the men of Israel assembled themselves unto King Solomon at the feast in the month Ethanim which is the seventh month.

And all the elders of Israel came, and the priests took up the ark.

And they brought up the ark of the Lord, and the tabernacle of the congregation, and all the holy vessels that were in the tabernacle, even those did the priests and the Levites bring up.

And King Solomon, and all the congregation of Israel, that were assembled unto him, were with him before the ark, sacrificing sheep and oxen, that could not be told nor numbered for multitude.

And the priests brought in the ark of the covenant of the Lord unto his place, into the oracle of the house, to the most holy place, even under the wings of the cherubim.

1 Kings, 8:1-6.

5°: Perfect Master

It is a vast work that any man may do, if he never be idle: and it is a huge way that a man may go in virtue, if he never go out of his way by a vicious habit or a great crime: and he who perfectually reads good books, if his parts be answerable, will have a huge stock of knowledge.[96]

ALLEGORIC CHRONOLOGY:

Following the previous degree, twelve days after King Solomon ordered the construction of the Hiram's mausoleum.

LEGEND AND COMMENTS:

Adoniram manages to carry out the order of King Solomon, to build the mausoleum of Hiram Abiff, in nine days. Three days later, the funeral ceremony in his tribute was conducted by King Solomon, with the assistance of Adoniram and Zabud, and assistance from Zerbal and Stolkin.[xxix] King Hiram of Tyre also makes a point of being present to pay his honor to his dear compatriot. During the ceremony, Zabud talks to King Solomon, his friend, about life and death. In the Bible, more precisely in 1 Kings, Zabud is briefly mentioned as the son of Nathan (the prophet), chief officer (something corresponding to a general), and a friend of King Solomon. The ceremony is symbolically closed on the fifth hour of the afternoon, with the sun already signaling for the night.

MORAL:

Death and Family. Perfect Master is invited to reflect on the uncertainty of life and, when facing the certainty of death, he is reminded of the pecuniary responsibilities before the family. At this point, it is important to consider that the Masonic affiliation itself means, among many other things, an extension of the concept of family, considered its fraternal character. Thus, this responsibility falls not only on the Freemason's home but also on that of his freemason brothers. The degree of Perfect Master is also a call to the conscience of the brothers' responsibility for the orphaned nephews.

As this life is short and fleeting, Scottish Rite suggests that the only thing left behind is good deeds; therefore, honesty and work should prevail over idleness, and no Freemason should receive wages that are not due to him. Hiram Abiff was a great example of an honest worker and that is why he was honored by everyone, from kings to apprentices. He was the Perfect Master, not us. Let us imitate his example.

SYMBOLOGY:

[xxix] In the French version there is no mention of Zabud. It is Stolkin who leads the reflections.

A cinerary urn, a symbol of death, and a branch of acacia, a symbol of the immortality of the soul, are the most striking symbols of this degree. Its coat of arms is illustrated by a cubic stone, which refers to the idea of perfection.

BIBLICAL PASSAGE:

And King Solomon raised a levy out of all Israel; and the levy was thirty thousand men.
And he sent them to Lebanon, ten thousand a month by courses: a month they were in Lebanon, and two months at home: and Adoniram was over the levy.
And Solomon had threescore and ten thousand that bare burdens, and fourscore thousand hewers in the mountains;
Beside the chief of Solomon's officers which were over the work, three thousand and three hundred, which ruled over the people that wrought in the work.
And the king commanded, and they brought great stones, costly stones, and hewed stones, to lay the foundation of the house.
5:18And Solomon's builders and Hiram's builders did hew them, and the stonesquarers: so they prepared timber and stones to build the house.
I Kings, 5:13-18.

6°: Intimate Secretary

(...) first controlling your own temper, and governing your own passions, you fit yourself to keep peace and harmony among other men, and especially the brethren. Above all remember that Masonry is the realm of Peace, and that "among Masons there must be no dissension, but only that noble emulation, which can best work and best agree".

> Wherever there is strife and hatred among the brethren, there is no Masonry; for Masonry is Peace, and Brotherly Love, and Concord.[97]

ALLEGORIC CHRONOLOGY:

Following the previous degree, during the brief stay of King Hiram of Tyre as a guest of King Solomon, after the tribute to Hiram Abiff.

LEGEND AND COMMENTS:[xxx]

King Hiram of Tyre takes advantage of his presence in Israel, on the occasion of the tribute to Hiram Abiff, to visit the cities and fields in Galilee promised by King Solomon as payment for the human and material resources provided for the construction of the Temple. Disappointed by what he sees, he quickly returns to Jerusalem, to King Solomon's palace, and enters the courtroom, with hard and hurried steps, without waiting to be properly announced. His face is charged with rage.

King Solomon, still in mourning for Hiram Abiff, is alone, with only his Captain of the Guard, Zerbal, in his post at the western door, far enough away to not see and hear what may happen there. From the anteroom, Zabud watches King Hiram of Tyre enter the courtroom and the apparent state he was in. Aware that King Solomon was alone, he feared for his safety and decided to discreetly enter the courtroom and hide in a position close to the throne, so that he could defend his king from possible attack.

During the hearing, Hiram of Tyre, a little nervous, tells that he passed through the cities and fields that Solomon had promised as payment for the human and material resources provided by Tyre for the construction of the Temple, and he felt deceived, for the state it was in was not worth what was owed to him.

While speaking, King Hiram of Tyre notices the presence of a hidden intruder in the room, revealing his presence and, when judging him as someone curious or a spy, yells at the guards to arrest and punish him.

At that moment, the Captain of the Guard, when approaching the East, argues with King Hiram of Tyre in favor of Zabud, explaining that

---

[xxx] It is interesting to note the similarity of this legend with that of the Elected Master's degree of the Cryptic Masonry (York Rite).

Zabud voluntarily sought to protect his king from a possible rage. It was not curiosity or espionage, but fervor and zeal for his friend, King Solomon.

King Hiram of Tyre appears somewhat embarrassed by the situation, while King Solomon introduces Zabud to him as his close, always devoted, and loyal friend. King Solomon also reports that he intended to rebuild the cities and plant the fields before handing it over as payment.

Calmer and more enlightened, King Hiram of Tyre sees that he had rushed and let himself be carried away by wrath. He decides to renew the covenant with Solomon and both commit to taking care that it is eternal. Finally, they decide to choose Zabud as Intimate Secretary, replacing the deceased Hiram Abiff, who had served them as such.

MORAL:

Fervor and Zeal. Some believe that there is no better way to teach than by example, and the Scottish Rite legends explore this very well. This time, the example is in Zabud's fervor (commitment, dedication) and zeal (care) towards his friend and king, Solomon. The Scottish Rite, to that degree, calls on its Intimate Secretaries to act in the same way for the cause of Freemasonry and all just causes to be embraced. A Freemason must be committed to his work, be it his profession, or to family, neighbor, and God (volunteer work, like Freemasonry). He must care for the people around him and the institutions to which he belongs.

Another lesson to be learned with this degree is the search for self-control, not letting a negative feeling speak louder than reason or guide your thoughts, words, and actions. The legend also reinforces that golden rule, the Benefit of Doubt, to avoid hasty judgments, such as that of King Hiram of Tyre, when passing through the cities and fields promised by Solomon, without knowing his intention to improve before handing it over.

SYMBOLOGY:

The triple delta or triple triangle is the jewel of that degree. It appears in the shape of three triangles intertwined in some versions of the coat of arms, merging the three into a triangle, with one end of each touching the other, in the versions of the degree jewel. In the case of jewelry, there are versions in which the triangles are engraved, each with

Phoenician letters, Hebrew letters, or symbols of the sun, moon, and mercury.

Some authors argue that these recordings signify the three theological virtues: Faith, Hope, and Charity. Others claim to be the Sun, the Moon, and the Worshipful Master. And there are still those who claim to be King Solomon, King Hiram of Tyre, and Hiram Abiff. Considering the Phoenician letters,[xxxi] present in the oldest rituals, the most plausible theory is that it is the initials of Alliance, Promise, and Perfection (perfect conclusion or fulfillment). These three words would summarize the outcome of the degree, to which Hiram of Tyre and Solomon renew the alliance, committing each one to fulfill its parts to guarantee the perpetuity of the agreement. So, too, the the relationship (alliance) between the Freemason and Freemasonry, in which the Freemason swore oaths (promises), to which he must seek the strictest fulfillment (perfection).

BIBLICAL PASSAGE:

And it came to pass at the end of twenty years, when Solomon had built the two houses, the house of the Lord, and the king's house.

(Now Hiram the king of Tyre had furnished Solomon with cedar trees and fir trees, and with gold, according to all his desire) that then King Solomon gave Hiram twenty cities in the land of Galilee.

And Hiram came out from Tyre to see the cities which Solomon had given him; and they pleased him not.

And he said, What cities are these which thou hast given me, my brother? And he called them the land of Cabul unto this day.

And Hiram sent to the king six core talents of gold.

I Kings, 9:10-14.

[xxxi] Why Phoenician? Because Hiram of Tyre and Hiram Abiff were Phoenicians.

7°: Provost and Judge

Every wrong done by one man to another, whether it affect his person, his property, his happiness, or his reputation, is an offence against the law of justice. The field of this Degree is therefore a wide and vast one; and Masonry seeks for the most impressive mode of enforcing the law of justice, and the most effectual means of preventing wrong and injustice.[98]

ALLEGORIC CHRONOLOGY:

Following the previous degree, a few days after the departure of King Hiram of Tyre, who had renewed his alliance with King Solomon.

LEGEND AND COMMENTS:

The temple is still unfinished and the work is being delayed. Conflicts among workers are more and more frequent, mainly due to the absence of the charismatic and conciliatory leadership of the late Grand Master, Hiram Abiff. To make up for that absence, King Solomon appointed seven Provosts and Judges who would form a court, to meet in the Middle Chamber of the Temple and carry out conciliation and judgments when necessary. They were to judge Phoenicians and Jews without distinction and the court records would be filed and locked in an ebony box.

There are versions in which Chief Provost is Titus, Prince of Harodim, for being the oldest of the seven. The court would also have personages like Adoniram and his father. It is a legacy of the French version.

In Pike's version and many others, the chief of the court is Azarias, who is the son of Nathan (Nathan was Solomon's brother) and brother of Zabud (general and friend of the king). Zabud also having been chosen and appointed by the king as Provost and Judge. In other words, the "president" of the court and one of the other six members were the king's nephews. This choice of characters proved to be useful, since, in this case, the legend of this version says that Naboth tries to convince Zabud to favor him before the court, in the name of the friendship they have. Thus, he implies that Zabud himself had been favored with the appointment as Provost and Judge, for his friendship with the king, and that it would not hurt to pass the favor on, favoring a friend now. Zabud, offended, loses patience with Naboth.

MORAL:

Justice, Impartiality, and Equity. These are the teachings of the Provost and Judge degree. Freemasons must always act justly, listen impartially, and decide fairly. Thus, a Freemason must always seek to be fair in his dealings with other people, never seeking to benefit at the expense of others. You should listen and dialogue impartially when, in a leadership position, you are mediating a conflict or discussion between two brothers (regardless of friendship, closeness, or affinity that you have more or less with one of them). Finally, it will ensure that any decision to be made is proportional to the issue under analysis.

SYMBOLOGY:

A golden key illustrates the jewel as well as the coat of arms of the degree. This is the key to the ebony box, where the records of the cases considered by the court of Provosts and Judges were kept. It symbolizes the discretion that the Freemason must maintain regarding the confidences made by friends and brothers. Another important symbol of the degree, present in its coat of arms along with the key, is the balance, referring to justice.

BIBLICAL PASSAGE:

> *Judges and officers shalt thou make thee in all thy gates, which the LORD thy God giveth thee, throughout thy tribes: and they shall judge the people with just judgment.*
>
> *Thou shalt not wrest judgment; thou shalt not respect persons, neither take a gift: for a gift doth blind the eyes of the wise, and pervert the words of the righteous.*
>
> *That which is altogether just shalt thou follow, that thou mayest live, and inherit the land which the LORD thy God giveth thee.*
>
> Deuteronomy, 16:18-20.

8°: Intendant of the Building

A Mason's contentedness must by no means be a mere contented selfishness, like his who, comfortable himself, is indifferent to the discomfort of others. There will always be in this world wrongs to forgive, suffering to alleviate, sorrow asking for sympathy, necessities and destitution to relieve, and ample occasion for the exercise of active charity and beneficence.[99]

ALLEGORIC CHRONOLOGY:

Following the previous degree, a few days after the creation of the court of Provosts and Judges.

LEGEND AND COMMENTS:

The absence of Grand Master Hiram Abiff, and consequently his final plans and experience in directing and controlling the hierarchy of workers, ended up paralyzing the construction workers of the Temple, still unfinished. King Solomon, unable to find a skilled successor to complete the Herculean mission on his own, listened to the advice of the prophet Sadoc and of Ahishar, his steward, and appointed five builders who had been pupils of Hiram Abiff as intendants. One of them would serve as superintendant (Adoniram), and each of the other four would be the intendant of an architecture and construction department: brass (Yehu, Phoenician), wood (Stolkin, Jew), stone (Zelec, Phoenician), and gold (Gareb, Jew).[xxxii]

Upon taking them in, King Solomon orders them to follow the illustrious example of Hiram Abiff, his precious teachings, and, above all, two of his most evident precepts: benevolence towards all and charity towards the needy.

MORAL:

Benevolence and Charity. Although each intendant takes on an architecture and construction department, which leads to technical and operational responsibilities, King Solomon makes it clear during his inauguration as to the nature and priority of the other responsibilities contracted. The moral responsibilities of the intendants over those they govern should be the primary objective of each intendant. The physical construction of the Lord's Temple cannot be done at the expense of social construction.

[xxxii] In the Brazilian version, as well as in the French, there are also five intendants, but they are not nominated. And each of the five is responsible for an Order of Architecture: Ionic, Doric, Corinthian, Tuscany and Composite. Pike's version, on the other hand, brings interesting information, which is the division of the 4 intendants under Adoniram into 2 Jews and 2 Phoenicians, considering the massive participation of Phoenician workers in the work.

When conflicts between workers broke out after the death of Grand Master Hiram Abiff, King Solomon hastened to create a court of Provosts and Judges to reconcile or judge them. This was the emergency solution to the crisis; however, in all his wisdom, King Solomon knew that the next step would be to prevent such conflicts, restoring not only the direction but especially the attention, support, and motivation the workers lacked.

It is not by chance that the motto of this degree in some versions is "one for all and all for one", a motto credited to the famous writer Alexandre Dumas (probable freemason). Benevolence is the goodwill and sincere generosity of the one who leads towards those under his command (one for all), while charity is the act of love for the needy neighbor (all for one). Benevolence is the mortar of social construction, while charity is that of moral construction. A material temple without these foundations, however beautiful, will be forever empty.

SYMBOLOGY:

The scale, this time not as a symbol of justice, but of balance, in the sense of constancy, stability, and harmony, which is what an Intendant of the Building is expected to promote among his workers, thus also achieving a balance between material construction (professional work, matter) and social construction (volunteering, ethic).

BIBLICAL PASSAGE:

And Solomon the son of David was strengthened in his kingdom, and the Lord his God was with him, and magnified him exceedingly.

Then Solomon spake unto all Israel, to the captains of thousands and of hundreds, and to the judges, and to every governor in all Israel, the chief of the fathers.

So Solomon, and all the congregation with him, went to the high place that was at Gibeon; for there was the tabernacle of the congregation of God, which Moses the servant of the Lord had made in the wilderness.

But the ark of God had David brought up from Kirjathjearim to the place which David had prepared for it: for he had pitched a tent for it at Jerusalem.

II Chronicles, 1:1-4.

9°: Elu of the Nine

(...)defend weakness against strength, the friendless against the great, the oppressed against the oppressor! Be ever vigilant and watchful of the interests and honor of your country! and may the Grand Architect of the Universe give you that strength and wisdom which shall enable you well and faithfully to perform these high duties![100]

ALLEGORIC CHRONOLOGY:

In sequence to the previous degree, a few days after the inauguration of the Intendants of the Building.

LEGEND AND COMMENTS:

This degree deals with the discovery of the whereabouts and punishment of the first of Hiram Abiff's three assassins. It is the first among the high degrees of A&ASR criticized by some authors, especially those linked to the Rectified Scottish Rite - RER, for being considered "degrees of revenge". In this sense, Albert Pike recorded his discomfort with the situation faced by the ninth degree:

> Innovators and inventors overturned that primitive simplicity. Ignorance engaged in the work of making Degrees, and trifles and gewgaws and pretended mysteries, absurd or hideous, usurped the place of Masonic Truth. **The picture of a horrid vengeance, the poniard and the bloody head, appeared in the peaceful Temple of Masonry**, without sufficient explanation of their symbolic meaning (emphasis added).[101]

Here is an observation: in most Latin rites, among them the majority of versions of A&ASR, the third degree only addresses the legend of Hiram Abiff until the discovery of his body, already decomposing, and his removal from the improvised grave for him to receive due funeral honors; while the third degree in Anglo-Saxon rites and rituals reveals later events, such as the capture and trial of the three murderers. In the case of A&ASR, these subsequent events involving the death of Hiram Abiff, the capture and trial of the murderers, which did not exist in the Master Mason degree, are presented in 9th and 10th degrees.

Shortly after the discovery of Hiram Abiff's body, the proper burial of his remains, and convinced that the culprits would be the three fellows craft who had fled, King Solomon requests wide disclosure in the kingdom of his request to citizens for useful information that they could lead to the killers. Then, during an assembly of Temple construction workers, a pastor appears, Pharos, requesting to speak to the king. He reports seeing three men who match the description, hiding in a cave near the coast of Joppa (currently Jaffa).[xxxiii]

King Solomon then chooses nine masons he trusts to accompany Pharos to the cave, intending to arrest and bring the murderers to trial, appointing one of them, Yehu-aber, to lead the group. After getting organized, they leave for the trip as soon as it gets dark, guided by Pharos, arriving at the coast of Joppa just before dawn. They decide to get some sleep, before heading to the cave in search of the traitors; however, the leader of the nine, Yehu-aber, anxious and wanting to avenge Hiram Abiff, uses the rest of the others of the group to go alone to the cave. Guided by the flame of a candle arranged inside the cave, he comes across one of the assassins, Jubelum, sleeping, having a dagger near his feet. Yehu-aber, without hesitation, takes the dagger and strikes a blow to the head and another to the heart of the murderer who, in his last breath, babbles "revenge done".

Upon leaving the cave and seeing his bloody hand, Yehu-aber heads for a stream[xxxiv] that runs right by, to wash his hands and quench his thirst. Tired and sleepy, he falls asleep there. A few minutes later, when the other eight chosen arrived outside the cave, they came across Yehu-aber, sleeping. Upon waking him up, he says he avenged Hiram Abiff, then returns to the interior of the cave, separating Jubelum's head from the body and taking it, along with the dagger, with the other eight on the journey back to the palace.

In this part of the legend, there is some variation between the versions. Some say that King Solomon was angry with Yehu-aber that took the king's opportunity to execute Jubelum in front of the other masons, and the other eight who accompanied him had to intercede on his behalf so that King Solomon could understand that the final result would be the same and that the mission was partially completed successfully. In other versions, King Solomon praised Yehu-aber's bravery and dedication, pointing him out as the "Elu" of the Nine.

[xxxiii] In some versions, instead of a shepherd, Pharos is a fisherman, which would be more common in Joppa, a coastal and port region at the time. The distance between Joppa and Jerusalem is approximately 30 miles.

[xxxiv] In some versions, it is a water spring.

Regarding the name of the protagonist of this degree, a clarification is in order. In many versions, Yehu-aber is transliterated in Latin languages in another way, like Joabert.[xxxv]

MORAL:

Combating Ignorance. Initially, it appears to be somewhat difficult to defend a degree of the charge of being a "degree of revenge" when, at the height of its narrative, it is said that revenge has been done. Thus, it may be easier to accept and assume that it is a degree of revenge, failing to debate whether or not it is revenge, to debate whether this type of revenge would be justified or not; if the *lex talionis* is not just the natural law of action and reaction acting, guaranteeing the compensation of a vile and violent act, especially when in the name of the country; or whether, despite containing vengeance, the degree would not be intended to teach other lessons.

From this "tight spot" of revenge, the Supreme Council, Southern Jurisdiction, USA emerges, pointing the cave as the famous allegory of Plato's Cave and interpreting Jubelum as the personification of ignorance. That would be the daily killer in our society, which deserves to be hunted down and ended. Freemasons would thus be called upon to combat prejudice and spiritual despotism, consequences of ignorance.

The understanding of many authors is that being on a mission ordered by the king, a murder in this situation is like a soldier who kills an enemy in a war or a policeman who kills a criminal. These would be deaths justified by the "exercise of duty". Pike is one of those authors who interpreted the ninth degree through the prism of patriotism. For him, being "elected" among the nine is representative of being rewarded for his fidelity, obedience, and devotion to the country.

Some versions contribute to the issue, by pointing to the dark interior of the cave as the "inner self", the conscience, where vices, defects, and prejudices have been deep hidden, and, with the dagger (of the moral), the Freemason must hurry to kill them, so that he can leave that darkness (to evolve) and quench his thirst in the spring or stream (the source of truth, of wisdom). Thus, these versions have a less civic interpretation than the previous one, but much more moral and consistent with the purpose of the Scottish Rite to be a college of morality.

[xxxv] Arturo de Hoyos confirms that Joabert and Yehu-aber are spellings of the name of the same character in: De Hoyos, Arturo. 2016. *Scottish Rite Ritual, Monitor & Guide*. 2016. 3rd. edition, Corrected. Washington, D.C.: Supreme Council, 33°, S. J., p. 161.

SYMBOLOGY:

The dagger, which is the jewel of the ninth degree, is a symbol of the fight against ignorance, intolerance, and fanaticism, these symbolized by the murderers.

BIBLICAL PASSAGE:

And Solomon stood before the altar of the LORD in the presence of all the congregation of Israel, and spread forth his hands toward heaven:

And he said, LORD God of Israel, there is no God like thee, in heaven above, or on earth beneath, who keepest covenant and mercy with thy servants that walk before thee with all their heart:

Who hast kept with thy servant David my father that thou promisedst him: thou spakest also with thy mouth, and hast fulfilled it with thine hand, as it is this day.

Therefore now, LORD God of Israel, keep with thy servant David my father that thou promisedst him, saying, There shall not fail thee a man in my sight to sit on the throne of Israel; so that thy children take heed to their way, that they walk before me as thou hast walked before me.

And now, O God of Israel, let thy word, I pray thee, be verified, which thou spakest unto thy servant David my father.

1 Kings, 8:22-26.

10°: Elu of the Fifteen

To diffuse useful information, to further intellectual refinement, sure forerunner of moral improvement, to hasten the coming of the great day, when the dawn of general knowledge shall chase away the lazy, lingering mists of ignorance and error, even from the base of the great social pyramid, is indeed a high calling, in which the most

> splendid talents and consummate virtue may well press onward, eager to bear a part. From the Masonic ranks ought to go forth those whose genius and not their ancestry ennoble them, to open to all ranks the temple of science, and by their own example to make the humblest men emulous to climb steps no longer inaccessible, and enter the unfolded gates burning in the sun.[102]

ALLEGORIC CHRONOLOGY:

Following the previous degree, six months after the death of Hiram Abiff's first murderer.

LEGEND AND COMMENTS:

"Revenge is a dish best served cold"... This narrative is the continuation of the previous degree, of the Elected of the Nine. King Solomon ordered the head of Jubelum (or Abiram or Abairam or Akirop) to be embalmed to await the capture of the other two assassins. However, it has been approximately six months since then for a new report to make another mission possible. The information was that the other two killers were in Gath,[xxxvi] working as masons.

Solomon then summoned his nine workers who had served him on the previous mission, and, as they were two murderers and the imprecision of the location to find them, he thought it would be good to add six more to the nine, resulting in a total of 15, to capture them and bring them alive.

In Gath, the group decides to split itself into five smaller groups, three in each, to cover a greater search radius. After five days, Ben-Dekar, Yehu-Aber, and Stolkin found the two murderers, who were surrendered and taken to Jerusalem, where they slept in prison and the next day were executed. They had their heads cut off and the three heads were exposed on the arches of Jerusalem's gates. The bodies were left outside the city walls to be devoured by animals, birds, and insects.

As a way of paying tribute to the good work of the three companions who found and surrendered the murderers, King Solomon then created the Order of the "Elected of the Fifteen" and first granted it to the three.

[xxxvi] This part of the legend is similar to a biblical passage, from 1 Kings 2:39, which reports that two slaves from Shimei fled to Gath.

MORAL:

Combating Intolerance and Fanaticism. Being a degree that only continues the plot of the previous degree, concluding the revenge started with the ninth degree, its moral message is the same. Pike only adds that, just like the first murderer, executed in the ninth degree, personified Ignorance, the other two, executed in this tenth degree, are symbols of Intolerance[xxxvii] and Fanaticism. Ignorance, Intolerance, and Fanaticism are vices that every Freemason, especially in the Scottish Rite, must combat, first internally (killing them inside themselves, from their "cave"), and then externally.

As for the debate on these "degrees of revenge" and what it would represent for Freemasonry, observing from an educational perspective, it is necessary to use examples to better illustrate my opinion, even if irrelevant: When telling the good old story from the child who pretends to drown in the pool until the day he drowns, does the narrator intend to teach not to trust children or not to lie? And when you tell the story of Little Red Riding Hood, do you want to teach cheating and abusing children or not trusting strangers? Likewise, if we reduce the hiss of politically correct speech by those who have complained so much that these degrees have revenge and revenge goes against everything that Freemasonry teaches, we can easily observe that it is not revenge itself that is taught by the narratives, but that the wicked do not prosper and justice takes time, but it does not fail.

SYMBOLOGY:

The three severed heads on the arches of the city gates illustrate the coat of arms and versions of the apron of this degree.

BIBLICAL PASSAGE:

And David said to Solomon, My son, as for me, it was in my mind to build an house unto the name of the LORD my God:

But the word of the LORD came to me, saying, Thou hast shed blood abundantly, and hast made great wars: thou shalt not build an house unto my name, because thou hast shed much blood upon the earth in my sight.

[xxxvii] In some versions, there is Tyranny or Ambition instead of Intolerance.

Behold, a son shall be born to thee, who shall be a man of rest; and I will give him rest from all his enemies round about: for his name shall be Solomon, and I will give peace and quietness unto Israel in his days.

He shall build an house for my name; and he shall be my son, and I will be his father; and I will establish the throne of his kingdom over Israel for ever.

1 Chronicles, 22:7-10.

11°: Sublime Master Elected (NMJ) or Elu of the Twelve (SJ)

For if any people thinks that it is a grander, a more beneficial, or a wiser policy, to invent subtle expedients by stamps and imposts, for increasing the revenue and draining the life-blood of an impoverished people ; to multiply its naval and military force ; to rival in craft the ambassadors of foreign states ; to plot the swallowing up of foreign territory ;

> to make crafty treaties and alliances; to rule prostrate states and abject provinces by fear and force ; than to administer unpolluted justice to the people, to relieve the condition and raise the estate of the toiling masses, redress the injured and succor the distressed and conciliate the discontented, and speedily restore to every one his own ; then that people is involved in a cloud of error, and will too late perceive, when the illusion of these mighty benefits has vanished, that in neglecting these, which it thought inferior considerations, it has only been precipitating its own ruin and despair.[103]

ALLEGORIC CHRONOLOGY:

Following the previous degree, a few days after the execution of the murderers of Hiram Abiff.

LEGEND AND COMMENTS:

In this third and final degree of "Elu", after becoming aware of complaints from the provinces regarding the collection of high taxes, King Solomon decides to choose 12 of those 15 chosen from the last mission, to serve as governors (or viceroys) of the 12 tribes of Israel. He grants them the title of Princes Ameth[xxxviii] or Princes of Truth, giving them the right to collect taxes and represent him in the management of the provinces. An Order was then created to house them called "The Twelve Chosen".

The twelve chosen were, in Pike's version: Geber ben Uri, Shimei ben Elah, Yehu-aber ben Hur, Yosaphat ben Paruah, Ben Dekar, Banah ben Hushai, Stolkin ben Hesed, Ahiman, Zerbal ben Abinadab, Bana ben Ahilud, Abner ben Geber, Ahinadab ben Iddo.

When we consider that the term "ben", in Hebrew, means "son" and the old custom of using it between names, thus indicating offspring, we can understand its appearance in almost all names reported in Pike's version. The only exceptions are Ben Dekar and Ahiman. In this regard, two assumptions should be made. The first that Dekar would have a single child, therefore known only as "Ben Dekar", which would be the equivalent of "Dekar II" or "Dekar Jr.". The second, that Ahiman, like Hiram Abiff, was the son of a widow, and his father was not named.

[xxxviii] Hebrew word that means Truth. This translation is also given in most versions; however, the Brazilian ritual states that Ameth in Hebrew translation means "faithful man at all times".

There is in the Pike version of this degree a small instruction that brings an interesting view. In it, it is stated that these three degrees of "Elu" or "Elected" (Chosen), which, in the case of A&ASR, is degrees 9th, 10th, and 11th, may be, in some way, present in other rites. In the York Rite it would be summarized in a scene of the third degree, whereas in the Modern Rite it would be condensed in a single degree, simply called "Elu" or "Elected" (4th degree of the Modern Rite).[104]

MORAL:

Service and Truth. The 11th degree, even with its short storyline, keeps these two important lessons. Serving is an act of love and, although civil servants chosen by the people on many occasions give signs or evidence of not doing so, it is in this way that the Scottish Rite teaches that civil service or any service provided must be seen to others: as an act of love. Love generates fidelity and zeal. Realizing that the tax collection system was generating injustices, King Solomon tried to replace it. To this end, he chose twelve "sublime knights" from among those who had shown their service with care and dedication. "When one is willing to serve, he never lacks opportunities".[105] This was the case with those twelve chosen ones, who were entitled as Princes of Truth.

The title was no accident. Truth should guide your work as civil servants. In this sense, these princes would have to be truthful, sincere to the people so that they could earn their trust. This includes transparency in the collection and the austere use of the amounts collected, charging according to the means and the exemption of the poorest, striving to do everything correctly.

In this way, we, as adherents of the Scottish Rite, must be true, sincere, transparent, and fair to all those to whom we provide voluntary or professional services, always carrying out our duties in the best possible way.

SYMBOLOGY:

One of the symbols of this degree is the sword, which represents the Truth. The other is the flaming heart, a symbol of zeal and devotion to a cause, even if it involves suffering and sacrifice.

BIBLICAL PASSAGE:

And the word of the Lord came to Solomon, saying,

Concerning this house which thou art in building, if thou wilt walk in my statutes, and execute my judgments, and keep all my commandments to walk in them; then will I perform my word with thee, which I spake unto David thy father:

And I will dwell among the children of Israel, and will not forsake my people Israel.

So Solomon built the house, and finished it.

1 Kings, 6:11-14.

12°: Master Architect

Thorough, faithful, and honest endeavor to improve, is always successful, and the highest happiness. To sigh sentimentally over human misfortune, is fit only for the mind's childhood; and the mind's misery is chiefly its own fault; appointed, under the good Providence of God, as the punisher and corrector of its fault. In the long run, the mind will be happy, just in proportion to its fidelity and wisdom.[106]

ALLEGORIC CHRONOLOGY:

Following the previous degree, a few days after the inauguration of the twelve chosen as viceroys of the twelve tribes.

LEGEND AND COMMENTS:

It has been more than six months since King Solomon installed his four intendants and their superintendent, Adoniram. During this period, the king observed Adoniram's good work at the head of the work and with his intendants, his dedication, knowledge, and expertise. Thus, King Solomon decided to grant him the title of Grand Master Architect, previously granted to Hiram Abiff, and give him the mission of systematizing the education of the masons, to achieve uniform work.

MORAL:

Works and trusts. It summarizes the moral of this degree. When Adoniram received the superintendence mission, he sought to improve himself and dedicate himself to properly fulfill it. Then Solomon rewarded him for this by making him a Grand Master Architect. In other words, who not only does his job as if it were a routine but seeks to learn every day, evolve, and improve the world around him, will achieve glory and victory, receiving due honors and rewards for his efforts.

Bringing this lesson to our Masonic life, there is no merit in the freemason, who for years has practically not been lacking in the Lodge, but always occupying the same position and presenting in it the same performance as always. If Freemasonry is a school and we are in it to evolve, then leave our comfort zone and accept different missions from our Worshipful Masters, such as occupying positions that we have not yet occupied and that require knowledge or skills that we have not yet mastered, it should be something natural. Otherwise, it is as if a child asks to study only Portuguese at school because he does not like or does not do well in other subjects. How could he evolve like that?

This type of stance in the Lodge impedes a brother's Masonic evolution, not allowing himself to prepare himself for one day to direct it. In the same sense, Dermott states that:

> (...) no man ought to be nominated or put in such election, but such as by his known skill and merit, is deemed worthy of performance, viz. He must be well acquainted with all the private and public rules and orders of the craft.[107]

SYMBOLOGY:

The degree bears a series of architectural symbols, including the five columns of the five orders of architecture, illustrating the scenario of Grand Master Architect. The new symbols, which differ from the others, are the North Star,[xxxix] always fixed and immovable, representing God as the center of the Universe and our faith in Him (trust); and the Morning Star, appearing to the east, referring to the perfection of the dawn and, thus, symbolizing the perfection of the Masonic light and the evolution that it provides when it symbolically goes from the West to the East, in search of light (work).

BIBLICAL PASSAGE:

And it came to pass, when Solomon had finished the building of the house of the Lord, and the king's house, and all Solomon's desire which he was pleased to do,

That the Lord appeared to Solomon the second time, as he had appeared unto him at Gibeon.

And the Lord said unto him, I have heard thy prayer and thy supplication, that thou hast made before me: I have hallowed this house, which thou hast built, to put my name there forever; and mine eyes and mine heart shall be there perpetually.

And if thou wilt walk before me, as David thy father walked, in integrity of heart, and in uprightness, to do according to all that I have commanded thee, and wilt keep my statutes and my judgments:

[xxxix] The North Star was the guide of the navigators, due to its immutable position, which reinforces the meaning of trust, faith.

Then I will establish the throne of thy king-dom upon Israel forever, as I promised to David thy father, saying, there shall not fail thee a man upon the throne of Israel.

1 Kings, 9:1-5.

13°: Royal Arch of Solomon (SJ) or Master of the Ninth Arch (NMJ)

The law of retribution presses upon every man, whether he thinks of it or not. It pursues him through all the courses of life, with a step that never falters nor tires, and with an eye that never sleeps. If it were not so, God's government would not be impartial; there would be no discrimination; no moral dominion; no light shed upon the mysteries of Providence.[108]

ALLEGORIC CHRONOLOGY:

In sequence to the previous degree, without determining days.

LEGEND AND COMMENTS:

This degree starts a narrative completed at the next degree, the 14th. Together, it is considered by many Scottish Rite authors, including Albert Pike, the main degrees granted in the Lodge of Perfection. It is not by chance that the group of degrees to which it belongs, from the 4th to the 14th, is called "Ineffable Degrees", due to the legend that started in this 13th degree.

This legend is built on the foundations of an older legend, from Enoch: Behold, Enoch had a dream which he sought to realize. From the peak of a mountain, he dug a nine floor crypt. Each floor was supported by an arch. In the deepest floor of the crypt, he deposited the name of the Great Architect of the Universe, engraved in a golden triangle, which was sealed to a face of an agate cube, resting on a luminous pedestal of white alabaster.

This ineffable name of God, initially known only as Enoch, would have been lost until God himself spoke it to Moses, who also engraved it on a gold piece and deposited it in the Ark of the Covenant. Its pronunciation was taught to Aaron and Joshua to be transmitted to the future high priests of Israel; however, it was lost after Joshua's death. The gold piece kept in the Ark, on the other hand, would have been melted by the Philistines, in the Samuel's reign. The name had been lost again.

Thus, the legend of the 13th degree says that the King Solomon ordered the construction of a palace to function as the court of justice (for the Provosts and Judges, 7th degree) next to the ruins of the Temple of Enoch. With the mission of planning the work, three intendants (Intendant of the Buildings, 8th degree), Adoniram (formerly Superintendent, now Grand Master Architect), Stolkin, and Yehu-aber, went to the ruins. During the analysis of the ground, one of them, Yehu-aber, founds a curious stone with a large iron ring attached to it. Upon removing it, a small entrance was discovered, which led to a gallery with another entrance, and another, until it reached under the ninth arch of the crypt. On that last floor was the cube with a golden triangle on the luminous pedestal, from the legend of Enoch.

In appreciating the cube, Adoniram would have shown his gratitude to Yehu-aber for having found the initial entrance, saying "Hamalec Gebalim", which means "Chief of the men of Gebal". Gebal was a city famous for its stone carvers and where Yehu-aber came from. From this word, "Gebalim", which means "men of Gebal", almost a synonym for "stone cutters" since the city was a quarry, the word Jabulom[xl] would derive, as well as "Giblim".

Aware of the immeasurable value of the discovery, but unable to decipher what was engraved in the triangle, they brought to the attention of King Solomon and Hiram of Tyre, who was in a meeting together, after the new alliance (Intimate Secretary, 6th degree). Solomon recognizes the word and shows it to Hiram of Tyre, who also recognizes it as the true word of Master Mason and as the ineffable name of God, until then only known by the two kings and the late Hiram Abiff, who had agreed never to communicate to others without the three being present.

King Solomon then tells Adoniram and the two intendants about the legend of Enoch, which had been told to him by his father, David. Finally, he decides to grant the three the title of Royal Arch Masons and invites them to deposit, with the two kings, the cube in a special place: his secret crypt, located below the Holy of Holies and where he met with Hiram of Tyre and Hiram Abiff until his death, also built under nine arches inspired by the legend of Enoch. Thus, when the deposit was made, the three faithful workers learned the correct pronunciation of the ineffable name, three times three.

A few days later, the construction of the Temple was completed and it was finally dedicated. Soon after the ceremonies and celebrations, King Solomon took advantage of the meeting of all the illustrious of Israel to grant them the new degree, now entitled "Grand Elected Perfect and Sublime Mason"[xli] and, consequently, the true word of Master Mason, before losing. A total of 27 brethren became members of this select degree: the twelve Princes Ameth; the nine Chosen of the Fifteen; Zerbal, who succeeded Adoniram as Grand Master Architect; the three who received the degree first hand: Adoniram, Stolkin, and Yehu-aber; and the two kings: Solomon and Hiram of Tyre.

Some were the Master Masons who, however, having completed their work on the construction of the Temple of Solomon, also wanted to

---

[xl] In some versions, Jabelom.

[xli] While in the 13th degree only the story is told that the most illustrious and deserving brothers were initiated in the degree of Grand Elected Perfect and Sublime Mason, this initiation is reproduced in the 14th degree.

receive the true word of the Master, since they only had the substitute. In response, the king advised them to continue to work patiently until the time to be honored with the real word. Not satisfied with the answer, they went to the ruins of the Temple of Enoch, hoping to find secrets or, at least, valuables there, as the rumors said about Adoniram, Stolkin, and Yehu-aber.

After a day of searching, they found the curious stone with an iron ring. They suspended it and spotted the entrance to the first crypt. Some went down through the entrance, while others waited outside. After a few minutes, the outsiders felt an earthquake, followed by a crash. That was when a fireball came out of the cavity. They ran while the earth they stepped on sank, swallowing the debris of the temple on its surface.

Due to the legends involved in this degree, it can be found under different names, even in the Scottish Rite: Royal Arch of Solomon, Master of the Ninth Arch, Royal Arch of Enoch, Royal Arch of Solomon, etc.

MORAL:

Truth and Retribution. The luminous pedestal illustrates the reason, given by God to man, while the three masons who found it symbolize examples of Freemasons, who must always seek knowledge and the truth; however, this degree speaks not only of the search for truth but also for freedom, which needs to be won and guaranteed because, when it is lost, the knowledge and the truth is lost with it. That was how the word, even deposited in the Ark of the Covenant, was lost. Where there is no freedom, the truth is lost.

The legend deals with what Pike calls the Law of Retribution. This universal law is also called the Law of Action and Reaction or the Law of Cause and Effect. So, if you do good things, then at some point good things happen to you. In the narrative, the three workers who dedicated themselves so much in the previous degrees and the two kings who renewed their alliance with each other were rewarded with the encounter of the lost word. Those who did not deserve it, but longed for it; the vain, greedy, unjust, ungodly. These were rewarded with a painful death, without the possibility of a dignified burial, and without the admiration of good men.

SYMBOLOGY:

The agate cube, a symbol of perfection, with the gold plate engraved with the ineffable name of God. This must be the "treasure" hunted by the Freemason adept of the Scottish Rite: its improvement, that is, its evolution towards the Great Architect of the Universe.

BIBLICAL PASSAGE:

And God spake unto Moses, and said unto him, I am the Lord:
And I appeared unto Abraham, unto Isaac, and unto Jacob, by the name of God Almighty, but by my name JEHOVAH was I not known to them.
And I have also established my covenant with them, to give them the land of Canaan, the land of their pilgrimage, wherein they were strangers.
And I have also herd the groaning of the children of Israel, whom the Egyptians keep in bondage; and I have remembered my covenant.
Wherefore say unto de children of Israel, I am the Lord, and I will bring you out from under the burdens of the Egyptians, and I will rid you out of their bondage, and I will redeem you with a stretched out arm, and with great judgments:
And I will take you to me for a people, and I will be to you a God: and ye shall know that I am the Lord your God, which bringeth you out from under the burdens of the Egyptians.
Exodus, 6:2-7.

14°: Perfect Elu (Grand Elect Perfect and Sublime Mason)

The hope of success, and not the hope of reward, should be our stimulating and sustaining power. Our object, and not ourselves, should be our inspiring thought. Selfishness is a sin, when temporary, and for time. Spun out to eternity, it does not become celestial prudence. We should toil and die, not for Heaven or Bliss, but for Duty.[109]

ALLEGORIC CHRONOLOGY:

Experience in details of a specific moment just mentioned in the previous degree, with reports of times later, when the Temple was destroyed.

LEGEND AND COMMENTS:

Initially, it is interesting to note a curious detail regarding the name of the degree. In the revised version of the Mother Supreme Council of the World (or Southern Jurisdiction), its name is "Grand Elect Perfect and Sublime Mason", without a comma between "Elected" and "Perfect and Sublime". That is, the brother is not qualified as elected and/or perfect and sublime. He is elected as Perfect and Sublime. "Elected" does not have an adjective function, such as "Perfect" and "Sublime", but rather a verb in the past participle, which is the same function that the term occupies in the titles of the "Elu" degrees: Elected of the Nine, Elected of the Fifteen, Chosen of the Twelve. In other words, the brother is one of the grand (in the sense of "distinguished") who is elected (in the sense of "chosen") as the Perfect and Sublime Mason. It is for this reason that the degree is also commonly called "Perfect Elu" in these jurisdictions, but never "Perfect and Elected" or even "Perfect or Elected".

Other versions include other spellings: "Grand, Elected, Perfect and Sublime Mason" (a single title with an additive collection of 4 attributes: 1. Grand, 2. Elected, 3. Perfect, and 4. Sublime); and the most common, "Grand Elected, Perfect and Sublime Mason" (a single title with an additive collection of 3 attributes: 1. Grand Elected, 2. Perfect, and 3. Sublime).

In any case, the degree is known as the Degree of Perfection, since the brother reaches the perfection (conclusion) of the legend of the third degree, finding what had been lost, after having completed his work, which was the construction of the perfect work: the Solomon's Temple. It must be taken into account that a Master Mason experiences an enormous emptiness when he is raised: the Grand Master is dead, the temple is unfinished and the word is lost. Until, in the 14th degree, when justice for the death of the Grand Master was achieved, the temple was completed and dedicated, and the word was finally found and granted. It is not by chance that the body that this degree concludes and represents its apex is also called the Lodge of Perfection.

As for the legend, in an excerpt from the 13th degree narrative, the story is told that, after the completion and dedication of the Temple (it is estimated that in 1004 BC), King Solomon selected that other 22 brethren who joined him, King Hiram of Tyre and the three Masons of the Royal Arch (therefore, in a total of 27) in the degree that came to be called the Grand Elect Perfect and Sublime Mason. Then, other Master Masons who did not enter the degree claimed the right to receive the real word, without success.

The 14th degree provides exactly the experience of that mentioned initiation, carried out in the secret crypt. In it, the bread and wine are divided, obtaining a strong symbolic appeal among the brothers.

After this initiation and the end of the Temple dedication festivities, it is reported that the other masons not initiated in this new degree began to grant the other degrees that they knew without due care and control, even allowing for innovations and irregularities. Even King Solomon went astray, intoxicated with so much fame and wealth, which led him to multiply the women in his Harem and to worship other gods, no longer worrying about preserving the Royal Art. Only the Perfect Elus kept the degree and its practices intact and restricted their access to the usual restricted number. The result could not be different: in 13 generations (just over 400 years) Israel's prosperity has come to an end, and Jerusalem and the Temple have been destroyed (it is estimated that in 587 BC).

Then, at dawn, a group of Perfect Elus went to the ruins of the Solomon's Temple, in search of rescuing the cube containing the golden triangle with the word and, thus, preserving it from a possible discovery by an unworthy person. After excavating an access and reaching the ninth arch, they came across the body of Galahad,[xlii] chief of the Levites and a respected member of the Degree of Perfection. His body was on the pedestal with the cube, as if trying to protect it.

When deliberating, they decided to erase the engravings on the gold triangle, remove it from the cube and break it into pieces. Then, the cube and the pedestal were placed in a corner of the secret crypt and Galahad's body received proper treatment and ceremonies dedicated to a Perfect Elu.

MORAL:

[xlii] This name, Galahad, may not have been chosen at random, as it is the name of a character from Arthurian legends, being one of the knights of the round table and considered the purest knight of all, having reached the Holy Grail. Thus, it would be possible to make a parallel between the symbolism of the cube with the ineffable name and the sacred chalice.

Justice, Right, and Truth. In this degree, Justice is represented by the color white; the Right for the blue; and Truth by crimson, which is a strong red, more drawn to purple, and known as the color of fire.

White is a sign of purity, strictly linked to the principle of justice, which must be clear, indisputable. The blue reminds us of the sky, with its countless shades of blue between morning and night. In this sense, the word "Right" refers to "Correct". Thus, one must seek to be as sure as the blue of the sky, and still be correct day and night, that is, at all times, without exception. Crimson, on the other hand, was considered the color of fire, which faces and purifies anything, like the Truth.

The revised version of Pike carries the sentence: "Live virtuously (Truth), act worthily (Right) and decide justly (Justice)". And the 1883 version read: "Justice in action and execution. Right in decision and adjudication. Truth in doctrine and legislation".

A Perfect Elu must seek to be just, correct and true in all his actions, especially towards Freemasonry. He must preserve the Truth, not "relativizing" it, lest it become something false and cease to be truth; granting it only to those worthy, who won such a right with morals and work; doing justice, honoring the dedication and efforts of those who came before and bequeathed such a sublime treasure and mission to us.

The legend of this degree holds another important teaching. The plot brings real fragility even to the victories believed to be more lasting and to the constructions considered to be more solid, especially when ethical leadership is not the foundation and moral principles as guides. If, with the Temple of the Lord to conclude, many workers were almost lost on the way (7th and 8th degrees), what to expect with its completion and without any other challenge to be overcome? With the king himself, considered the wisest among men, giving himself up to vices? The result could not be otherwise. Freemasonry and its degrees were corrupted, the nation fell from grace and the Temple was destroyed. Thus, the maxim is reinforced that everything in this life is temporary, especially when it is not protected by the shield of morality and work.

Such is the importance of this degree in the structure of the Scottish Rite that it has its ring, indicating that the cycle started in the third degree has been completed (a circle of perfection). It is golden, engraved on the outside with an equilateral triangle containing the Hebrew letter Yod in its center. Inside, the motto *Virtus Junxit Mors Non Separabit* is traditionally engraved, which means "What virtue has united, death will not separate". This motto suggests that the freemason who passes through the 14th degree creates an indissoluble moral bond with Freemasonry, the depth of which reaches his immortal soul.

As the 33rd degree endowment is restricted to a few, both in the Southern and Northern Jurisdiction of the United States and in many other countries, the 14th degree ring is the only ring that most Scottish Rite members will have in their lifetime.

SYMBOLOGY:

The main symbol of the degree is the golden triangle engraved with the Ineffable Name in Sanskrit in the center and with the corresponding Phoenician letters in the corners. This model would justify the reason that the three intendants who found the piece in the 13th degree were unable to decipher the message, which was only understood by King Solomon (sage, supposedly knowledgeable of several languages) and King Hiram of Tyre (Phoenician).

Another important symbol of the degree is the pentagram containing a radiant triangle in its center, in which the Hebrew word *shalamot* is engraved, which means "perfection" and "complete".

BIBLICAL PASSAGE:

And he said, I beseech thee, shew me thy glory.

And he said, I will make all my goodness pass before thee, and I will proclaim the name of the Lord before thee; and will be gracious to whom I will be gracious, and will shew mercy on whom I will shew mercy.

And he said, Thou canst not see my face: for there shall no man see me, and live.

And the Lord said, Behold, there is a place by me, and thou shalt stand upon a rock:

And it shall come to pass, while my glory passeth by, that I will put thee in a clift of the rock, and will cover thee with my hand while I pass by:

And I will take away mine hand, and thou shalt see my back parts: but my face shall not be seen.

Exodus, 33:18-23.

Ineffable Degrees Considerations

The saga started in the third degree has an end. In it, the initiate exercises, at all times, his symbolic role as an operative mason, a builder of the Solomon's Temple. However, in each of its phases, stages, or narratives, the initiate performs a different function, between the protagonist, supporting actor, or spectator.

The Ineffable Degrees begin moments after the death of Grand Master Hiram Abiff, when King Solomon reinforces the guard of the Holy of Holies to protect the secrets kept there (or below). We followed the construction of the Hiram Abiff mausoleum and his funeral ceremonies. Thereafter, a new alliance between Kings Solomon and Hiram of Tyre is signed, with a new secretary. However, conflicts between masons and delays in the work increased because absence of Hiram Abiff, remedied with the creation of a court and the appointment of new leaders for such work. Within a few months, Solomon is successful in finding and executing those responsible for Hiram Abiff's murder. And after justice has been achieved, the replacement of Hiram Abiff as Grand Master Architect is made. The universe then favors Masonry with the finding of the lost word and the completion of the Temple construction.

To better analyze these stories that make up the Hiramic adventure of the building of Solomon's Temple, let us start with the concept of monomyth, also known as Hero's Journey, by anthropologist Joseph Campbell who, as a mythologist, identified a pattern in which classic myths fit, originally published in 1949.[110] This standard was later adopted for the development of new myths, such as the Star Wars and Matrix sagas. Thus, the twelve stages that make up the Hero's Journey were identified in the Hiramic monomyth or legend:

STAGES OF THE HERO'S JOURNEY	STEPS OF THE HIRAMIC LEGEND
1. Ordinary world (normal situation in the story context).	The candidate becomes an Apprentice (1st degree) and, later, a Fellow Craft (2nd degree) during the construction works of the Solomon's Temple.
2. Call to adventure (a problem that arises, ending normality).	Hiram Abiff is murdered and the Master's word is lost (3rd degree).

3. Refusal of the Call (period in which the hero has not yet decided to try to solve the problem)	The guard of the Holy of Holies is strengthened (4th degree). A mausoleum is built and funeral ceremonies are performed. Grief prevails over any desire for justice (5th degree).
4. Meeting the mentor or outside help	After an initial conflict, Solomon's encounter with Hiram of Tyre results in a new alliance for the construction of the Temple (6th degree).
5. Crossing the Threshold ("wind of change" that signals that the time has come to face the challenge or battle)	Conflicts between masons begin to affect the progress of the building and to highlight the impact of the absence of Hiram Abiff. This causes Solomon to create a court of justice. It is perceived that justice regarding the death of the Hiram Abiff also needs to be done for the masons to return to normal (7th degree).
6. Tests, allies and enemies or The Belly of the Whale (situation that appears to make the hero's life even more difficult)	Hiram Abiff's absence reaches the peak of its reflection when the construction works of the Temple are halted due to lack of proper planning and direction, and Solomon is unable to find a suitable replacement, needing to choose five intendants to handle the work that was previously done by one. Something urgently needs to be done to leverage masons' moral and motivation, or the Temple will be tainted by chaos and will not be completed (8th degree).
7. Approach To The Inmost Cave (first success)	Solomon offers a reward for any information about the killers' whereabouts. An informant takes a group of nine chosen to a cave in Joppa and one of the chosen nine hastens to kill one of the three assassins (9th degree).
8. Ordeal (greater challenge and success)	After a few months, new information takes fifteen chosen to Gath in search of the other two killers. They are captured, brought to justice, convicted and executed (10th degree).

9. Reward	The success of the Hiram Abiff assassins' search mission led Solomon to select twelve of the fifteen chosen to serve as princes in each of his twelve tribes (11th degree).
10. The Road Back (rededication)	Having achieved justice by Hiram Abiff and the construction work in full force and vigor, Solomon appoints a new Grand Master Architect, Adoniram (12th degree).
11. Resurrection Hero (final test with risk of death and use of skills accumulated throughout the journey)	With difficulties and risk of death, three intendants explore the nine floors of Enoch's crypt and recover the lost word, which is the Ineffable Name of God (13th degree).
12. Return with the Elixir (return with the final reward, which helps to return to the normality of the "ordinary world")	After the recovery of the lost word, the construction works of the temple are concluded and the same is, finally, consecrated. In celebration, some illustrious chosen ones are initiated in the mysteries of the lost word (14th degree).

When decoding the Hiramic Legend, you realize how interesting this odyssey presents itself to the viewer's eyes, without leaving anything to be desired for the already mentioned successful Hollywood franchises, built on similar basic structures. The Hiramic Legend has two fundamental differences, which make it unique compared to other myths, one related to its environment and the other to its end. The first is the participation of the viewer in parts of the drama, experiencing a kind of basic psychodrama and reaching different levels of catharsis. The second and most important is its purpose, which, far from the simple entertainment of the film industry, has an ethical and moral character.

Thus, the Freemason who attends the Ineffable Degrees adds to the basic moral principles accumulated in the symbolic degrees other important lessons related to secrecy and fidelity; death and family; fervor and zeal; justice, impartiality, and equity; benevolence and charity; combating ignorance, intolerance, and fanaticism; service to others; search for the truth; work and trust; retribution law; among other beautiful lessons of morality veiled in their narratives.

4.3. The Chapter of Rose Croix and its Capitular Degrees

Introduction to Capitular Degrees

Having passed the stage of ineffable degrees (4th to 14th degree), the freemason becomes eligible to enter a body called the Chapter of Rose Croix, in which degrees from 15th to 18th are awarded. Its name, Rose Croix, is about the last degree granted in it, the 18th, Knight of the Rose Croix, similarly to what happens with the previous body, from The Lodge of Perfection, which alludes to the 14th degree, known as the Degree of Perfection.

Some believe and defend the idea that Freemasonry descends from the Rosicrucianism, pointing to the Chapter of Rose Croix and its last degree, Knight of the Rose Croix, as evidence; however, this degree only appeared in the second half of the 18th century, when Freemasonry was already a reality in dozens of countries and already experienced a plurality of rites and rituals. The reverse theory would be more plausible, that the Rosicrucianism descends from Freemasonry, considering that the first known Rosicrucian Order is the *Societas Rosicruciana in Scotia*, founded in 1800, in Edinburgh, and restricted to freemasons.[111]

In countries of Latin origin, it is common to group the degrees considering only the body in which they are granted. Thus, there are symbolic degrees (1st to 3rd), granted in a Symbolic Lodge (or Blue Lodge); ineffable degrees (4th to 14th), granted in a Lodge of Perfection; chapter degrees (15th to 18th), awarded in a Chapter of Rose Croix; the philosophical degrees (19° to 30°), granted in a Council of Kadosh; administrative degrees (31st and 32nd), granted in a Consistory; and an honorary degree (33rd), granted by a Supreme Council.

We also can group degrees according to its content, however, which impacts especially on the degrees granted in the Rose Croix Chapter, exposing its transience character. For this view, the 15th and 16th degrees are called Historical Degrees, still maintaining a relationship, even if chronologically a little distant, with the events narrated in the ineffable degrees; while the 17th and 18th degrees are considered, by their content, already as philosophical degrees,[xliii] closer to the chivalry degrees taken as philosophical that are granted in the Council of Kadosh.

[xliii] Some authors choose to call the 17th and 18th degrees "doctrinal degrees", so as not to confuse them with those granted in the Council of Kadosh.

15°: Knight of the East, of the Sword, or of the Eagle

He who endeavors to serve, to benefit, and improve the world, is like a swimmer, who struggles against a rapid current, in a river lashed into angry waves by the winds. Often they roar over his head, often they beat him back and baffle him. Most men yield to the stress of the current, and float with it to the shore, or are swept over the rapids; and only here and there the stout, strong heart and vigorous arms struggle on toward ultimate success.[112]

ALLEGORIC CHRONOLOGY:

Approximately in 537 B.C., decades after the destruction of Solomon's Temple mentioned in the previous degree.

LEGEND AND COMMENTS:

Initially, it is necessary to understand the name of the degree, similar to the case presented in the previous degree. The correct name of the degree is "Knight of the East, of the Sword, or of the Eagle". The use of the conjunction "or" in the presented model is of an alternative coordinative classification, which means that the elements must be considered separately and exclusively. Thus, the degree can be called "Knight of the Orient" or "Knight of the Sword" or "Knight of the Eagle", the most common being the use of only the first term, "Knight of the Orient".

In some jurisdictions, however, it is called "Knight of the Orient, Sword, and Eagle", possibly due to French influence. The use of "and" in this sense is additive coordinating conjunction, which requires the elements to be considered together. This would theoretically inhibit the possibility, following the norms of the language, to call it only "Knight of the Orient", as occurs in most jurisdictions; however, the degree is called this way, "Knight of the Orient", in several excerpts from different versions of the degree, showing the error in the title of the degree in such jurisdictions.

This degree illustrates facts alleged to have occurred in 537 BC, fifty years after the destruction of Jerusalem and the first Temple by Nebuchadnezzar of Babylon, which was supposed to have happened in 587 BC. Despite the dates estimated by scholars on the topic indicate this 50-year interval (587 to 537 BC), the ritual mentions 70 years. If we reflect a little on this, the 50-year interval, in addition to being more precise in terms of theorists' estimates, makes more sense when we consider the mention of the liberation of those "children" from Israel, taken captive to Babylon, to work on the reconstruction of the city of Jerusalem and the Lord's Temple. Manual labor would not be appropriate for elderly people over 70 years of age. This seemingly illogical point of the ritual can be questioned by any observant candidate. The justification for using 70 years is biblical:

> In the first year of his reign, Daniel understood by books the number of the years, whereof the word of the Lord came to Jeremiah the prophet, that he would accomplish seventy years in the desolations of Jerusalem (Daniel, 9:2).
> And this whole land shall be a desolation, and an astonishment; and these nations shall serve the king of Babylon seventy years (Jeremiah, 25:11).
> For thus saith the Lord, That after seventy years be accomplished at Babylon I will visit you, and perform my good word toward you, in causing you to return to this place (Jeremiah, 29:10).

The degree narrative reports that Zerubbabel, regarded as a prince of Solomon's lineage, has an audience with King Cyrus II of Persia, who had conquered Babylon, to convince him to free the captive Jews so that they could return to Jerusalem and rebuild the Temple. Cyrus, who had had a dream on the subject, decided to comply with Zerubbabel's request, including committing himself to finance the construction.

In his dream, there was a lion ready to jump and devour him. Cyrus tried to run, but his feet did not obey him. Then he saw Nebuchadnezzar and Balthasar, kings of Babylon, fallen and bound with chains. Above them, the name of Jehovah shone. Next to the name shining and the clouds illuminated around it, an eagle appeared, who approached Cyrus and told him to give freedom back to the enslaved or his crown would pass to the hands of strangers.

King Cyrus gives ample powers for Zerubbabel to return with his people to Jerusalem and carry out the work of rebuilding the city and the temple. He then returns to Zerubbabel his sword, also granting him a seal, as a symbol of the authority he was conferring on him as his representative in Israel. Still, Cyrus presents Zerubbabel with the distinctive prince necklace. On the way back, crossing a bridge over a river, Zerubbabel and his people are attacked. They resist and win the battle, concluding their journey to Jerusalem.

Passing through Gadara,[xliv] they found a bridge, where they were attacked by Babylonian settlers based in Samaria. Gadara was on the east side of the Jordan River and was inhabited predominantly by non-Jews, with Samaria[xlv] being on the west side of the river.

[xliv] Currently it is called Umm Qais, a city in Jordan. The old name, Gadara, probably derives from the Hebrew word "gader", which means "border".

[xlv] Samaria was Israel's capital before David invaded Jerusalem and made it the new capital. It is currently part of the West Bank.

MORAL:

Fidelity and Perseverance. Zerubbabel is an example of fidelity to duty and perseverance in carrying out his mission, even in the face of so many difficulties. And each Scottish Rite Freemason must remain faithful to the duty assumed to combat ignorance, intolerance, and fanaticism, in addition to that sacred duty of charity. He must persist, not allowing the occasional discouragement of one or the other brother and the difficulties imposed on the way to prevent him from fighting (sword) and working (trolley) for a better world.

There is no way of avoiding the apathy, disbelief, indifference, and selfishness of some people around, transforming the visible social environment into the moral ruins of a city destroyed by the lack of love for others and education; however, this is what Freemasonry exists for: to touch the heart and mind of the freemason with principles and moral virtues, so that he becomes aware and motivates himself to make a difference in his social environment.

The social dimension of the non-Masonic world is so immense compared to Freemasonry that, if Freemasonry does not persist to fulfill its mission with mastery, it will be allowing inertia, the ills and profane vices to do the opposite way, impacting in such a way the Freemason may end up impregnating Freemasonry with these elements foreign to it.

Thus, for centuries that Freemasonry, and especially the Scottish Rite, have played the role of Zerubbabel, being faithful to its duty and persistent in the face of all difficulties, to provide each freemason with the possibility and tools necessary to (re)build his inner moral temple (the symbolic Temple) amid the ruins of society, in many respects, deteriorated (destroyed Jerusalem).

SYMBOLOGY:

The bridge is a symbol of "freedom to pass", which can also be interpreted as "freedom to think", that is, freedom of conscience.

The jewel of the degree is formed by three concentric triangles, representative of the French motto of "Freedom, Equality, and Fraternity" and, according to Pike's version, also of "Law, Order, and Subordination". Inside the jewel, there are two crossed swords, symbols of Honor and Loyalty. With them, man seeks justice and attains his freedom.

There is also the symbol of a trowel crossed with a sword because, symbolically, the followers of Zerubbabel would have the sword in one hand (for freedom) and the trowel in the other (to rebuild). It also represents the union of Chivalry (warriors) with Freemasonry (builders) in favor of the great work.[xlvi]

BIBLICAL PASSAGE:

Now in the second year of their coming unto the house of God at Jerusalem, in the second month, began Zerubbabel the son of Shealtiel, and Jeshua the son of Jozadak, and the remnant of their brethren the priests and the Levites, and all they that were come out of the captivity unto Jerusalem; and appointed the Levites, from twenty years old and upward, to set forward the work of the house of the Lord.

Then stood Jeshua with his sons and his brethren, Kadmiel and his sons, the sons of Judah, together, to set forward the workmen in the house of God: the sons of Henadad, with their sons and their brethren the Levites.

And when the builders laid the foundation of the temple of the Lord, they set the priests in their apparel with trumpets, and the Levites the sons of Asaph with cymbals, to praise the Lord, after the ordinance of David king of Israel.

Ezra, 3:8-10.

16°: Prince of Jerusalem

[xlvi] This is, in fact, the first Scottish Rite degree whose original name bears the title "Knight".

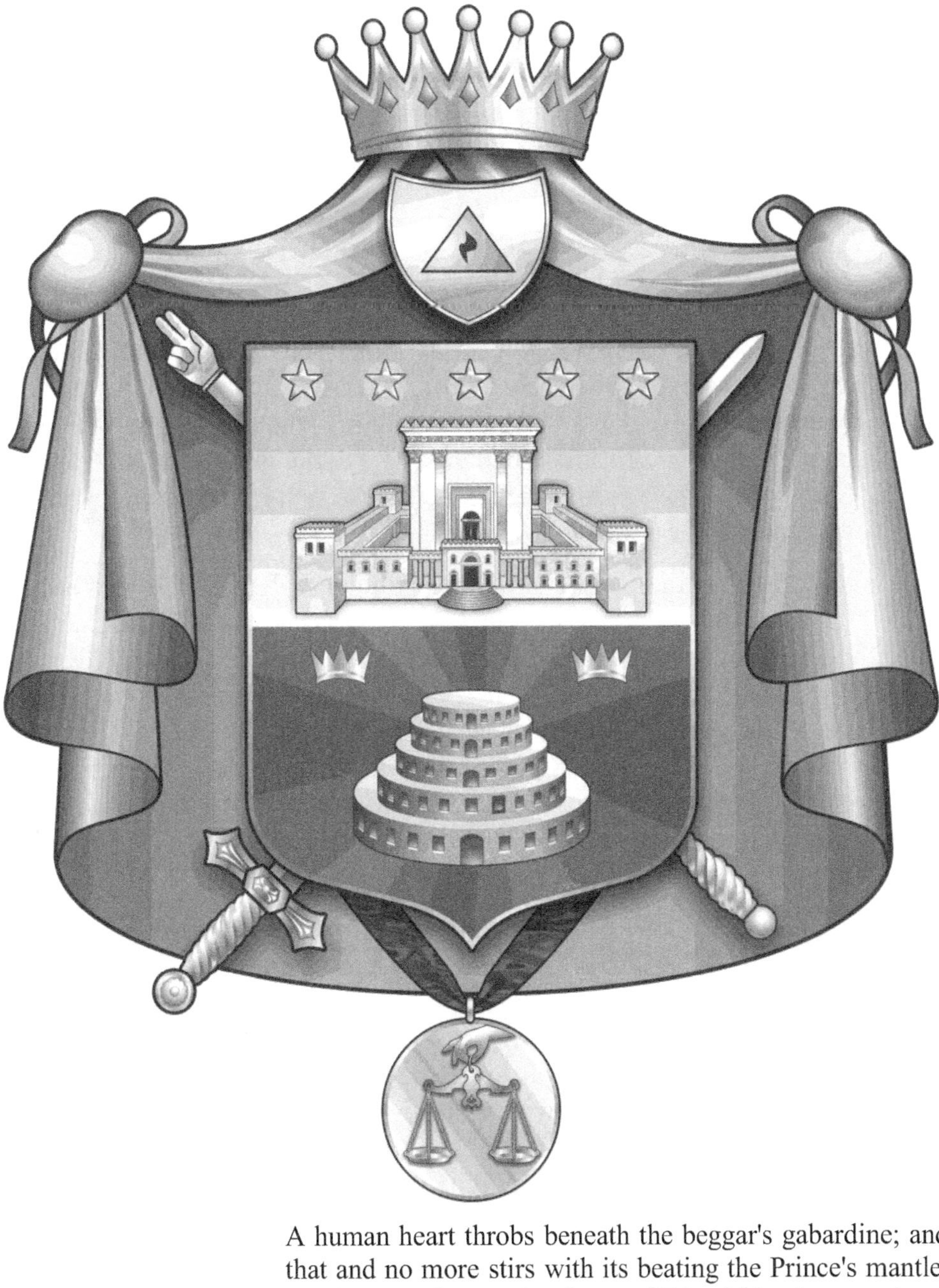

A human heart throbs beneath the beggar's gabardine; and that and no more stirs with its beating the Prince's mantle. The beauty of Love, the charm of Friendship, the sacredness of Sorrow, the heroism of Patience, the noble Self-sacrifice, these and their like, alone, make life to be life indeed, and are its grandeur and its power. They are the priceless treasures and glory of humanity; and they are not things of condition. All places and all scenes are alike clothed with the grandeur and charm of virtues such as these.[113]

ALLEGORIC CHRONOLOGY:

In sequence to the previous degree, between 522 and 486 BC.

LEGEND AND COMMENTS:

Zerubbabel and the Jews freed from Babylon arrive at the ruins of Jerusalem and, after building their quarters, begin the work of rebuilding the city and the Temple. Almost every day the work is interrupted by attacks, however, by foreign groups coming from outside the city, mainly the Samaritans.[xlvii] With each attack, the builders halt the work and take their swords to defend the city and the families who live there. Some of the residents, encouraged by the High Priest and the Prophet, assist in the local defense.

With battles, the number of warrior-builders decreases every day. In the meantime, Cyrus dies and Darius takes over as king. Zerubbabel realizes that the only hope of fulfilling the prophecy of rebuilding the Temple is to request an audience with Darius, the new king, and to convince him to embrace the cause, just as he did with Cyrus; however, outside the destroyed walls of Jerusalem, there is danger in every stretch, at least until they reach the eastern side of the river and find Persian troops.

Zerubbabel selects four princes to accompany him, as well as determines those who will assume duties in his absence, departing with them on the journey. Already in an audience with Darius, he is received with due honor to the position previously granted by Cyrus to him. Zerubbabel reports on the difficulties he has faced in the reconstruction work with the constant attacks of other peoples, especially the Samaritans. Darius, recognizing the wisdom and virtues of Zerubbabel, gives the princes that accompany him the same titles and benefits. He also determines that the construction will be financed by his treasury and that no one else will be able to attack Jerusalem and interrupt the reconstruction work, due to the risk of having wood logs removed from his house to be made a cross in which the offender will be nailed to it while the rest of your home will be demolished. Finally, Darius ratifies Zerubbabel as Governor of Israel and elevates Israel's status as a colony to part of the kingdom.

[xlvii] From Samaria, people who had fought in the vicinity of the bridge in the previous degree and who feared a new expansion of Israel.

From there, Zerubbabel manages to reorganize Israel and the reconstruction works of the city of Jerusalem and the Temple, with this second Temple being completed in six years.

MORAL:

Justice and Equity. These are the foundations of a Prince of Jerusalem. When the captives returned to Jerusalem, many conflicted with the Jews who remained there, mainly on account of immovable property. Who is entitled to land? That who dwelt with his family half a century ago and now returns; or the one who has spent the last few decades looking after and investing in it? The Princes of Jerusalem (deputy governors of Zerubbabel) had a responsibility to judge these cases, not uncommon, with justice and fairness. They were also, for the most part, Babylonian ex-captives. Despite this, they should not favor those who return from Babylon, treating everyone as equals and thinking of those who need it most.

But there is no point in maintaining domestic justice if external injustice reaches and impacts it; if all the peace and harmony provided by the internal order is constantly wounded by the external chaos. That is why the freemason cannot live only for himself and his family, without worrying about being charitable to the neediest people who are beyond the door of his home.

SYMBOLOGY:

The main symbol of this degree is a scale containing a dagger between the plates, five-pointed stars, and the letters "D" on one side and "Z" on the other. The balance represents justice, as Darius was just in honoring the commitment of his predecessor, Cyrus, and promised justice against Samaritans who disobey his order. The dagger recalls Ehud's attack on Eglon, king of the Moabites,[xlviii] who lived across the river and attacked Israel. The five stars represent the five Princes of Jerusalem who went to the audience with Darius. And the letters D and Z are the initials of Darius and Zerubbabel.

[xlviii] The Moabites' relationship with the Israelites was one of love and hate. Solomon was of Moabite descent, even if distant. Her father, David, was the great-grandson of Boaz, a Jew, with Ruth, a Moabite.

BIBLICAL PASSAGE:

Then Tatnai, governor on this side the river, Shethar-boznai, and their companions, according to that which Darius the king had sent, so they did speedily.

And the elders of the Jews builded, and they prospered through the prophesying of Haggai the prophet and Zechariah the son of Iddo. And they builded, and finished it, according to the commandment of the God of Israel, and according to the commandment of Cyrus, and Darius, and Artaxerxes king of Persia.

And this house was finished on the third day of the month Adar, which was in the sixth year of the reign of Darius the king.

And the children of Israel, the priests, and the Levites, and the rest of the children of the captivity, kept the dedication of this house of God with joy.

Ezra, 6:13-16.

17°: Knight of the East and West

Those speculations and fancies are useful to study; that knowing in what worthless and unfruitful investigations the mind may engage, you may the more value and appreciate the plain, simple, sublime, universally acknowledged truths, which have in all ages been the Light by which Masons have been guided on their way; the Wisdom and Strength that like imperishable columns have sustained and will continue to sustain its glorious and magnificent Temple.[114]

ALLEGORIC CHRONOLOGY:

After the year 1118, Vulgar Era (AD), without date determination.

LEGEND AND COMMENTS:

McClenachan understood this degree as the first of the "Modern" degrees as opposed to the degrees of what he called Ancient Masonry.[115] The term "Ancient" would be in the sense of antiquity and not that old known rivalry between "Ancients" and "Moderns" in 18th century England. His conception was based on the reasoning that Ancient Masonry was the one whose legends are directly related to the construction and reconstruction of the Solomon's Temple, which is addressed up to the previous degree, 16th, Prince of Jerusalem; while Modern Freemasonry presents allegories related to events after the destruction of the second Temple or, as some scholars prefer to describe, related to the construction of the "third temple", which would be in a figurative sense, of an interior, moral construction.

From this degree, the builder who predominated in the symbolic degrees and ineffable degrees, and who had become a kind of warrior-builder in the last two degrees, Knight of the East (15th) and Prince of Jerusalem (16th), he abandoned the craft and its operative symbology (Ancient Masonry), with the degrees migrating to a more chivalrous approach. For this reason, McClenachan, Pike and so many others considered the 17th degree as the first Philosophical Degree (in fact), despite being on the list of Chapter Degrees.

This 17th degree is strictly connected to the subsequent degree, of the Knight of Rose Croix, so that only in the next degree can this be fully understood. Something similar to what happens between the 13th and the 14th degrees.

Its narrative is related to that Order founded in 1118, by eleven knights, to protect Christian pilgrims in Jerusalem, which would later be called the Order of the Poor Knights of Christ and the Temple of Solomon, better known as Order of the Temple or, still, Order of the Templars. This relationship, however, is not made explicit in most versions, which is content to illustrate a knight from the West (Europe) who arrives in the East (Holy Land). In any case, the fact that the content of the degree revolves around the book of Revelation and John the Evangelist, its author,[xlix] indicates the Templar essence, since its knights were devotees of Saint John the Evangelist.

The initiation mentions the book of the seven seals of God. The knights, eager to discover the secrets and mysteries kept in the book, decide to seek the Ineffable Name, which has been lost again, with which the seals of the new law can be opened.

In honor of the seven seals, there are seven duties or attributes that a knight must seek to be worthy of knowing the Truth: Beauty (or Harmony), Dignity, Wisdom (or Intelligence), Power, Honor, Glory, and Strength. Three are the original pillars of Freemasonry: Wisdom, Strength, and Beauty. And these seven columns would still be based on seven virtues. In the Southern Jurisdiction, USA (and also in France and Brazil), they are Union, Honor, Duty, Loyalty, Courage, Discretion, and Silence.

Some Latin versions have a point of attention. In them, the members of the degree are considered Parthenian (from Parthenope), that is, native to the region where today is Naples, in Italy. It was not possible to find any direct relation between Parthenope and the Scottish Rite, the degree of Knight of the East and the West, or with the Order of the Templars that justified such mention.

About this mystery, the version of McClenachan (old version in Northern Masonic Jurisdiction) brings information that can explain it. In it, he says that " *Your Masonic age is very ancient, and you are termed a Patmian, as coming from Patmos*".[116]

Probably "Patmian", from "Patmos" was mistakenly translated as "Parthenian", from "Parthenope" in these versions. Unlike Parthenope, Patmos makes perfect sense concerning the allegory of the degree, since it was the place of John's exile, where he would have written the book of Revelation.

MORAL:

Virtues and Truth. Symbolically, the Truth is concealed by blindfolds, veils, or seals. This is because it needs to be discovered, deserved, and only the virtuous can deserve it. But what are these virtues of the virtuous? The rituals seem to agree with some, such as Union, Discretion, Loyalty, Duty, and Silence.

[xlix] However, there are strands of theologians who defend the possibility that John of Patmos, author of the Book of Revelation, is not the same John who wrote a Gospel.

The Union means understanding that we are a cog in our society and we need each other to live and be happy. Discretion is the duty to be reserved and restrained. Loyalty refers to the word given and commitments made. Duty is the feeling that must reign before the regulations of the institutions to which you are affiliated and the obligations taken by oaths, and Silence, to never reveal to a profane what must remain veiled, as well as not to utter words that give a profane reason to censor him.

SYMBOLOGY:

The book with the seven seals, with a lamb on it, is the main symbol of this degree; followed by the heptagon containing the initials of the seven virtues of a Knight from the East and the West.

BIBLICAL PASSAGE:

And I saw in the right hand of him that sat on the throne a book written within and on the backside, sealed with seven seals.

And I saw a strong angel proclaiming with a loud voice, Who is worthy to open the book, and to loose the seals thereof?

And no man in heaven, nor in earth, neither under the earth, was able to open the book, neither to look thereon.

And I wept much, because no man was found worthy to open and to read the book, neither to look thereon.

And one of the elders saith unto me, Weep not: behold, the Lion of the tribe of Juda, the Root of David, hath prevailed to open the book, and to loose the seven seals thereof.

Revelation, 5:1-5.

18°: Knight Rose Croix

Man is once more taught to look upward to his God. No longer to a God hid in impenetrable mystery, and infinitely remote from human sympathy, emerging only at intervals from the darkness to smite and crush humanity : but a God, good, kind, beneficent, and merciful: a Father, loving the creatures He has made, with a love immeasurable and exhaustless ; Who feels for us, and sympathizes with us, and sends us pain and want and disaster only that they may serve to develop in us the virtues and excellences that befit us to live with Him hereafter.[117]

ALLEGORIC CHRONOLOGY:

In sequence to the previous degree, without determining the time.

LEGEND AND COMMENTS:

This degree has received different names. As an example, we can mention Sovereign Prince Rose Croix of Heredom; Perfect Prince of H-R-D-M; Knight of the White Eagle or Pelican; and Knight of the Eagle and Pelican. Besides, it is a degree common to several rites.

In it, as in the previous degree, the esoteric speaks louder than the allegorical. The knight continues to seek to recover the true word, then lost. The Masonic symbology of the transformation of rough stone into cubic, parallel to the alchemical symbology of the transformation of lead into gold, is now replaced by the mystical symbology of the transformation of the cross (death), from which a rose is born (life). In the case of the knight, his transformation is moral and, in showing himself to be deserving, it is in this degree that he finds the word, but in a new form, for being a new era under a new law.

In this new law, the three original Masonic pillars, which supported the ancient Temple, of Wisdom, Strength, and Beauty, are now replaced by the three theological virtues of Faith, Hope, and Charity. They are deeply inculcated, crowning Charity (Love) as the master of others and, therefore, the greatest obligation of every Knight of Rose Croix. Jesus is pointed out as an example of this virtue, regardless of creed, by accepting such suffering and sacrificing himself in the name of the Law of Love. In his honor, the true word becomes INRI, short for "*Iesus Nazarenus, Rex Iudeorum*" (Jesus of Nazareth, King of the Jews), but also short for "*Igne Natura Renovatur Integra*" (Fire renews the whole nature), the alchemical motto "*Igne Nitrum Rosis Invenitur*" (the salt of dew is extracted by fire), and the hermetic sentence "*Iam, Nour, Ruach, Iabeshah*" (water, fire, air, earth).

Considering the sacrifice of Jesus as an illustration of the main lesson of this degree, the Christian symbolism of a pelican is adopted, who legendarily injures his chest to offer his flesh and blood as food for its children. Thus, the Last Supper has significant relevance for the Knights of Rose Croix Degree, who observe the Thursday of Holy Week, also called Maundy Thursday, the symbolic day of the Last Supper, to share bread and wine in a mystic banquet.

The observance of Scottish Rite's Ceremony of Remembrance and Renewal, concerning Christian members, who may need to attend religious commitments on the date, is often carried out on a date different from that of Maundy Thursday, either on a weekend close to the same or close to the March Equinox.

Still, it should be remembered that, at that same time, there is the celebration of the Pessach and the Persian New Year (*Jamshedji Navroz*). Thus, at each Mystic Banquet of the Scottish Rite, it must be remembered that we count in our ranks with brothers of the most different creeds and ethnicities and that the celebration of the Knights of Rose Croix Degree is above all, in the name of peace and the union of the peoples, recognizing that we all have the same divine origin, from a single God, which makes us brethren. Hence the symbolism of the Flaming Star, which shines on all men, without distinction, representing the Truth and whose rays of light are philosophy, which is not limited to dogmas.

It is necessary, however, to register the theory that the first versions of this degree pointed to the Flaming Star as a symbol of the Star of Bethlehem, which had revealed the birth of Jesus (dawn of a new era and a new law), gaining this more ecumenical interpretation and enlightenment from the Mother Supreme Council of the World.

MORAL:

Charity. The Scottish Rite does not claim to become a charity in the current mold, since charity is not its purpose of existence and institutional mission. On the other hand, the 18th degree comes to show that, for the Scottish Rite, a charity may not be the end, but it is, with absolute certainty, the means for the freemason's moral evolution. Without charity, that is, without loving and caring for others, there is no virtue or even faith that can be sustained. And the hope of a better world, of peace and harmony, dies.

The lessons of this degree must remind the freemason that charity is not necessarily philanthropy. Since charity is a reflection of love for one's neighbor, any philanthropy that is not motivated by this feeling is not a charity. On the other hand, listen to who needs to be heard; a smile and a hug to those in need; or good advice to those who are confused; they are true acts of charity, of love, although they are not characterized as material philanthropy.

Still, the lesson of the pelican or Jesus goes further in the lesson of charity, as it teaches that pure charity is not just giving what is left over but giving what is often lacking. It is sharing. This lesson becomes more and more difficult to be taught and learned each day, considering the current consumer culture, which is taking great strides in not only tolerating but socially justifying and approving increasingly selfish and individualistic behaviors.

Declaring that each member of the human species is your brother and should be loved and supported as such, that you should sacrifice yourself and take from yourself (like the pelican) to give to those who have nothing, sounds like Communism to some, who reject such an idea and prefer to adopt new "Christian" conceptions, such as the Prosperity Theology, founded initially on the famous healing cults and growing televangelism, which gave impetus to some churches that promote the idolatry of its own religious leaders.

Thus, before anyone wants to surrender to the political polarization syndrome that prevails today and accuse the Scottish Rite of being "left-handed" or "communist", it is emphasized that the Knight of Rose Croix degree, having arisen in the 18th century, is before the emergence of Marx and his theory. Still, it is a time when the lessons of loving your neighbor and sharing bread were praised more than the promise of heaven made of gold waiting for the rich of the earthly life.

SYMBOLOGY:

The main symbols of this degree are the pelican, symbol of the purest charity; the flaming star, the symbol of Truth and philosophy; and the Rose Croix, a symbol of moral and spiritual evolution.

BIBLICAL PASSAGE:

And the first day of unleavened bread, when they killed the passover, his disciples said unto him, Where wilt thou that we go and prepare that thou mayest eat the passover?

And he sendeth forth two of his disciples, and saith unto them, Go ye into the city, and there shall meet you a man bearing a pitcher of water: follow him.

And wheresoever he shall go in, say ye to the goodman of the house, The Master saith, Where is the guestchamber, where I shall eat the passover with my disciples?

And he will shew you a large upper room furnished and prepared: there make ready for us.

And his disciples went forth, and came into the city, and found as he had said unto them: and they made ready the passover.

And in the evening he cometh with the twelve.

Mark, 14:12-17.

Chapter Degrees Considerations

Similar to the symbolism of the Rose Croix, which represents the birth of a new era and the emergence of a new law, based on love, this mason from the Lodge of Perfection, forged by tools and construction work, dies to be reborn as a knight, thus inaugurating the degrees of chivalry, called in the Scottish Rite as philosophical degrees. Thus, the four degrees of the Chapter of Rose Croix play this role of transition between the mason and the knight, the old and the new, the before and after Christ.

The mason coming from the ineffable degrees already faces, in the 15th degree, his first battle, on the River Jordan's banks. In 16th degree, the sword is already on an equal footing with the trowel. Thus, there is a kind of builder-warrior. Then, in the 17th degree, there were only ruins of that time that the masons built and rebuilt. And the knight or prince present among its broken columns has no intention of raising it physically, but only metaphorically, dedicating himself to building his inner temple of virtues, and seeking and defending his truth and finally, reaching the desired virtuosity, in the 18th degree that knight or prince discovers his "holy grail", which is the new true word, in this new era under a new law. Upon receiving it, he begins to dedicate his life to loving and helping others.

As for this prince status, mention is made in the 17th degree, which is intensified in the 18th, including the use of the term in some versions of its title, such as Sovereign Rose Croix Prince of Heredom, and Perfect Prince of H-R-D-M. This is clear evidence of the strong influence that the already discussed Ramsay's Oration had on the emergence of these degrees, in particular, the following excerpt:

> (...) our founders had been simple workers in stone, or merely curious geniuses who wished to perfect the arts. They were not only skillful architects, desirous of consecrating their talents and goods to the construction of material temples; but also religious and **warrior princes** who intended to enlighten, edify and protect the living temples of the Most High. (emphasis added) (Ismail, K. *Debatendo Tabus Maçônicos*. 2016. Londrina: A Trolha, p. 158).

It should be noted that in the historical degrees, the first two capitular degrees (15th and 16th), the typical temporal location of the ineffable degrees is kept. Still, with these, there is a certain historical connection. The next two degrees of the Chapter (17th and 18th), doctrinal (or pre-philosophical), present some abstraction in this temporal sense, losing the chronological links between the legends.

Another observation that deserves mention is regarding the protagonism of the Word: Lost in the last degree of the blue lodge, it is recovered at the end of the Lodge of Perfection. Then, lost again, a new Real Word is discovered at the end of the Chapter of Rose Croix. That is, the conclusions of each of the first three bodies of the Scottish Rite are closely related to the Word. In the case of the 18th degree, Jesus of Nazareth, King of the Jews, is placed on the same level as Jehovah and, to a degree that has the cross as one of his main symbols and as part of its title, whose sacrifice of Jesus serves as an allegory, and the love your neighbor is its main teaching, there is a great effort by the ritualists of the different versions to give it a less Christian and more ecumenical or syncretistic guise, which has been effective throughout of all these years.

In a way, this reality can be observed, on some scale, in each degree of Scottish Rite. The initiate can identify more or less with its allegories and symbols, but, armed with reason and free from ignorance, intolerance, and fanaticism, he will always be able to absorb some moral teaching. If the way and its format have limitations, the message transmitted does not have them. Thus, as a system of morality, its legends and symbology do not claim to be dogmatic, indisputable, and blindly followed, but only to invite reflection on the ethical and moral lessons hidden in them.

In this case, the lessons taught or reinforced in the degrees of the Chapter of Rose Croix are of fidelity and perseverance; justice and equity; virtues (union, discretion, loyalty, duty, and silence) and truth; and undoubtedly the most important of all, charity.

4.4. The Council of Kadosh and its Degrees

Introduction to the Council of Kadosh Degrees

Kadosh is the transliteration of a word in Hebrew that means "sacred" and is used in the Bible when referring to temples or sacred sites. Thus, a Knight Kadosh is a Knight of the Temple, that is, a Templar, which is more explicit in the last degree of the Council of Kadosh, which simulates an investiture to the Order of the Temple.

The name of the body is appropriate when referring to the so-called philosophical degrees, inaugurated from the 17th degree onwards, clearly, a degree of Templar inspiration, despite granted in the Chapter of Rose Croix, which proved to be a transition body between the physical temple and the metaphorical (hence the "philosophical" aspect), the old and the new testament, the old and the new law, the mason and the knight.

Speaking of knights, the Council of Kadosh's degrees have a strong content of courage and religiosity, especially those that simulate an endowment to three orders of chivalry, specifically the 27th, 29th, and 30th degrees. Still, having been developed in France in a period of gnostic and occult effervescence, the degrees are quite mystical in comparison to the ineffable ones, especially the 24th and 28th degrees, eminently hermetic.

The Council of Kadosh is the body that gathers the highest number of degrees among all the Scottish Rite's bodies. It is also the body where most of the degrees that were not part of the Rite of Heredom are centered. Thus, it can be understood that it is thanks to the degrees of the Council of Kadosh that the A&ASR is the A&ASR because it is in this body that it differs from the others.

19°: Grand Pontiff

Therefore faint not, nor be weary in well-doing! Be not discouraged at men's apathy, nor disgusted with their follies nor tired of their indifference! Care not for returns and results; but see only what there is to do, and do it, leaving the results to God! Soldier of the Cross! Sworn Knight of Justice, Truth, and Toleration! Good Knight and True! Be patient an3 work![118]

ALLEGORIC CHRONOLOGY:

Undetermined.

LEGEND AND COMMENTS:

Still exploring the apocalyptic content presented in the previous degree as a backdrop, in this 19th degree, the candidate becomes a high priest of the Order of Melchizedek and is considered a "bridge builder" (hence the title "pontiff", from the Latin *pontifex*). Thus, that traditional Masonic mission to complete the construction of the temple is replaced by the vision of the New Jerusalem,[1] that is, of a world in peace and harmony. It is the bridge, between the destroyed and divided Jerusalem for the New Jerusalem, that is, from this imperfect world and divided between light and darkness to a world of pure light and perfection, that the brother must build as a member of the Order of Melchizedek. The stones to build this bridge are the good deeds (charity) and the tools used are the virtues.

To better understand the term "Order of Melchizedek", the Bible should be used, more precisely in Hebrews, 5: 4-10:

> And no man taketh this honour unto himself, but he that is called of God, as was Aaron.
> So also **Christ** glorified not himself to be made an high priest; but he that said unto him, Thou art my Son, today have I begotten thee.
> As he saith also in another place, Thou art a priest for ever after the **order of Melchisedek**.
> Who in the days of his flesh, when he had offered up prayers and supplications with strong crying and tears unto him that was able to save him from death, and was heard in that he feared;
> Though he were a Son, yet learned the obedience by the things which he suffered;
> And being made perfect, he became the author of eternal salvation unto all them that obey him;

[1] Called by some authors from Heavenly Jerusalem. It appears in the Book of Revelation as the city destined for the believers. It has no temples and it is always daytime, even without sun, because God illuminates it. A river of clear water crosses it and in its center is the Tree of Life.

> Called of God an high priest after the **order of Melchisedek** (emphasis added).

Melchizedek is probably the most enigmatic character in the entire Bible. By order of God, Abraham would have sought guidance from Melchizedek, a man of divine appearance, without ancestry or descent or known beginning and end of life, and paid to tithe to him, who was king (of Salem) and high priest at the same time (as later Jesus was also considered). Thus, he is the first biblical character to exercise the priesthood.

In the aforementioned biblical passage, Jesus is considered to be the high priest of the Order of Melchizedek, that is, that he was not of the Order of Aaron. The Order of Aaron was a priesthood of the Levite lineage, of sinners who offered sacrifices and supplications. The Order of Melchizedek, in which Jesus was qualified, was something superior, of a non-Levite priesthood, based on the purity of thoughts and actions.

Some believe that Jesus is the reincarnation of Melchizedek. Others, that Melchizedek would have been a non-incarnate (but temporary bodily) appearance of Jesus centuries before his birth. Still, some defend the theory that Melchizedek was Shem, Noah's firstborn. And, finally, those who believe that he was just a character with similarities to Jesus, which earned him the comparative mention in Hebrews.

Finally, the other title option of the degree, " Sublime Scotch Mason", suggests that the plot may also be symbolic of the Jacobite desire for the restoration of the Stuart dynasty.

MORAL:

Virtue, Sincerity, Moderation, Truth, Justice, and Tolerance. These are the moral tools so that the Grand Pontiff can fulfill his duty to collaborate in the construction of a bridge to the New Jerusalem, without forgetting that the construction is slow, but the destruction is fast and, therefore, in addition to building it must be preserved.

When qualifying the candidate as of the Order of Melchizedek, the intention is not to compare him to Jesus, but to consider that, not being of the Levite lineage, it is up to the brother to seek to develop his symbolic priesthood through his good words, actions, faith and devotion, seeking to be fair and tolerant towards the people around you; for he will not be judged by the family he was born in, clan or lineage, but by his choices and attitudes.

SYMBOLOGY:

The New Jerusalem: city in square format, walled, with a large tree in the center, floating on clouds.

BIBLICAL PASSAGE:

And the wall of the city had twelve foundations, and in them the names of the twelve apostles of the Lamb.
And he that talked with me had a golden reed to measure the city, and the gates thereof, and the wall thereof.
And the city lieth foursquare, and the length is as large as the breadth: and he measured the city with the reed, twelve thousand furlongs. The length and the breadth and the height of it are equal.
And he measured the wall thereof, and hundred and forty and four cubits, according to the measure of a man, that is, of the angel.
And the building of the wall of it was of jasper: and the city was pure gold, like unto clear glass.
And the foundations of the wall of the city were garnished with all manner of precious stones. The first foundation was jasper; the second, sapphire; the third, a chalcedony; the fourth, an emerald;
The fifth, sardonyx; the sixth, sardius; the seventh, chrysolite; the eighth, beryl; the ninth, a topaz; the tenth, a chrysoprasus; the eleventh, a jacinth; the twelfth, an amethyst.
Revelation, 21:14-20.

20°: Master of the Symbolic Lodge (SJ) or Master ad Vitam (NMJ)

As Master of a Lodge, you will therefore be exceedingly careful that no Candidate, in any Degree, be required to submit to any degradation whatever; as has been too much the custom in some of the Degrees: and take it as a certain and inflexible rule, to which there is no exception, that real Masonry requires of no man anything to which a Knight and

> Gentleman cannot honorably, and without feeling outraged or humiliated, submit.
>
> (...) As Master, you will teach those who are under you, and to whom you will owe your office, that the decorations of many of the Degrees are to be dispensed with, whenever the expense would interfere with the duties of charity, relief, and benevolence (...).
>
> (...) As Master of a Lodge, you are to inculcate these duties on your brethren. Teach the employed to be honest, punctual, and faithful as well as respectful and obedient to all proper orders: but also teach the employer that every man or woman who desires to work, has a right to have work to do; and that they, and those who from sickness or feebleness, loss of limb or of bodily vigor, old age or infancy, are not able to work, have a right to be fed, clothed, and sheltered from the inclement elements (...).[119]

ALLEGORIC CHRONOLOGY:

Between 465 and 424 BC, sometime during the reign of Artaxerxes I, that is, chronologically after the 16th degree.

LEGEND AND COMMENTS:

This 20th degree of the Scottish Rite has a similar origin to the 5th degree of the York Rite, in which there is the so-called Induction into the Oriental Chair and the members are treated as Past Masters. This becomes even clearer when observing that the degree is called in many Supreme Councils, among them that of the North Jurisdiction of the USA, "Master *ad Vitam*". The title of Master *ad Vitam* has the same meaning as Past Master since the Latin term "*ad Vitam*" (for life) is commonly used from the end of a successful mandate,[li] in this case, of a Worshipful Master in a blue lodge. Some authors report that this degree served, in fact, as an installation ceremony in some French lodges in the 18th century.[120] [121]

In the Supreme Council of the Northern Jurisdiction of the USA, this degree gained George Washington as protagonist. The other title of the degree, Sovereign Prince of Freemasonry, refers to another example of leadership, Zerubbabel, recognized as the Sovereign Prince among the

[li] Under the influence of this degree, it is common to adopt the title "Grand Master Ad Vitam" by the Past Grand Masters of many Grand Lodges in Latin America.

princes of Israel, and responsible for the work of rebuilding the Lord's Temple.

The innovation of the first title of the degree, from Master ad Vitam to "Grand Master ad Vitam", or even, "Grand Master of all lodges", found in some versions, is not justified given the history of the degree's appearance, its original utility (installation of Worshipful Masters) and its ritualistic content. The appearance of this variation was probably motivated by the allegorical interpretation that Zerubbabel served as Grand Master of the Temple reconstruction, and not as Worshipful Master. However, it is the second title, by Sovereign Prince, which is based on the allegory of Zerubbabel, while the first title, Master *ad Vitam*, as several scholars have reported, was functional and not allegorical. Thus, perhaps Pike was correct about the process of innovation of this and other titles, as well as the ritualistic before its revision, and which persists in several Latin versions:

> An empty and sterile pomp, impossible indeed to be carried out, and to which no meaning whatever was attached, with far-fetched explanations that were either so many stupid platitudes or themselves needed an interpreter; **lofty titles, arbitrarily assumed, and to which the inventors had not condescended to attach any explanation** that should acquit them of the folly of assuming temporal rank, power, and titles of nobility, made the world laugh, and the Initiate feel ashamed (emphasis added).[122]

The degree teaches that a Master of the Lodge: must not impose his belief on anyone; he must always give the benefit of the doubt; he must not lie to the brethren; he must spread the Masonic lights (nine, symbolized by nine lit candles) to the apprentices and fellows of the Craft, in addition to the instructions of the rituals and the examination of questions and answers; and he must not accept the position if he is not prepared to carry it out, which includes knowing the history, philosophy, and morals of Freemasonry. You must "listen patiently, judge deliberately and serenely, and decide impartially", the Bible has the role of reminding you that: "(...) for with what judgment ye judge, ye shall be judged: and with what measure ye mete, it shall be measured to you again" (Matthew, 7: 2).

MORAL:

Masonic values are presented to the freemason using five squares and three triangles, whose bases, united, form an octagon. The first square symbolizes prudence, temperance, purity, and sobriety. The second square symbolizes **heroism**, firmness, moderation, and zeal. The third square symbolizes probity, **honor**, fidelity, and punctuality. The fourth square symbolizes disinterest, lenience, forgiveness, and patience. The fifth and final square symbolizes **charity**, kindness, **generosity**, and detachment. The first triangle symbolizes gratitude to God, love for humanity, and trust in human nature. The second triangle symbolizes **veneration for God**, devotion to family and friends, and **patriotism**. The third and last triangle symbolizes **truth**, **justice**, and **tolerance**.

Just by observing these 29 virtues, he will have the moral conditions to enlighten the brothers of the Lodge with the nine lights or virtues of Veneration (to God), Charity, Generosity, Heroism, Honor, Patriotism, Justice, Tolerance, and Truth.

It can be seen that the nine lights (bold) are among the 29 virtues to be observed by the Worshipful Master. This means that he must show himself far more virtuous from what he should instill in his followers, as a High Priest who must have infinitely greater devotion than the members of his congregation. This is the secret of leadership. A heroic act that becomes public is unlikely to generate other heroic acts, but it encourages various acts of altruism and courage. A company director who is polite and a philanthropist may not turn his employees into charitable gentlemen, but he will create an organizational environment of education and solicitude.

SYMBOLOGY:

The octagon formed by the base of five squares and three triangles, representing the 29 virtues of a Worshipful Master; and nine lit candles, symbolizing the nine virtues to be transmitted to the members of the Lodge.[lii]

BIBLICAL PASSAGE:

[lii] I suppose this symbol of nine lit candles for nine virtues may have inspired Frank Sherman Land to develop the symbolism of the Seven Cardinal Virtues of the Order of DeMolay, represented by seven lit candles. The fact that some of these DeMolay cardinal virtues are common or similar to these of the 20th degree weighs in favor of this assumption.

And in the days of Artaserxes wrote Bishlam, Mithredath, Tabeel, and the rest of their companions, unto Artaxerxes king of Persia; and the writing of the letter was written in the Syrian tongue, and interpreted in the Syrian tongue.

Rehum the chancellor and Shimshai the scribe wrote a letter against Jerusalem to Artaxerxes the king in this sort:

Then wrote Rehum the chancellor, and Shimshai the scribe, and the rest of their companions; the Dinaites, the Apharsathchites, the Tarpelites, the Apharsites, the Archevites, the Babylonians, the Sunsachites, the Dehavites, and the Elamites,

And the rest of the nations whom the great and noble Asnapper brought over, and set in the cities of Samaria, and the rest that are on this side the river, and at such a time.

Ezra, 4: 7-10.

21°: Noachite, or Prussian Knight

There is but one rule for the Mason in this matter. If there be virtues, and he is called upon to speak of him who owns them, let him tell them forth impartially. And if there be vices mixed with them, let him be content the world shall know them by some other tongue than his. For if the evil-doer deserve no pity, his wife, his parents, or his children, or other innocent persons who love him may (...).[123]

ALLEGORIC CHRONOLOGY:

At an undetermined moment, probably between the end of the 12th century and the beginning of the 14th century.

LEGEND AND COMMENTS:

The Vehmgericht, better known as Holy Vehme or simply Vehm, can also be translated as Vehmic Court. It is a kind of secret court that existed in Westphalia, with constant activity during the 14th and 15th centuries, and whose members were known as "free judges". It functioned as a secret society, including an initiation, the fraternal nature among the members, and modes of recognition. It was common for some members to hide the affiliation from their family members, many of the meetings were restricted to insiders, and there was secrecy about the executioner who would apply the penalty, which was often death. His motto was *Fiat Justicia, ruat Coelum*, which means "May justice be done, even if Heaven falls", whose authorship is credited to Lucius Calpurnius Piso Caesoninus, who was the father-in-law of Julius Caesar.

The region of Westphalia, which was once independent and is now part of Germany, belonged to Prussia during the 18th and early 19th centuries. This degree having arisen around 1762, justifies his other title, Prussian Knight. Furthermore, it should be noted that, when the degree was developed, Frederick II was the king of Prussia (1740-1786) and, as is known, he was chosen by the eleven gentlemen of Charleston, founders of the Scottish Rite (especially by Frederick Dalcho), as its patron, which justifies the survival of the degree in the selection of the founders.

This degree presents the allegories that would illustrate the supposed initiation ritual of the Vehmic Court: the story of Noah (hence the title of the degree, Noachite) and the tower of Babel, which had Phaleg, Shem's grandson, as an architect and Grand Master. With the confusion of languages caused by God, Phaleg would have gone into exile in the region of Westphalia and built a pyramid-shaped temple there to beg for divine mercy. In many versions, this is not explicit.

The legend of Noah is closely related to the Masonic allegory, which historically explores this common concept of Abrahamic religions and even other religions, of a just and obedient man who allies with God to survive with his family in the Flood and follow His most basic commandments. This relationship reaches such a point that Dermott refers to "Noachite" as a synonym for "freemason" and points to the first three laws of Noah's covenant as the cement of the Lodge, that is, what unites us as brothers, regardless of professed faith. They would be the renouncement of idols, the veneration of one God, and not killing.[124]

In the same way, the legend of the Tower of Babel is an allegory historically explored in Freemasonry, having as reference what is considered by the English as the oldest Masonic document in the world: the Regius Manuscript, supposedly from the year 1390. In it, King Nimrod, grandson of Ham, is considered to be the first Grand Master of Freemasonry and responsible for the construction of the Tower.[liii] This is also repeated in the Thistle Manuscript 1756.[125]

There are also versions of this degree, such as those of both US jurisdictions, that present a judgment of the Vehmic Court, assembled under the light of a full moon, led by a Prussian Teutonic Knight[liv] named Adolf, who returns from the Crusades and finds his goods and lands taken by another knight. The matter is taken to the free judges, who end up judging in favor of the plaintiff and condemn the defendant to death. Adolf ends up donating his recovered goods, as was already his intention. These versions have more adherence to 17th, 18th, and 19th degrees, enabling the resumption of that sense of continuity that the Scottish Rite's member got used to experiencing up to the 16th degree.

MORAL:

Justice and Charity. To this degree, the need that society and its members have for a free and impartial judiciary is evident. For Pike, there is, in fact, no democracy without this legal guarantee. Besides, there is a vision about the harsh reality behind charity: there are many in need because there are many injustices. Thus, preventing and combating injustice is also an act of charity; however, it is not up to the freemason who joins the Scottish Rite to dress in the robe of the punisher and condemn other people, even more publicly. He must be discreet when making complaints to the competent authority, either to a manager about

---

[liii] And not Phaleg, as in the Scottish Rite, which would be a primitive version of Hiram Abiff, as Melchizedek would be of Jesus (in the 19th degree).

[liv] The Teutonic Order or Germanic Order was one of the orders that, together with the Templars and Hospitallers, served in the Crusades. Initially, it aimed to provide medical care to Germanic pilgrims, since the overburdened Hospitals gave preference to the English and French over these. Finally, it ended up getting closer to the Templar model, also assuming the role of military order.

the misconduct of an employee or to a judge regarding an infraction or crime committed by a third party.

SYMBOLOGY:

The full moon, which occupies the upper part of the coat of arms of the degree, remembering that the Prussian Knights met in the light of the moon; and the arrow with its tip pointing downwards overlapping the triangle, symbolizing the will of God imposed on the Tower of Babel, illustrating the lower part of the coat of arms.

BIBLICAL PASSAGE:

And the Lord said, I will destroy man whom I have created from the face of the earth; both man, and beast, and the creeping thing, and the fowls of the air; for it repenteth me that I have made them.

But Noah found grace in the eyes of the Lord.

These are the generations of Noah: Noah was a ***just man and perfect***[lv] *in his generations, and Noah walked with God.*

And Noah begat three sons, Shem, Ham, and Japheth.

The earth also was corrupt before God, and the earth was filled with violence.

And God looked upon the earth, and, behold, it was corrupt; for all flesh had corrupted his way upon the earth.

(emphasis added) Genesis, 6: 7-12.

[lv] Just and Perfect. This Noachite term, linked to Ancient Freemasonry, survives, as a usual term among Freemasons to refer to something strictly Masonic in Latin countries, and in rituals that qualify a Blue Lodge as "just, perfect, and regular".

22°: Knight of the Royal Axe, or Prince of Libanus

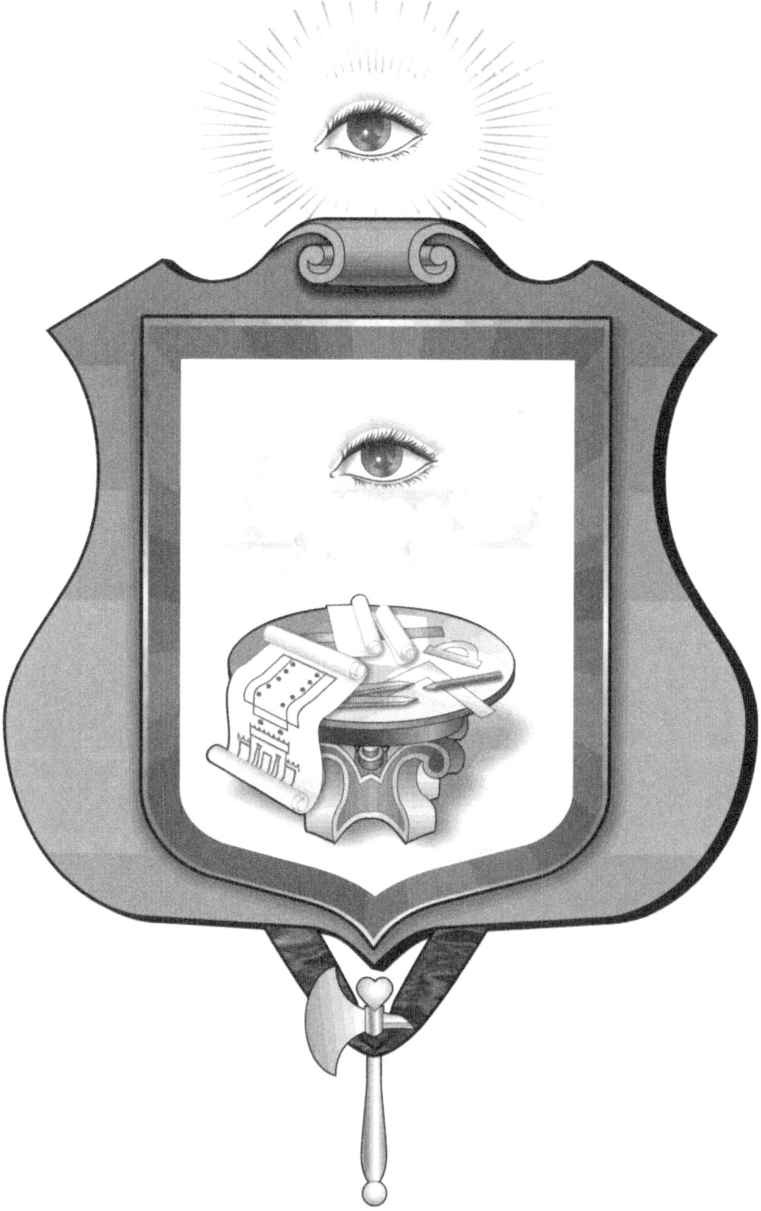

SYMPATHY with the great laboring classes, respect for labor itself, and resolution to do some good work in our day and generation, these are the lessons of this Degree, and they are purely Masonic. Masonry has made a working-man and his associates the Heroes of her principal legend, and himself the companion of Kings. The idea is as simple and true as it is sublime. From first to last, Masonry is work. It venerates the Grand Architect of the Universe. It commemorates the building of a Temple. Its principal emblems are the working tools of Masons and Artisans. It preserves the name of the first worker in brass and iron as one of its pass-words. When the Brethren meet together, they are at labor. The Master is the overseer who sets the craft to work and gives them proper instruction. Masonry is the apotheosis of WORK.[126]

ALLEGORIC CHRONOLOGY:

Before 500 BC in an indefinite period.

LEGEND AND COMMENTS:

This degree is basically about work. The allegory is based on the lumberjack work of the Phoenicians, especially those of Tyre, who supplied the cedars of their forests to Babylon, Egypt, and Israel, the latter in particular for the construction of the Temple. The meeting is allegorical of a kind of acceptance to the Phoenician college of craftsmen, similar to the Roman *Collegia Fabrorum* that would have appeared some centuries later. There is also a three-headed serpent in the degree, called idleness (the enemy of work), whose heads represent drunkenness, impurity, and gambling.

The French version goes a little further and illustrates the initiation to the Phoenician College of Craftsmen with the legend of Adam, who would have eaten the forbidden fruit and been expelled from Eden, having to, from then on, work to survive. And when he leaves Eden, he takes with him a seedling of the Tree of Life, which gives rise to the cedars of Lebanon.

This version brings a controversial point to the scholars of the rite, as it presents work as a punishment, while the moral of the degree starts from the understanding of work as a means of approaching God as much as praying.

The second title of the degree, Prince of Libanus, can be understood by an interpretation presented by Pike for the term Prince, which would be " who aims to be Chief, [Princeps[lvi]], first, leader, among his equals, in virtue and good deeds".[127]

[lvi] *Princeps*. Latin word that means leader.

MORAL:

Work. There is no way to interpret this degree without remembering the popular maxims that "work dignifies man" and "an idle mind is the devil's workshop". In this sense, Brother Voltaire noted that "work saves us from three great evils: boredom, vice and need".

This view of the work is not restricted to the philosopher and adages, but is also supported by the three great Abrahamic religions: Judaism, Christianity, and Islam: "And also that every man should eat and drink, and enjoy the good of all his labour, it is the gift of God"(Ecclesiastes 3:13); "Now he that planteth and he that watereth are one: and every man shall receive his own reward according to his own labour" (1 Corinthians 3:8); "For the like of this let the workers work" (Quran, 37:61). And in Freemasonry it could not be different: the candidate, as soon as he becomes an apprentice, already receives his work tools symbolically.

One must see beyond the simplistic approach that work dignifies man, as it is through it that family support is provided. This view is mistaken in the sense that, in this case, it would not be the work itself that would dignify the man, but his material reward: the salary. To make this mistake would be dishonorable, neglecting and mocking both the man and his work, for limiting the result of the work to a salary, leading to suggest that the man only works to earn his pay.[lvii]

Work produces more than just the worker's wages. Work generates a product or service that is demanded by someone else or by society. The work generates skill and experience for the one who performs it. The work creates not only commercial but also social relationships. Work results in learning and knowledge. Work provides pleasure when done well. Work establishes partnerships. And this is exactly what the allegory of this degree is about: the intangible fruits of work. Demand and social relations (construction of the Temple), learning and knowledge (College of Craftsmen and division by degrees), and the establishment of partnerships (such as between Hiram of Tyre and Solomon of Israel).

Taking the work of a tailor, for example, he cannot make a suit without the farmer who plants and harvests the cotton, the trucker who transports the cotton to the textile factory, the factory workers who transform it into the fabric, the trucker who delivers the fabric to the

[lvii] *Homo Economicus*. Nineteenth-century economist concept, which summed up man to a being who sought maximum gain with minimum effort and only worked to be able to supply his needs and finance his pleasures.

wholesaler, and finally, the wholesaler who supplies it to the tailor. Not to mention the other utensils used to make a suit, such as buttons, which involve so many other stages of work and workers. Thus, it is thanks to the work of many workers that the tailor can do his work. And this work cycle does not stop there, since the suit produced by the tailor will dress another professional, who depends not only on the tailor but on many other professionals to survive and be able to perform his work, on which other workers may depend, including the tailor.

In this way, wages are just a cog in the gigantic and complex machine of work, which connects countless numbers of men of good will and allows them to serve each other, without distinction. Look at yourself and see the immensity that surrounds you. See each object and accessory you are using right now. Look at the environment around you and try to imagine how many workers from around the world were involved in producing all of these things. Also note the electrical energy that probably keeps on some utensil from that environment in which it is connected.

Now, think of the vast production and transport networks and the millions of workers involved in them to allow all these to exist and function around you; not to mention the interior of the walls, where you may find water services, internet, telephone, etc. Without a doubt, we can say that millions of workers from your city, state, country and even (or mainly) from other countries were and are involved in the production and supply of the products and services that currently surround you.

Sometimes, the rush of daily life does not allow us to stop for a few minutes and make this reflection. Simply look around and understand how we are all dependent on the work of countless unknown workers and we should be grateful for the work of each one, who not only dignifies them, but also ourselves. So, perhaps, we can see our own work, not as a punishment, but also as a way of serving (and loving) others; giving, discreetly or hiddenly, our collaboration for the happiness of humanity.

SYMBOLOGY:

The ax, a work tool that also serves as a weapon, thus showing itself to be more noble than the sword. Other work tools presented in the degree are the saw (handsaw), a symbol of patience and persevering determination; and the planer, which removes inequalities from a surface, inequalities that can be interpreted as the result of ignorance.

The antagonism of the three work tools is illustrated by the three-headed snake, Idleness, whose heads represent drunkenness, impurity (of thoughts and actions) and gambling. These three addictions are historically related to absenteeism.

BIBLICAL PASSAGE:

Now the serpent was more subtle than any beast of the field which the LORD God had made. And he said unto the woman, Yea, hath God said, Ye shall not eat of every tree of the garden?

And the woman said unto the serpent, We may eat of the fruit of the trees of the garden:

But of the fruit of the tree which is in the midst of the garden, God hath said, Ye shall not eat of it, neither shall ye touch it, lest ye die.

And the serpent said unto the woman, Ye shall not surely die:

For God doth know that in the day ye eat thereof, then your eyes shall be opened, and ye shall be as gods, knowing good and evil.

And when the woman saw that the tree was good for food, and that it was pleasant to the eyes, and a tree to be desired to make one wise, she took of the fruit thereof, and did eat, and gave also unto her husband with her; and he did eat.

And the eyes of them both were opened, and they knew that they were naked; and they sewed fig leaves together, and made themselves aprons.

Genesis, 3:1-7.

23°: Chief of the Tabernacle

Nature is as free from dogmatism as from tyranny; and the earliest instructors of mankind not only adopted her lessons, but as far as possible adhered to her method of imparting them. They attempted to reach the understanding through the eye; and the greater part of all religious teaching was conveyed through this ancient and most impressive mode of "exhibition" or demonstration. The Mysteries were a sacred drama, exhibiting some legend significant of Nature's change, of the visible Universe in which the divinity is revealed, and whose import was in many respects as open to the Pagan, as to the Christian.[128]

ALLEGORIC CHRONOLOGY:

During the Exodus, supposedly in the 13th century BC.

LEGEND AND COMMENTS:

In this degree, the candidate plays the role of a Levite to be consecrated to the priesthood in the tabernacle period (Exodus), by the hands of Aaron and his sons, Eleazar and Ithamar. He becomes a Son of Light and learns that he must exercise his priestly duties always with clean hands, a pure heart, and a sincere desire to serve others and God.

The tabernacle is understood in the hermetic sense that "that which is above is like that which is below". Thus, it is the microcosm of the universe. At its center is the Holy of Holies (*Sanctum Sanctorum*, in Latin, *Kadosh Kadoshim*, in Hebrew), which contains the Ark of the Covenant, the Menorah,[lviii] the censer, and the loaves of bread.

The colors of her veils represent the elements of life: white (earth), blue (air), red (fire), and purple (water); and the four attributes of God: beneficence (white), wisdom (blue), glory (red) and power (purple).

The lampstand of seven candles would be emblematic of the other seven stars then known: Sun, Moon, Mercury, Venus, Mars, Jupiter, and Saturn; and also of the seven archangels of the Jewish tradition, who are symbolically related to these stars: Michael (Saturn), Raphael (Mercury), Gabriel (Jupiter), Ariel or Auriel (Mars), Barachiel or Zerachiel (Sun), Gamaliel or Khamaliel (Venus), and Tsaphiel (Moon). Still, these seven stars are related to seven virtues: Faith (Sun), Hope (Moon), Charity (Venus); Force (Mars), Prudence (Mercury), Temperance (Saturn), and Justice (Jupiter).[lix]

[lviii] Menorah: seven-lamp lampstand that symbolizes the burning bush that Moses saw on Mount Sinai.

[lix] Here the names of the seven archangels and astral correspondences were adopted according to McClenachan (1914). However, it should be noted that, with the exception of the three main archangels, Michael, Raphael and Gabriel, there are variations in the names of the other four. Also, the correspondence of the archangels with the stars also suffers divergence between different authors and esoteric traditions.

Thus, there is a generic alchemical and astrological interpretation, in which colors and candles are related to the elements of nature and the observation of the sky; and a theological interpretation, in which they are related to God and his archangels. This meets the tastes from the most esoteric to the most religious of the members.

MORAL:

Faith, Hope, and Charity; Strength, Prudence, Temperance, and Justice. These seven virtues are separated into a group of three, known as theological virtues; and four, known as cardinal virtues. Theologically, one group is considered complementary to the other, similar to the view of the seven Liberal Arts or Sciences in *Trivium* and *Quadrivium* and the relationship between them.

The theological virtues of Faith, Hope, and Charity are already extensively addressed in previous degrees. The cardinal virtues, of Platonic origin, although it has already been addressed separately, only in this degree is presented together. This dedication to theological and cardinal virtues is the basis of Christian moral theology and is suited to the moral lessons of a degree illustrated as a priesthood.

SYMBOLOGY:

Hyssop branch, used at the time for cleaning places and people (purification); censer or thurible, whose smoke scared the flies from the blood of sacrifices (protection) and also represented the prayers going upwards; silver dagger, for sacrifices (forgiveness); and the seven-candle chandelier, Menorah (moralization).

BIBLICAL PASSAGE:

And the Lord spake unto Moses, saying,
On the first day of the first month shalt thou set up the tabernacle of the tent of the congregation.
And thou shalt put therein the ark of the testimony, and cover the ark with the vail.
And thou shalt bring in the table, and set in order the things that are to be set in order upon it; and thou shalt bring in the candlestick, and light the lamps thereof.

And thou shalt set the altar of gold for the incense before the ark of the testimony, and put the hanging of the door to the tabernacle.
Exodus, 40: 1-5.

24°: Prince of the Tabernacle

Nothing excites men's curiosity so much as Mystery, concealing things which they desire to know: and nothing so much increases curiosity as obstacles that interpose to prevent them from indulging in the gratification of their desires. Of this the Legislators and Hierophants took advantage, to attract the people to their sanctuaries, and to induce them to seek to obtain lessons from which they would perhaps have turned away with indifference, if they had

> been pressed upon them. In this spirit of mystery they professed to imitate the Deity, who hides Himself from our senses, and conceals from us the springs by which He moves the Universe. They admitted that they concealed the highest truths under the veil of allegory, the more to excite the curiosity of men, and to urge them to investigation.[129]

ALLEGORIC CHRONOLOGY:

During the Exodus, in sequence to the previous degree.

LEGEND AND COMMENTS:

The degree of Prince of the Tabernacle is a kind of continuation and deepening of the previous degree, Chief of the Tabernacle, exploring a cosmopolitan character of the idea of the priesthood. In the beginning, the candidate wears the Cloak of Apollonius, carries the Lamp of Trismegistus in one hand and the Rod of the Patriarchs in the other. These are occultist symbols, mentioned by Éliphas Lévi in his best-known book, Dogma and Ritual of High Magic, which relates initiation in the Occult Sciences to initiation into Priestly Art.

It is known that Éliphas Lévi was an important reference for Albert Pike, especially when it came to Kabbalah. However, the presence of these three occult symbols in the Northern Masonic Jurisdiction's former version and others versions not influenced by Pike suggests that these symbols were not included in the degree by Pike under Levi's influence, as some presume, but actually, it belonged to the degree previously, before Lévi and Pike, which indicates an occult French origin.

Apollonius of Tyana is a controversial character. Magician, alchemist, philosopher, professor, vegetarian, miracle worker, polymath, but accused of charlatanism and rival of Jesus by some religious. His cloak would be a symbol of religious and intellectual freedom.

Hermes Trismegistus (or Hermes, the Thrice-Greatest) was an Egyptian priest and philosopher who would have written dozens of books, not only about philosophy and theology but the most of the different sciences known at the time. Before the great Greek thinkers, such as Plato and Aristotle, it is believed that his philosophy may have served as a basis and inspiration for these. For these reasons, his symbolic lamp is emblematic of reason.

The Patriarchs are Abraham, Isaac, and Jacob. The rod would have passed from Abraham, the first patriarch; for Isaac, the second; and from this to Jacob, the third. According to Haggadah,[lx] the rod was made from the Tree of Life of the Garden of Eden,[lxi] having been used by Adam, Noah, Shem, and Enoch before reaching the Abraham's hand. After being used by him, his son (Isaac) and his grandson (Jacob), would have belonged to Joseph, recovered by Jethro and given to Moses, who shared it with Aaron. This rod was reportedly deposited with the Ark of the Covenant and was later lost when the Temple was destroyed. The rod is a shepherd's tool, to assist him in walking in the field and leading the flock, and, for this reason, he has become a priestly tool. It is a symbol of faith.

In the sense of the aforementioned cosmopolitan character of the degree, it seeks to explore common concepts in the most different traditions and religions, such as the dogmas of the existence of God and the immortality of the soul, starting from the theory that harmony means balance, and balance is based in polarization, duality, opposites united by the center.

Duality is present in the ideas of light and dark, concave and convex, full and empty, attraction and repulsion, objective and subjective, faith and reason. But in some sense, even some triads can be seen as opposites united by the center. In the case of the famous Masonic triad of Wisdom, Strength, and Beauty, there is wisdom at one extreme and strength at the other, and by pondering both, harmony or beauty, which is balance, is achieved.[lxii] The same occurs between childhood and old age, which has a longer adult life as an intermediary. In the symbology of this degree, there is Faith (rod) in one hand and Reason (lamp) in the other, and among them, in the center of the balance, freedom (mantle).

So, in the end, the good (the beautiful, the harmony) prevails. Due to the nature of duality, however, it is necessary to worsen to improve. There is a famous phrase that illustrates this concept well: "The darkest hour is just before the dawn". And this degree presents examples from different traditions of that universal law. In Norse mythology, there is Balder, killed by Loki and who returns after Ragnarök. In Egyptian

---

[lx] Haggadah: Hebrew narration used on the night of Pesach (Passover), which reports the liberation of the Jews from Egypt.

[lxi] Tree of Life: Mentioned in the 22nd degree as having given rise to Lebanese cedars.

[lxii] This interpretation also finds support in Eastern traditions. For example, the new Japanese era, which started on May 1, 2019, has been named "Reiwa", which can be translated as "beautiful harmony".

mythology, Osiris, killed by Seth and resurrected by Isis. In the Christian belief, Jesus, betrayed by Judas, died, who was resurrected on the third day. In Masonic legend, we have Hiram Abiff, who does not need summaries. In these examples and so many others, there was a death to achieve a rebirth; a sacrifice to have an evolution; a fall to rise.

This is the universal law of duality. Because, to win a fair (balanced) game, an equal opponent is necessary. And this is at the heart of the Monomyth or Hero's Journey theory, presented at the end of the ineffable degrees and valid in all these mythologies.

MORAL:

The veiled secret of this degree is related to the search for Truth, which can only be realized if the freemason knows how to combine and balance, in harmony, faith with reason. And to achieve this balance, there must be religious and intellectual freedom, without one sphere invading the territory of the other, so that each person can, in an intimate way, dose faith and reason, without imposing their dose on others, since each one has his own template.[lxiii]

It is for this reason that Freemasonry "seeks truth but does not define truth".[130] And it is also for this reason that I must not specifically develop this moral discussion between faith and reason beyond this point, for the risk of suggesting my dose of that elixir, the template for the construction of my inner temple, which would do little or nothing in another construction.

SYMBOLOGY:

The Lamp of Trismegistus, a symbol of Reason; the Cloak of Apollonius, a symbol of Religious and Intellectual Freedom (dependent on Civil liberty), and also of knowledge (including self-knowledge), knowledge and freedom are closely related: "know yourself"[lxiv] and " And ye shall know the truth, and the truth shall make you free";[lxv] and the Rod of the Patriarchs, symbol of the Faith.

[lxiii] Template is a model of specific dimensions to trace, verify and control shapes and / or measures in a work.

[lxiv] Socrates

[lxv] John 8:32.

BIBLICAL PASSAGE:

And Moses reared up the tabernacle, and fastened his sockets, and set up the boards thereof, and put in the bars thereof, and reared up his pillars.

And he spread abroad the tent over the tabernacle, and put the covering of the tent above upon it; as the Lord commanded Moses.

And he took and put the testimony into the ark, and set the staves on the ark, and put the mercy seat above upon the ark;

And he brought the ark into the tabernacle, and set up the veil of the covering, and covered the ark of testimony; as the Lord commanded Moses.

Exodus, 40: 18-21.

25°: Knight of the Brazen Serpent

There are, it is true, dangers inseparable from symbolism, which countervail its advantages, and afford an impressive lesson in regard to the similar risks attendant on the use of language. The imagination, invited to assist the reason, usurps its place, or leaves its ally helplessly entangled in its web. Names which stand for things are confounded with them; the means are mistaken for the end: the instrument of interpretation for the object; and thus symbols come to usurp an independent character as truths and persons.[131]

ALLEGORIC CHRONOLOGY:

In sequence to the previous degree, still during the Exodus.

LEGEND AND COMMENTS:

Considered in some versions (among them, that of the Southern Jurisdiction) as a degree in line with the Sufism,[lxvi] which includes brief quotations from the Koran and the mention of God as Allah, his allegory is the episode reported in Numbers, Chapter 21, in which Moses, during the Exodus, made, instructed by God, a bronze serpent to heal those people bitten by serpents.

According to the aforementioned biblical passage, this sculpture of the serpent would be wrapped around a rod. This rod was supposed to have the shape of a Tau or an Ankh, an Egyptian symbol of life and immortality, whose shape is that of a Tau with a kind of ring on top.

Thus, there is the duality of the previous degree (24th) in a literally reflective sense, because the death by the bite of a serpent, which crawled and hid before attacking, was avoided when looking at the symbol of life wrapped by another serpent. In other words, the hidden attack of darkness was defeated by the explicit defense of light.[lxvii] The serpent plays, by itself, this dual role. A representative of sin, it is divinity in different traditions. Likewise, symbolic of death, his ability to "change his skin" earned it the representation of immortality in different places and ages, especially by the famous Ouroboros symbol.

The serpent wrapped around a rod as related to healing is an ancient symbol and not restricted to the Old Testament. In Ancient Greece, the same symbol was known as Rod of Asclepius, considered the Father of Medicine, and this science adopts it as its official symbol. Consequently, the snake also became a symbol of the Pharmacy, with the caduceus (rod) being replaced by a cup.

[lxvi] Sufism is a kind of Islamic gnosis or mysticism that involves a certain level of religious syncretism.

[lxvii] As in the Law of Retribution, or Action and Reaction, or Cause and Effect, studied in the 13th degree.

Some are the authors who relate this allegory of the episode of the bronze serpent to the Order of Knights of the Hospital of Saint John of Jerusalem, as a reminder of the care they should have with the unfortunate pilgrims in the Holy Land.

MORAL:

Do not worship. That is the veiled lesson of this degree. The bronze serpent against the real serpents is not an allegory whose symbolic purpose is duality, which fulfills only its secondary role, but not primary. The heart of the matter is in the constant danger provided by symbolism, which is to confuse the symbol with its meaning, that is, the middle with the end. For this is exactly what happened to many of the Jews, who, over the years, began to venerate the Bronze Serpent and burn incense for it (2 Kings, 18:4).

This was one of the great questions raised by some of the so-called Church Reformers, who warned that symbols and images were losing the role of simple instruments of interpretation to become objects of worship. Instead of proposing education, however, as a solution for a better understanding of symbols, their impressions, and representations, some chose to preach their abolition, ignoring the fundamental role of archetypes at different levels of individual and collective consciousness.

The freemason adept of the Scottish Rite, a rite so rich in symbols, is expected to not confuse a symbol with its meaning; starting to prefer the material, fragile and temporary form than the thesis that it only partially represents.[lxviii] It is from these constant dangers (these snakes) that the freemason must protect himself, get vaccinated, and, in case of already bitten, heal.

SYMBOLOGY:

The snake coiled around the rod and a lamp is symbols of this degree. Both are symbols related to care and healing, having survived to the present day as representative of Medicine and Nursing.

BIBLICAL PASSAGE:

[lxviii] And as a thesis, it is always susceptible to Dialectic, to continuous improvement.

And the Lord sent fiery serpents among the people, and they bit the people; and much people of Israel died.

Therefore the people came to Moses, and said, We have sinned, for we have spoken against the Lord, and against thee; pray unto the Lord, that he take away the serpents from us. and Moses prayed for the people.

And the Lord said unto Moses, Make thee a fiery serpent, and set it upon a pole: and it shall come to pass, that every one that is bitten, when he looketh upon it, shall live.

And Moses made a serpent of brass, and put it upon a pole, and it came to pass, that if a serpent had bitten any man, when he beheld the serpent of brass, he lived.

Numbers, 21: 6-9.

26°: Prince of Mercy, or Scottish Trinitarian

We do not undervalue the importance of any Truth. We utter no word that can be deemed irreverent by any one of any faith. We do not tell the Moslem that it is only important for him to believe that there is but one God, and wholly unessential whether Mahomet was His prophet. We do not tell the Hebrew that the Messiah whom he expects was born in Bethlehem nearly two thousand years ago; and that he is a heretic because he will not so believe. As little do we tell

> the sincere Christian that Jesus of Nazareth was but a man like us, or His history but the unreal revival of an older legend. To do either is beyond our jurisdiction. Masonry, of no one age, belongs to all time; of no one religion, it finds its great truths in all.[132]

ALLEGORIC CHRONOLOGY:

At the end of the first century, more precisely sometime between the years 93 and 96 A.D., during the rule of the Roman emperor Domitian, who ruled from September 14th, 81 to September 18th, 96.

LEGEND AND COMMENTS:

Arturo de Hoyos interprets that this is the third of the so-called Mysteries Degrees, being the 24th degree of Jewish mystery (purification), the 25th degree of Muslim mystery (initiation), and this 26th would be of Christian mystery (realization).[133]

It is known that Emperor Domitian, after a period of consolidation of the empire, in which he focused his efforts to stabilize the economy and reduce social inequalities; dedicated himself to "romanization", that is, to the promotion of official Roman culture and religion, condemning Christianity. It was during this period that John the Evangelist was exiled in Patmos (17th degree), and it is during this period that this legend takes place.

With the prohibition and persecution of Christianity in this period of Domitian, early Christian practice is illustrated in this degree as a kind of Freemasonry, with degrees, secret meetings in catacombs, modes of recognition, and teachings through symbols and allegories. Thus, the Christians of that time are called in some versions of this degree "Christian Freemasons" and "children of the truth",[lxix] and the candidate receives the experience of being one of those in such an adverse time, when it was necessary to use a tessera[lxx] with the mark of a fish to be admitted to the works and participate in the bread and wine sharing ceremony, as a symbol of Realization (redemption, regeneration, improvement) and Charity (love of neighbor, brotherly love).

[lxix] Most versions return to expose the term "Ameth", presented in the 11th grade and which means "Truth".

[lxx] Small identification piece widely used in Ancient Rome, which was made of wood, metal, bone or ivory and engraved in high and low reliefs.

In this sense, the Christian Trinity is interpreted through the prism of the Masonic Trinity of Wisdom, Strength, and Beauty, as three attributes of a single God. Still, the "Christian Freemason" is given three letters, I, H, and S, the initials of which are the Latin terms *Iesus Hominum Salvator* (Jesus Savior of Men) and *Imperium, Harmonia, Sapientia* (Strength, Beauty, Wisdom). Over time, these initials began to gain new interpretations, such as *In Hoc Signo* (For This Sign) and English, "In His Service".

Originally, it is said in the degree that God entered into a Triple Covenant with men, granting them three graces (hence the term "Mercy"): the first via Abraham, which was circumcision; the second through Moses, which was the bronze serpent; and the third via Jesus, which was his passion and death. The version of the Southern Jurisdiction, USA, always concerned with non-Christian adherents of the rite, also brings an alternative version for Jews and Muslims of the three graces: the first via Noah, never to destroy the earth again;[lxxi] the second via Abraham, of the emergence of nations that believe in a single God from him; and the third through His Prophets so that His Word echoes among men forever.

As for the title of the degree, Prince of Mercy, the authors are almost unanimous in interpreting it based on these three graces granted by the three covenants between God and men. Finally, the second option of the title of the degree, Scottish Trinitarian, suggests a Jacobite origin or interpretation for the degree, and the Christians persecuted by the Roman emperor could also symbolize the Stuarts' followers, also persecuted.

MORAL:

Search for Truth and religious tolerance. What Abrahamic religions have in common would be a glimpse of divine truth: There is only one God, who is the Great Architect of the Universe; and it is from Him that all souls are born, who are immortal and have free will. To expect something more than that of others is to be intolerant of the search for the individual and intimate truth that each being, in his free will, has the divine right to do.

[lxxi] Already covered in the 21st degree.

Before judging someone else's beliefs, it must be considered that it is impossible to make a fair judgment, which is biased by our own beliefs and prejudices. On this topic, Pike declares that:

> Birth, place, and education give us our faith. Few believe in any religion because they have examined the evidences of its authenticity, and made up a formal judgment, upon weighing the testimony. Not one man in ten thousand knows anything about the proofs of his faith. We believe what we are taught; and those are most fanatical who know least of the evidences on which their creed is based. Facts and testimony are not, except in very rare instances, the ground-work of faith. It is an imperative law of God's Economy, unyielding and inflexible as Himself, that man shall accept without question the belief of those among whom he is born and reared; the faith so made a part of his nature resists all evidence to the contrary; and he will disbelieve even the evidence of his own senses, rather than yield up the religious belief which has grown up in him, flesh of his flesh and bone of his bone.
>
> (...)The truth comes to us tinged and colored with our prejudices and our preconceptions, which are as old as ourselves, and strong with a divine force. It comes to us as the image of a rod comes to us through the water, bent and distorted. An argument sinks into and convinces the mind of one man, while from that of another it rebounds like a ball of ivory dropped on marble. **It is no merit in a man to have a particular faith, excellent and sound and philosophic as it may be, when he imbibed it with his mother's milk. It is no more a merit than his prejudices and his passions** (emphasis added).[134]

Thus, however knowledgeable a subject can consider himself about his faith, with rare exceptions he cannot deny the fact that he inherited it from his family and that, if he had been born in another family, in another country, he would probably profess another belief and he would have an opinion as adverse about his present faith as he might have today about someone else's faith.

Nothing has killed more people in all human history than religion. Only through cognitive acceptance, religious humility, a rational faith regarding its limitations and biases, can men live in peace with each other and experience the happiness of humanity, linked by the fraternal bond of that glimpse of truth in which men of goodwill agree.

We are born good and, as we grow and age, we accumulate prejudices. The Masonic ideal is the restoration of man to his natural state of goodness and tolerance. However, we are surrounding ourselves with so many "absolute truths" that it becomes impossible to accept the fact that some of them may be partial truths, if not false truths. And it is not up to Freemasonry to point out what is true and what is not, but to encourage its search based on reason and not preconception. In any case, Freemasonry asks for maximum tolerance, inside and outside its Masonic bodies, so that this sincere search for the truth can be carried out without persecutions and condemnations like those of the past and, unfortunately, also of the present.

SYMBOLOGY:

The triangle, symbol of the Trinity, be it Christian or Masonic. In addition to this, there is the flaming heart engraved with the initials IHS.

BIBLICAL PASSAGE:

And God said, This is the token of the covenant which I make between me and you and every living creature that is with you, for perpetual generations:
I do set my bow in the cloud, and it shall be for a token of a covenant between me and the earth.
And it shall come to pass, when I bring a cloud over the earth, that the bow shall be seen in the cloud:
And I will remember my covenant, which is between me and you and every living creature of all flesh; and the waters shall no more become a flood to destroy all flesh.
Genesis, 9: 12-15.

27°: Knight Commander of the Temple

Times change, and circumstances; but Virtue and Duty remain the same. The Evils to be warred against but take another shape, and are developed in a different form.

(...)The characters, religions and military, attention to the sick and wounded in the Hospital, and war against the Infidel in the field, are no longer blended ; but the same duties, to be performed in another shape, continue to exist and to environ us all.[135]

ALLEGORIC CHRONOLOGY:

At an undetermined time between 1198 and 1525.

LEGEND AND COMMENTS:

The most common title of this degree is Knight Commander of the Temple. It has also been called the Teutonic Knight of the House of Saint Mary of Jerusalem.[lxxii]

Although the 17th degree allegorically represents the trajectory of a crusader, being considered the first philosophical degree, many authors (e.g.: McClenachan) consider this degree, the 27th, as the first strictly chivalry degree (as an investiture in a specific Chivalry Order).

An interesting detail is that in the Southern Jurisdiction, USA (Mother Supreme Council of the World), this degree occupies the 28th position, thus inverting the order with the degree of Knight of the Sun, which started to be granted before, as a logical matter that, for that jurisdiction, it justified bringing the Knight (or Grand) Commander of the Temple closer to two other later degrees that are eminently Orders of medieval chivalry. However, the original order of the degrees of the rite is maintained here and still adopted by the majority of the Supreme Councils of the world.

To this degree, the knight faces the fragility of this earthly life and vows to defend the honor of women, not to ignore the sick and afflicted, and to serve others. Still, he commits to observe five virtues: Humility, Temperance, Chastity, Generosity, and Honor. Also, the degree has the characteristic of stamping the double-headed eagle for the first time. However, not the double-headed eagle of Scottish Rite, but that of Prussia.

MORAL:

Bravery and altruism. These two virtues are fundamental to a knight and are timeless.

Bravery does not fit only on the battlefield, but can be observed in the citizen who, when a fire siren sounds, is not the first to run out of the room, but is concerned with helping those with some mobility difficulties; or the fireman, who does not for money, but out of a sense of duty, enters a burning building or rescues isolated in floods; or a doctor, who,

[lxxii] On Teutonic Knights, see the 21st degree.

after so many hours on duty, does not hesitate to do everything to save the life of another stranger.

Many professions today have bravery (or should have) inherent, but acts of bravery can be performed by all good men. For that, it is not necessary to have the luck to be in the right place at the right time, because the world we live in is still full of injustices, with flags and causes to be defended, and good battles to be fought. One who was even tired of his workday devotes time and efforts to the causes he considers fair, whether for flora, fauna, and impaired minority or against an undue government proposal, while so many are accommodating in the inertia of his routines.

Just as some flags and causes demand the combatant knight, our society still maintains a considerable portion of citizens in need and social risk. Among children, the elderly, and adults, there are countless abandoned, helpless, unfortunate, sick, forgotten in shelters, hospitals, and streets throughout the city. There is an even greater number of citizens in better conditions, but who have become accustomed to closing their eyes and, in many cases, turning their faces away from them. A Knight Commander of the Temple, a symbolic Teutonic Knight of the present day, cannot afford this luxury. While his predecessors risked their lives for the dying, the least that is expected of a freemason invested in this 27th degree is that the indifference to the suffering of others, if it exists, die in your heart, springing in his place a disinterested love for others, that leads to the selfless behavior that our society so badly needs.

SYMBOLOGY:

The clearest symbols of the degree are two crosses. The first is the Teutonic Cross and the second is the Cross of Lorraine. The latter stars in the coat of arms of the degree and deserves further explanation here, thus avoiding confusion with similar crosses, such as the Caravaca Cross.

The currently known Cross of Lorraine was a donation from the Bishop of Crete to Lord Jean de Allaye, of Anjou,[lxxiii] who was returning from one of the crusades in the Holy Land. He donated it (or sold it) to his land abbey, Anjou, and later, for many years, came under the protection of the Jacobins of Angers. Over time, it became known as Cross of

[lxxiii] Anjou is a former French province whose capital was Angers. It was a county and later a duchy. The region had a strong historical relationship with Scotland and was a place of concentration of exiled Jacobites in France.

Anjou. Only in the 15th century did Jean II of Anjou, the descendant of the crusader Jean de Allaye, by a marriage become Duke of Lorraine. His son, René I, adopted the Cross in his heraldry and his grandson, René II, consolidated it as a symbol of the Duchy of Lorraine, which led to the cross becoming known as the Cross of Lorraine.

Perhaps you are asking yourself: And what is the relationship of this cross with the Teutonic knights? Edviges d'Anjou was born out of the House of Anjou, who, as a descendant of the House of Piast, came to become the sovereign queen of Poland.[lxxiv] Edviges, who is now a Catholic Saint, with a lot of diplomacies and investing in the creation of hospitals, won the respect of the Teutonic Knights, who ruled much of the border regions in what was known as the State of the Teutonic Order. Besides, in the 18th century, the Anjou region was practically a stronghold for the Jacobites exiled to France, which would explain the adoption of the cross when the degree was developed.

In short, the Cross of Lorraine is related to the Crusades, to France, to the Jacobites, and the Teutonics.

BIBLICAL PASSAGE:

In the seventh month, in the one and twentieth day of the month, came the word of the Lord by the prophet Haggai, saying,
Speak now to Zerubbabel the son of Shealtiel, governor of Judah, and to Joshua the son of Josedech, the high priest, and to the residue of the people, saying,
Who is left among you that saw this house in her first glory? and how do ye see it now? is it not in your eyes in comparison of it as nothing?
Yet now be strong, O Zerubbabel, saith the Lord; and be strong, O Joshua, son of Josedech, the high priest; and be strong, all ye people of the land, saith the Lord, and work: for I am with you saith the Lord of hosts:
According to the word that I covenanted with you when ye came out of Egypt, so my spirit remaineth among you: fear ye not.

[lxxiv] She adopted the title of "King" and exercised all the powers of one.

Haggai, 2: 1-5.

28°: Knight of the Sun, or Prince Adept

Thus, from every direction, from metaphysics, aesthetics, and morality above all, we rise to the same Principle, the common centre, and ultimate foundation of all truth, all beauty, all good. The True, the Beautiful, the Good, are but diverse revelations of one and the same Being. Thus v/e reach the threshold of religion; and are in communion with the great philosophies which all proclaim a God; and at the same time with the religions which cover the earth, and all

> repose on the sacred foundation of natural religion; of that religion which reveals to us the natural light given to all men, without the aid of a particular revelation. So long as philosophy does not arrive at religion, it is below all worships, even the most imperfect; for they at least give man a Father, a Witness, a Consoler, a Judge. By religion, philosophy connects itself with humanity, which, from one end of the world to the other, aspires to God, believes in God, hopes in God. Philosophy contains in itself the common basis of all religious beliefs; it, as it were, borrows from them their principle, and returns it to them surrounded with light, elevated above uncertainty, secure against all attack.[136]

ALLEGORIC CHRONOLOGY:

Undetermined.

LEGEND AND COMMENTS:

That partial and veiled lesson about symbols in the 25th degree becomes explicit and full in this, which is considered to be the last philosophical degree (with the 17th degree as the first): Symbols are necessary because some truths cannot be expressed in words. Thus, a symbol can hide as well as reveal a truth.

In this eminent alchemist, kabbalistic and occultist degree, the candidate has the opportunity to live a symbolically supernatural (or spiritual) experience, by witnessing a council of seven messengers angels or Malachim (Cassiel, Sachiel, Zamael, Michael, Hanael, Raphael, and Gabriel) chaired by Father Adam, called in some versions "Father of Fathers", and with the help of Brother Truth.

The symbol given to you is a pentagram. It is known that man was made by the image of God, the pentagram being a symbol of both, man and God, which refers to that hermetic teaching that "that which is above is like that which is below".

The brother is invited to review the symbols of such symbolic degrees and to interpret them with the knowledge acquired up to this degree. In the case of the pentagram, he is called to remember the five points of the fellowship of the 3rd degree and to understand that man, represented by the pentagram, is the fruit of the four elements of nature (earth, air, water, and fire) and his spirit. Then, the seven messenger angels continue with lessons that relate numerology (or mathematics) and geometry to God, His representations, and His Ineffable Name.

Still, Gabriel presents a version of the alchemical (or hermetic) image of Rebis, the perfect mythological being, created before Adam and Eve and from whose division they would have originated. He is half man and half woman, having the five elements around him/her. The man's side has the sun and his arm holds a compass; while there is a moon on the feminine side, which holds a square.

Finally, Brother Truth exhorts about the light and its meaning of revealing the truth, interpreting that, just as the sunlight reveals the world to the man, he must seek the spiritual light so that he can reveal his soul. It also teaches that all symbols are derived from the Book of Nature, which is also mentioned in earlier passages of the degree.

Thereafter, the title of Knight of the Sun is understood, as it illustrates this search for truth (light, sun). Similarly, the title of Prince Adept is symbolically awarded to those who can interpret the symbols of the Book of Nature, and are therefore considered Princes (principals, leaders) among Freemasons, and Adepts (initiates) among men.

This Book of Nature is a metaphor by Galileo Galilei, who stated that Nature is a book written in mathematical characters, which corroborates with all the "sacred mathematics" revealed in the degree. Many were the religious and thinkers who understood the world as "two books": one, metaphorical, Nature, would be full of symbols, which would be better interpreted in the light of the Bible, which would be the second book; and both would have the same author, which is God. In other words, the world would reveal symbols and signs that can be properly interpreted to those who know how to read between the lines of the Bible using sacred mathematics as the key (which, for Pike, was Kabbalah[lxxv]). Thus, for Galileo, there would be no possibility for Science and Religion to come into conflict because any logical demonstration of Science that was rejected by a religious would mean that this religious did not know how to interpret the Bible correctly.

MORAL:

[lxxv] In his masterpiece, Morals and Dogma, Pike is thrilled with this degree to the point of dedicating more than two hundred pages to it, that is, more than one third of the work, writing almost a treatise on Kabbalah and the Occultism. And some scholars see a lot of Éliphas Lévi in those pages.

Natural Theology. Whereas the previous degrees reinforced the belief in a single and eternal God; in an immortal soul endowed with free will; in harmony as a balance between duality; this degree brings the concept that the natural world, in which we are all inserted, is the great work of God, and we have all the answers to man's questions in nature, including spiritual and moral ones, it is enough that the man knows how to decipher it (with science and reason).

This does not mean denying the revealed religion, but accepting and recognizing that the existence of God and the immortality of the soul can be reached through philosophical and not just theological means, achieving a morality based on reason and not on theologically imposed limitations. This idea, which has existed since antiquity and has remained alive among theologians of the most diverse religions over the centuries, has gained strength and notoriety since the Enlightenment, especially with the Kant's works.

The first formal evidence of natural theology, that is, an attempt to understand the existence of God philosophically, is in the Vedas which, coincidentally (or not), is used in the preface to this degree in the McClenachan version (former Northern Masonic Jurisdiction of the USA), and reading by Father Adam in the first version of Pike. There are still concepts of natural (or rational) theology in Judaism, Islam, in the works of the Jesuit Thomas Aquinas, and in different religions and traditions, which is explored in Pike's version. And a phrase that both versions and jurisdictions share is that " Nature is the primary, consistent, and certain revelation or unveiling of God ". In this sense, we can highlight some Pike's phrases in his chapter of Morals and Dogma dedicated to this degree:

> All this[lxxvi] is philosophy, the unavoidable conclusion of the human mind. It is not the opinion of Coleridge and Kant, but their science; not what they guess, but what they know. (...) The failure of fanciful religion to become philosophy, does not preclude philosophy from coinciding with true religion (...)The grand objects of Nature perpetually constrain men to think of their Author (...) Nature is full of religious lessons to a thoughtful man. (...) Beautifully, above the great wide chaos of human errors, shines the calm, clear

[lxxvi] About the evidence regarding the existence and nature of God.

> light of natural human religion, revealing to us God as the Infinite Parent of all, perfectly powerful, wise, just, loving, and perfectly holy too.[137]

SYMBOLOGY:

The pentagram is the main symbol of this degree. They are the four elements (earth, air, water, and fire), governed by the fifth element (spirit), thus representing the perfect man, and how nature (represented by the four elements) and divinity (spirit) are intimately and inseparably connected. This dual relationship of spirit and matter is also present in another symbol of the degree, the right triangle, which has the baseline as representative of matter; height as well as spirit; and the hypotenuse, largest, like balance.

BIBLICAL PASSAGE:

And God said, Let there be lights in the firmament of the heaven to divide the day from the night; and let them be for signs, and for seasons, and for days, and years:
And let them be for lights in the firmament of the heaven to give light upon the earth: and it was so.
And God made two great lights; the greater light to rule the day, and the lesser light to rule the night: he made the stars also.
And God set them in the firmament of the heaven to give light upon the earth.
And to rule over the day and over the night, and to divide the light from the darkness: and God saw that it was good.
Genesis, 1: 14-18.

29°: Scottish Knight of Saint Andrew

If you, Sir E..., would be respectable as a Knight, and not a mere tinseled pretender and Knight of straw, you must practice, and be diligent and ardent in the practice of, the virtues you have professed in this Degree. How can a Mason vow to be tolerant, and straightway denounce another for his political opinions? How vow to be zealous and constant in the service of the Order, and be as useless to it as if he were dead and buried? What does the symbolism of the Compass

> and Square profit him, if his sensual appetite-s and baser passions are not governed by, but domineer over his moral sense and reason, the animal over the divine, the earthly over the spiritual, both points of the compass remaining below the Square?[138]

ALLEGORIC CHRONOLOGY:

On November 30, 1314, in Scotland.

LEGEND AND COMMENTS:

Also known only as Knight of Saint Andrew, a title adopted in many jurisdictions, this is the second strictly chivalry degree (with the status of Order of Chivalry). The Order allegedly was established by Scotsman Robert de Bruce, in 1314, to receive the Knights Templar exiled to Scotland.

It is known that in that period Robert de Bruce succeeded in the main battles against England, which guaranteed Scotland's independence. Among them, the Battle of Bannockburn stands out, which supposedly had the decisive participation of Knights Templar and would have motivated De Bruce to create the Order, which, since then, would have the King of Scotland as its Grand Master.

In this context, Prince Charles Edward Stuart, exiled in France, was supposed to be the Grand Master of the Order when, also supposedly, he would grant the Order to the so-called "Scottish Freemasonry" expanding on French soil.

MORAL:

Humility, Patience, and Renunciation. These are the three main principles of a knight of this Order. Charity, Mercy, and Generosity are considered essential qualities. And Virtue, Truth, and Honor are the commitments (paths) to be followed by each knight.

SYMBOLOGY:

The Saint Andrew's Cross, in the shape of an X, stands out as the main symbol of this degree. It is the symbol that forms the flag of Scotland, which has him as the patron. According to Catholic tradition, Saint

Andrew, who was to be crucified, requested that he be crucified on a cross like this, as he did not consider himself worthy of being crucified in the same way as Jesus. Saint Andrew's story also illustrates the principles of humility, patience, and renunciation, which must be inherent in a Knight of Saint Andrew.

BIBLICAL PASSAGE:

And he carried me away in the spirit to a great and high mountain, and shewed me that great city, the holy Jerusalem, descending out of heaven from God,

Having the glory of God: and her light was like unto a stone most precious, even like a jasper stone, clear as crystal;

And had a wall great and high, and had twelve gates, and at the gates twelve angels, and names written thereon, which are the names of the twelve tribes of the children of Israel:

On the east three gates; on the north three gates; on the south three gates; and on the west three gates.

Revelation, 21:10-13.

30°: Knight Kadosh, or Knight of the White and Black Eagle

The Blue Degrees are but the outer court or portico of the Temple. Part of the symbols are displayed there to the Initiate, but he is intentionally misled by false interpretations. It is not intended that he shall understand them; but it is intended that he shall imagine he understands them. Their true explication is reserved for the Adepts, the Princes of Masonry. The whole body of the Royal and Sacerdotal Art was hidden so carefully, centuries since, in the High Degrees, as that it is even yet impossible to solve many of the enigmas which they contain. It is well enough for the mass of those called Masons, to imagine that all is contained in the Blue Degrees; and whoso attempts to undeceive them will labor

> in vain, and without any true reward violate his obligations as an Adept. Masonry is the veritable Sphinx, buried to the head in the sands heaped round it by the ages.[139]

ALLEGORIC CHRONOLOGY:

In indefinite time, after March 18, 1314.

LEGEND AND COMMENTS:

This is the third and last degree considered strictly of chivalry, that is, it presents itself as an Order of Chivalry in which the candidate is symbolically invested. The other two are the 27th degree, from the Teutonic Order, and the 29th degree, from the Order of Saint Andrew. It is for this reason that in the Southern Jurisdiction, USA there is an inversion between the 27th and the 28th degree, with the "Knight Commander of the Temple" becoming the 28th in that version, so that these three degrees of investiture in chivalry orders are subsequently granted: 28th, 29th, and 30th degrees. In other jurisdictions, the degree of Knight of the Sun or Prince Adept (the darling of Pike), of hermetic nature (as is also the 24th degree, of Prince of the Tabernacle) remains as the 28th, separating the first from the second "Order of chivalry".

Arturo de Hoyos, the Grand Archivist and Grand Historian in the Southern Jurisdiction, further states that "the degree of Knight Kadosh derives from the same source of the York Rite Degree of Knight Templar, with which it has some affinities. The degree is the capstone of your experience in the Kadosh Council, and you will here assume your third degree of Knighthood".[140]

In addition to being the third and last degree of investiture in an Order of chivalry, this 30th degree is the first of the three Templar degrees, with the subsequent two also focusing on Templarism. While the candidate is symbolically invested as a Knight Templar in this degree, in the following two he experiences himself as one.

One of the curiosities regarding the degree, which is even observed in the next Templar degrees, is the prevalence of the Teutonic Cross in substitution to the Patte Cross (or Templar Cross). Some scholars suggest that this is an indication of the German origin of the degrees, from Strict Observance, or a tribute to the fact that German Templars were housed by Teutonics. In my experience as a Masonic researcher, I tend to believe in the most simplistic theories, such as the possibility of limited knowledge or confusion of the ritualist in the 18th century about the cross used by the Order of the Temple, since almost half a millennium had passed since its extinction and the access to information was not as easy and fast as it is today.

A striking point of the degree is the "Mysterious Ladder", usually presented as a "Double Seven-Step Ladder", with seven steps to go up and seven to go down. Its peak can be presented by the Latin motto "*Ne Plus Ultra*", which means that there is nothing else than here. In the Southern Jurisdiction, the steps to go up are Justice; Equity; Kindness; Good faith; Goodwill; Perseverance; and Wisdom (divided into Preparation, Intelligence, and Understanding). And the steps to go down are the already known Seven Arts or Liberal Sciences: Astronomy, Music, Geometry, Arithmetic, Logic, Rhetoric, and Grammar.

The heroism of Jacques de Molay,[lxxvii] the last Grand Master of the Knights Templar, is illustrated in this degree, which, in some other versions, features Squim de Florian, a knight templar, as his "judas". Following this analogy, Pope Clement V and King Philip IV occupy the respective roles that the High Priest (Church) and Pilate (State) had in the martyrdom of Jesus.

Squim (or Schin) de Florian, also introduced as Esquins (or Esquieu) de Floyrac, is a little-known character in the story of the end of the Order of the Temple. He would be a Béziers bourgeois who, imprisoned next to a Templar, supposedly listens to his laments about the crimes and sins committed by the Knights Templar, requesting an audience with the king to denounce them. Something very similar to the plea bargaining practice.

Squim de Florian knight templar affiliation is historically inaccurate. If he were, he would not need the confession of another Templar to denounce the Order, but he would do it by his knowledge and experience. Some defended the theory that he would be a Prior of Montfaucon who was not in prison, but would have gone, as a priest, to grant the sacrament of confession to the cloistered Templar. This would be even more unlikely, since a parish priest would not break the inviolable confidentiality of the confession, which is a common and canonical crime, especially for a king rather than an ecclesiastical authority.

Another historical figure that appears in some versions is Godofredo (or Geoffroi or, even, Geoffrey) of Charnay, also known by the

---

[lxxvii] In Latin: *Jacobus Burgundus Molensis*. It appears abbreviated as J. B. M. in parts of the degree paraphernalia.

nickname of Guy d'Auvergne, who was the Preceptor of the Order in Normandy. Many people think that Godofredo de Charnay and Guy d'Auvergne are different people. Guy d'Auvergne means "boy from Auvergne", with Auvergne being an ancient province in central France. When Godofredo, coming from Auvergne, was accepted into the Order via the Temple of Paris, he was just a young man and earned that nickname from the older knights, that remained over the years.

Still, these versions support the legend of the curse that Jacques de Molay would have poured on the king and the pope, in addition to its due fulfillment, inviting the new Templars to also avenge the former Grand Master, through the fight against political abuses and religious. These illustrate this legend well with the presence of the three skulls covered by a papal tiara, a crown, and a helmet. *Nekan Adonai*![lxxviii] In the same sense of the flag against political and religious abuses, there is, in the version of the Mother Supreme Council of the World, when the candidate needs to deliver a declaration of faith, in which he declares to believe in a Supreme Being, to fulfill Masonic duties. and defend democracy and the principle of equality.

It is interesting to note that the degree illustrates the entry into a post-Jacques de Molay Order of the Temple. Thus, it is a clandestine Order of the Temple, in the sense of operating in secret, and which supposedly would have given rise to Freemasonry. Thus, it crowns Ramsay's theory of the Templar origins of Freemasonry, which, despite being rejected by the Authentic School and the majority of respectable researchers on the subject, generated countless degrees in the most diverse rites, surpassing the allegorical limits and conquering loyal defenders and propagators among the brethren.

MORAL:

"To be just and true is the basis of all virtue and excellence".[141] But justice should not be confused with the punishment of those you find guilty, because the belief that there is the divine justice or the Law of Retribution (as already discussed in the 13th and 25th degrees) should be considered. The Knight Templar must fight against all kinds of oppression, injustice, and usurpation, especially political and religious despotism. He must also strive to free himself from the bonds of ignorance, addictions, and errors. Thus, instead of feeding personal

---

[lxxviii] *Nekan Adonai*: would be the transliteration of a term in Hebrew that can be translated as" Revenge, Lord".

vengeance, the Templar seeks to ensure that an injustice that has occurred to one person is not repeated with others. Thus, instead of seeking the unhappiness of one (revenge), the Knight Templar seeks the happiness of all (service).

Still, it is the essence of Knight Kadosh (or Knight of the Temple) not to be content to just do his duty mechanically or routinely, but to always try to overcome himself, trying to reach the summit of the evolutionary ladder, that is, that constant and tireless utopian search of perfection.

SYMBOLOGY:

The *Beaucéant* (standard) Templar, divided in two, half white and half black, is practically a rule in this degree. From there, you have a dagger half white and half black; a half-black double-headed eagle; and the black-and-white takes care of the entire degree. These colors indicated the duality of the Templar, who was a monk (white) and a warrior (black), that is, he exercised a sacred and an unholy function; one spiritual and the other material.

BIBLICAL PASSAGE:

At that time the Lord said unto me, Hew thee two tables of stone like unto the first, and come up unto me into the mount, and make thee an ark of wood.

And I will write on the tables the words that were in the first tables which thou brakest, and thou shalt put them in the ark.

And I made an ark of shittim wood, and hewed two tables of stone like unto the first, and went up into the mount, having the two tables in mine hand.

And he wrote on the tables, according to the first writing, the ten commandments, which the Lord spake unto you in the mount out of the midst of the fire in the day of the assembly: and the Lord gave them unto me.

Deuteronomy, 10: 1-4.

Council of Kadosh Degrees Considerations

The Council of Kadosh concentrates most of the degrees that did not appear in the Rite of Heredom and that came to compose the then newly created Ancient and Accepted Scottish Rite, making it different from everything that existed at the time, unique. After the transformation of a bricklayer into a warrior, experienced in the Chapter of Rose Croix, this warrior develops, throughout the degrees of the Council, his spiritual aspect, becoming a warrior monk, which culminates in the apex of this scale, when allegorically make one of those that best illustrate warrior monks: the Knights Templar.

While the mason polished his rough stone, he became more "polished" morally and intellectually; the warrior monk builds his inner temple (Kadosh) and fights his internal battles, thus seeking to rise spiritually, trying to reach that utopian peak (Ne Plus Ultra) of the spiritual ladder. Thus, the freemason opens his saga at the Council of Kadosh by building a bridge to New Jerusalem (19th), which, completed in the 30th degree, he hopes soon to be worth crossing, not facing the same fate as Moses, who fulfilled his mission to find Canaan but could not step on it.

This evolution provided by the Council of Kadosh, of the warrior who wants to approach his God is symbolically slow, step by step, and formed by lessons, tests, and atonements. While in a moment he is given the important teaching to be impartial when judging between two brothers (20th); in another, the feeling of being an innocent being judged is imposed on him (21st), thus fulfilling those wise words of the apostle: "For with what judgment ye judge, ye shall be judged: and with what measure ye mete, it shall be measured to you again".[lxxix]

The knight (warrior) is taught the value of work and its function of serving others (22nd), before making him a priest (or monk) (23rd), which could generate a certain pride and the undue desire to be served to those who are not prepared. This priest (monk) is entrusted with the esoteric secrets of duality and balance (24th), as well as the risks of idolatry (25th), and the three graces granted by God to man (26th). His priestly formation is concluded with a supernatural experience by which he is invited to face the faith in a more natural, philosophical, rational perspective (28th).

With the esoteric/spiritual base consolidated, this warrior follows his journey, as he needs to face his dragons, walk his rough ways, fight his own battles and those of those who cannot fight; in search of his grail, his elixir, the

---

[lxxix] Matthew, 7:2.

top of his mountain, his salvation, himself. He becomes a Teutonic Knight (27th), torn between charity and battle and redrawing the geopolitical map of the region where Germany and Poland are today. Subsequently, he helps Robert de Bruce to free Scotland from the English and is invested as Knight of Saint Andrew (29th). Fate leads him to be received in the post-Jacques de Molay Order of the Temple (30th), an order that he had already united at the beginning (17th), but which now acts in the shadows, more philosophical, and thirsty for a "good revenge" against political and religious abuses.

In this journey of more than two thousand years, this winner of Methuselah,[lxxx] this almost immortal symbolic being, a being that allegorically represents all of humanity, was, from an apprentice in the construction of the Solomon's Temple to a "modern" Templar, and went around the world through a path "between the cross and the sword". His evolution began since he was a bricklayer, the most "material" and "operative" work than existing; even a monk, the work closest to the "spiritual" and totally "speculative". In that way, he got lost, found himself, spilled blood, saved lives, and purified himself. At the beginning and the end, he suffered the loss of two beloved Grand Masters, Hiram Abiff and Jacques de Molay, equal in admiration, respect, and martyrdom. It seems that, after more than two thousand years between one murder and another, nothing has changed. History continues to repeat itself as Ouroboros or as a spiral. And between these two great losses, many fell. One of them, who became his Savior, had died for all, and in the centuries that followed thousands and thousands died "for Him", whether by the cross, by the sword, or by the fire.

Having learned to think, now following a natural and moral theology, and tired of seeing so many injustices and deaths ordered by bad rulers and false prophets, the immortal brother does not want to continue watching the same story. He senses earthly death when he can try to cross that bridge he built (or Jacob's Ladder), which leads to the New Jerusalem. He would like to see humanity happy, free, and prosperous; but he will entrust that mission to those new Knights Templar who will come after him and who begin to adopt a new name: Freemasons.[lxxxi]

[lxxx] Biblical character who supposedly lived 969 years.

[lxxxi] It is important to reinforce that, just as this "immortal brother" is fictitious (allegorical), the Templar origin of Freemasonry is also fiction. We should remember the teaching of the 25th degree, of not confusing the symbol with its meaning, absorbing the moral content of this plot and its narratives without taking them as absolute truths.

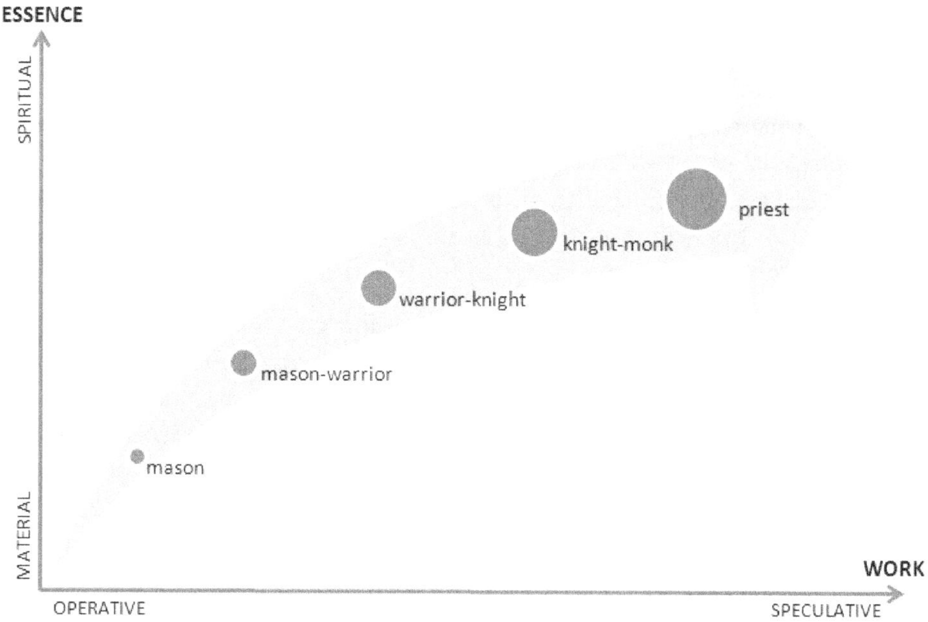

Figure: Allegorical evolution of the Scottish Rite member
Source: prepared by the author

4.5. The Consistory and its Degrees

Introduction to the Degrees of the Consistory

The Consistory of Princes of the Royal Secret is the smallest body of the Scottish Rite in numbers of degrees, granting only two: the 31st and 32nd degrees. These two degrees follow the Templar inspiration of the preceding degree.

The word Consistory is used to define an assembly of religious or a court, which is extremely suitable for the allegories of the 31st and 32nd degrees, in which the candidate will face his judgment after the earthly death (31st), and will circulate in a camp, where he will meet with prophets and gods (32nd).

Entering the Consistory is like reaching the portico of the Temple or the veil of the Holy of Holies. It is the small but significant range of space and time that separates you from your mission, your goal, your discovery, the end of your journey, the completion of a cycle.

31°: Inspector Inquisitor

It is entirely true to say that justice is the constitution or fundamental law of the moral Universe, the law of right, a rule of conduct for man (as it is for every other living creature), in all his moral relations. No doubt all human affairs, like all other affairs, must be subject to that as the law paramount; and what is right agrees therewith and stands, while what is wrong conflicts with it and falls. The difficulty is that we ever erect our notions of what is right and just into

> the law of justice and insist that God shall adopt that as His law; instead of striving to learn by observation and reflection what His law is, and then believing that law to be consistent with His infinite justice, whether it corresponds with our limited notion of justice, or does not so correspond. We are too wise in our own conceit, and ever strive to enact our own little notions into the Universal Laws of God.[142]

ALLEGORIC CHRONOLOGY:

In indefinite time, after the 30th degree.

LEGEND AND COMMENTS:

This degree is also known by another title, "Initiate of the Egyptian Mysteries" in the Mother Supreme Council of the World. This is because Albert Pike when revising his rituals, understood that the Supreme Court of the Knights Templar was allegorical of the particular judgment of each soul after death, a Catholic belief common to several older religions and traditions. The degree probably made some Christians uncomfortable, who believed that they should be judged exclusively by Jesus, but not by the spirits of Moses, two "false prophets", a pagan demigod, a dead foreign king, and an ancient philosopher. So, Pike used Egyptian mythology, which so clearly illustrates this judgment without running the risk of falling into the dangerous trap of the version being identified by Christian fundamentalists with any Christian religious denomination other than his own, or with Islamor Judaism, generating unnecessary dissonance. Thus, each brother can interpret the degree according to his faith, without the risk of judging the allegory of the same as a practicing conception different from him, which can generate a feeling of repulsion. In other words, the narrative goes from being dogmatic to being didactic. Again, good for Pike!

According to Egyptian mythology, those who died went to a court in which, initially, the negative confession was made, in which questions were asked and only those who were able to answer "no" to all of them would pass to the second stage of the trial. Then, his heart was placed on one of the dishes on a scale, while Maat, the goddess of Justice, was on the other dish (sometimes symbolized by a feather). If the heart was heavy, its owner would be condemned. That is, it was not enough to have a correct life, without breaking the commandments. If you have a heart heavy with anger, heartache and resentment, you will not move on.

Tresner risked an opinion on this Pike's choice:

> Almost every religion states or implies some sort of final judgment. Since the theme of the 31° is the importance of each person looking deeply into his own life and conscience and truly assessing the kind of person he has been, it was natural to include such a scene in this Degree. But why an Egyptian religious context, rather than Christianity or any of the other religions Pike could have selected? (...) by using a "dead" religion and the ancient setting of Egypt, Pike was able to signal that the Degree concerns universal ethics and morality, not really a "living" or present religion at all.[143]

Most Latin versions do not follow the Southern or the original versions. At the Court of True Judges, which would be the Vehmic Court already illustrated in the 21st degree, some Knights Templar, wandering after the death of Jacques de Molay, apply for admission. This would be a group that did not go to Scotland to help Robert de Bruce; nor to Portugal under the protection of King Dinis; but he went to Germany in search of the Holy Vehme, in the hope that there he would be able to receive a fairer trial than the French and, if absolved, could join this one to seek justice. During the narrative, a lesson on judicial power, justice, and equity is given. In some of these versions, the True Count, president of the court, presents the allegorical panel of the degree, which deals with the post-mortem judgment of Egyptian mythology, revealing this fragile but persistent link between these versions and that of the Mother Supreme Council of the World.

MORAL:

Forgiveness. This principle is part of justice, be it from this life or another. This is because, being imperfect beings, or, as Pike describes it, "men with bodies, and necessarily with bodily wants and animal passions", we are bound to make mistakes and, being also social beings, these mistakes can involve or impact other people and vice versa. As already taught in the 13th, however, then 25th, and the previous degree, the 30th, there is a universal natural law, the Law of Retribution, also known as the law of action and reaction or, still, the law of cause and effect. Thus, knowing that, in one way or another (and in this life or another), an offender, obligatorily, involuntarily and proportionally, will bear the consequences of his act; therefore, not to forgive, that is, any form of resentment, hurt and resentment arising from the error, is overreaction.

This is because, if the offender does not bear the consequences of his actions for the "justice of men", the "justice of God" he will not escape. And, in one or the other justice, we have the guarantee of the application of the principle of proportionality, that is, that the penalty, the effect, the consequence, the reaction, will be proportional to the error, to the action. Thus, not to forgive is to overreact, causing disproportion.

The one who does not forgive is lacking in his faith and reason. The belief in a God leads to the common understanding of the different religious denominations and also to the philosophy that, if God exists, He is omnipresent, omniscient, omnipotent, and just. Therefore, there is no divine impunity. In this context, any kind of hurt or resentment is a debt that one acquires for oneself and not for the target of that feeling, as very well illustrated in the allegory of weighing the heart.

SYMBOLOGY:

The scale, representative of justice and truth from the Egyptian mythology of Maat.

BIBLICAL PASSAGE:

If there arise a matter too hard for thee in judgment, between blood and blood, between plea and plea, and between stroke and stroke, being matters of controversy within thy gates: then shalt thou arise, and get thee up into the place which the Lord thy God shall choose;

And thou shalt come unto the priests the Levites, and unto the judge that shall be in those days, and enquire; and they shall shew thee the sentence of judgment:

And thou shalt do according to the sentence, which they of that place which the Lord shall choose shall shew thee; and thou shalt observe to do according to all that they inform thee;

According to the sentence of the law which they shall teach thee, and according to the judgment which they shall tell thee, thou shalt do: thou shalt not decline from the sentence which they shall shew thee, to the right hand, nor to the left.

Deuteronomy, 17: 8-11.

32°: Master of the Royal Secret (SJ) or Sublime Prince of the Royal Secret (NMJ)

It is enough for us to know, what Masonry teaches, that we are not all mortal ; that the Soul or Spirit, the intellectual and reasoning portion of ourself, is our Very Self, is not subject to decay and dissolution, but is simple and immaterial, survives the death of the body, and is capable of immortality ; that it is also capable of improvement and advancement, of increase of knowledge of the things that are divine, of becoming wiser and better, and more and more worthy of immortality ; and that to become so, and to help to improve and benefit others and all our race, is the noblest ambition and highest glory that we can entertain and attain unto, in this momentary and imperfect life.[144]

ALLEGORIC CHRONOLOGY:

In indefinite time, after the 31st degree.

LEGEND AND COMMENTS:

This is the third and last Templar degree, being, historically, the 25th and last degree of the Rite of Heredom and, also, the last effective degree of the Scottish Rite, since the 33rd degree is honorary. In fact, both in the US Jurisdictions and in many other countries, the tradition of restricting access to the 33rd degree to a few chosen on merit remains. In these realities, the 32nd degree is the limit for most members of the rite.

This degree is the conclusion of the long life journey of the Scottish Rite, symbolized by a camp through which the degrees, from the 1st to the 32nd, can be traversed. This camp is shaped like an enneagon, with a heptagon inside, which in turn has a pentagon inside it and an equilateral triangle containing a circle. Our hero, who received the old true word, hitherto lost, in the 14th degree; and the new true word, in the 18th degree; now take note of the Sacred Word of the Scottish Rite, in this 32nd degree: AUM.

AUM is the initials of Agni, Usha, and Mitra. Agni is the universal fire and light. Usha is the dawn in its first manifestation and Mitra is the morning star. Triads have been a common model of superior government since time immemorial. Since there are three, there is always a central, which is One, because it is the link of Union and a point of balance between the other two. This triad, related to the Sun, which served as the central symbol of the ancient peoples, their religions, and Masonic symbolism, reveals the so-called Sacred Doctrine, that the human spirit is a ray of Divine Light. This Sacred Doctrine is related to the Royal Secret, which is the Tree of Life, serving as a balance, a pillar in the middle between the famous two pillars of Freemasonry. This secret, which is the most sacred, is accessed with that key entrusted to the candidate in his initiation in the 4th degree.

This degree can be interpreted as a conclusion of the postmortem process of the previous one. The brother, who faced his judgment in the 31st degree, reviews his entire life or journey (camp). Then, understanding the whole and winning this process, he unveils the real meaning of life (Royal Secret, Tree of Life). In other words, he is now able to read that Book of Nature mentioned in the 28th degree. And this deciphering, discovery, the revelation of the Royal Secret, was made possible using a key that had been in his power for a long, long time: that key he received after the death of his first Grand Master, Hiram Abiff, and that he thought was the key to a sacred treasure.

It took him a lifetime of centuries and centuries to understand that the key (forgiveness) was his own heart, which needed to be emptied so that he could have the balance to cross the bridge, climb the ladder, evolve, and thus discover the Royal Secret, that is, the real meaning of life.

Perhaps you are asking yourself: Based on what we can assume that the candidate is symbolically dead in this degree? The answer is simple: Based, not only on the previous degree and its content but also on its symbology. Just look at the nine "commanders" at the "Templar" camp. In the Latin versions: Confucius, Zarathustra, Buddha, Moses, Hermes Trismegistus, Plato, Jesus, Muhammad, and Tomorrow. It is not a question of messenger angels (malachim) communicating with a living being, as in the 28th degree, but of thinkers, prophets, and gods, who have long passed through earthly life. This kind of apparition and communication only occurred in the previous degree, which illustrated the post-mortem personal judgment.

MORAL:

Symbolically there are no more moral lessons to be learned, as this degree is, in fact, your "solemn graduation session" at this school of morality and spirituality which is the Scottish Rite. And, following this analogy, the 33rd degree is the "prom", which celebrates and crowns its journey. So, instead of learning, commitments are made, here called vows.

The 32nd-degree candidate makes a total of five votes. The first is to combat despotism. The second, to fight fanaticism. The third, to defend religious freedom. The fourth, to love humanity. And the fifth and last, to exalt Freemasonry.

SYMBOLOGY:

The camp is the main symbol of this degree and geometrically summarizes the entire spiral saga of the Scottish Rite.

BIBLICAL PASSAGE:

And the Lord spake unto Moses and unto Aaron, saying,

Every man of the children of Israel shall pitch by his own standard, with the ensign of their father's house: far off about the tabernacle of the congregation shall they pitch.

But the Levites were not numbered among the children of Israel; as the Lord commanded Moses.

And the children of Israel did according to all that the Lord commanded Moses: so they pitched by their standards, and so they set forward, every one after their families, according to the house of their fathers.

Numbers, 2: 1-2/33-34.

Consistory Degrees Considerations

The Consistory is an extraordinary, metaphysical, sublime, transcendental experience. The Scottish Rite member, when developing morally up to the 22nd degree, starts, from the 23rd, to develop a natural, rational (and therefore also moral) theism, very explicitly in the 28th degree, followed by investiture in chivalry orders.[lxxxii] This moral, intellectual and spiritual evolution sets the stage for the experience kept in the consistory, by which the brother can anticipate his post-mortem judgment, reflecting on his whole life and, especially, on his moral "offenses" or "debts", which he must apologize for; in addition to the pardons he must grant to those who morally owe him, to clear that account. This moral duty is very well summed up in a brief passage from the first book of the New Testament: "Forgive us our debts, as we forgive our debtors" (Matthew, 6:12).

Thus, the degrees of the consistory form the meeting point of the end with the beginning. That's when that key entrusted after the first death (of Hiram Abiff) opens the final door. A final door that is inside (heart), and not in the East, in a mountain or cave. And that keeps a void (peace of mind) and not a material treasure. There is a light of its own and not that of the reflection of precious stones and noble metals. It is the union of "know yourself" with "that which is above is like that which is below": when opening his heart and seeing it light, empty of resentment, the freemason sees there the Divine Light (Sacred Doctrine) because there are no more edges and crusts (grudges and vices) to be thinned. Thus, he finds in himself that light that he sought his whole life when he went, from the West, towards the East and, being that divine light, he understands that he has found in himself (below, inside) God Himself (above, outside).

The Royal Secret, that is, the real meaning of life, reveals that the journey is more important than the arrival. The journey to the East is not to reach the East, since the light (sun) is in constant motion. It would be like chasing the end of the rainbow. The walk is to get to know, learn, live, evolve. In this path full of days and nights, joys and sorrows, bonanza and storms, peace and wars, the freemason gets to know himself better, looking inside himself and, mysteriously, finding there what he is looking for all over the world.

Yes, two Grand Masters died during that journey. The loss of a master and loved one is often difficult, especially when the loss is traumatic. But both

---

[lxxxii] Recalling that, in the Mother Supreme Council Mother of the World, the 28th degree occupies the 27th position, in order to keep the investiture together in the degrees referring to the three orders of chivalry or knighthood.

are avenged. The first is avenged in the 9th and 10th degrees in a brutal, passionate way; while the second is avenged in the 30th degree ideologically, through prevention so that this history does not repeat itself. There is a moral evolution there. Honoring someone's memory is no longer a feeling for oneself but others. Something clear between the ancient and the modern world, or, according to the Christian theological view, between the Old and the New Testament. Then comes the 31st degree to warn that the freemason must go beyond what is expected, to simply act so that injustices do not repeat themselves. He must do this without an ounce of hatred, bitterness, resentment. He must forgive and ask for forgiveness while still alive. It is extremely difficult, but this whole Masonic journey, if done sincerely, with an open mind and heart, prepared you for it. This is your last step of moral evolution in this earthly life.

When this journey is completed, the member who really understood the messages and meanings transmitted in all these degrees and briefly remembered on the 32nd, that is, a Prince Adept, Master of the Royal Secret, has no alternative but to commit himself to provide this journey to other members, continuing the Ouroboros cycle, better viewed as a spiral. He assumes the duty to invite the Master Masons of his Blue Lodge to join the High Degrees of the Scottish Rite and dedicates himself as an officer and leader of his High Bodies. With this, he not only guarantees the continuity of this extraordinary school but keeps in mind the important lessons of each degree and the reflections from them. This is his contribution to the happiness of humanity. This is the Sacred Doctrine that follows: do not let your inner light (which is Divine) become opaque, but more lustrous every day, and collaborate with other brothers so that they can find their lights. So, these lights can shine on other people through good deeds and examples.

4.6. The 33rd degree of the Scottish Rite

Introduction to the 33rd degree

We have reached the last degree the Scottish Rite. It is an honorary degree, awarded on merit to those who, serving as Sublime Princes of the Royal Secret (32nd degree) for a certain period, become eligible.

You lived, reinvented yourself, evolved, asked for forgiveness and forgave, and died. you were judged, approved, reviewed your life, and understood it, thus discovering the meaning of life. And now? What awaits you?

33°: Inspector General (SJ) or Sovereign Grand Inspector General (NMJ)

Like the Sun, it disseminates light and is the source of light; but, unlike that great luminary, which illuminates but one-half the globe at one and the same time, Masonry with its effulgence lights perpetually the entire Universe, and sends its rays of healing, consolations, and good cheer, dispelling ignorance, superstition, and error.[145]

ALLEGORIC CHRONOLOGY:

Undetermined.

LEGEND AND COMMENTS:

In certain jurisdictions, the 33rd degree is so restricted that it is only granted to the minimum number of officers needed to conduct the Supreme Council (only nine, in some countries, such as Scotland). Others create strict rules for granting it. As an example, we have the Mother Supreme Council of the World (Southern Jurisdiction), which created a species of 32.5° (or 32nd and ½), called Knight Commander of the Court of Honor - KCCH. This intermediate honorary degree between the 32nd and 33rd was created in 1870, by Albert Pike, as a way of recognizing those members of the 32nd degree who did not deviate from the work. A brother in the 32nd degree is eligible for KCCH after a minimum of 46 months of dedication and, while a KCCH, becomes eligible for 33rd after a minimum of another 46 months. Thus, there is a minimum of almost eight years of dedication and work between the 32nd degree and eligibility for the 33rd degree. This wait is usually longer by the few who are elected. This is because the number of nominations is also limited: for every 2,500 brothers initiated in the 32nd degree of a Valley, the Valley can appoint 6 (six) brothers Knights Commanders of the Council of Honor (KCCH) to be invested at the 33rd degree.

But there are exceptions: if the Valley can join 5,000 (five thousand) new members in the 32nd degree, it can nominate eight instead of six; Valleys previously considered small may nominate up to four KCCHs per year at 33rd degree, as long as they meet the target set for them; the Sovereign Grand Commander may nominate up to 10 (ten) KCCHs per year that meet the requirements to be invested at the 33rd degree; and 32nd-degree brethren who are not KCCHs are eligible for 33rd degree if the Supreme Council deems it to be in the best interest of the Scottish Rite.[146]

In the Supreme Council of the Northern Jurisdiction of the USA, there is no KCCH and there are 46 months of interstice between the 32nd and 33rd-degree eligibility. Investiture at the 33rd degree, however, is only carried out in odd years.

The Supreme Councils of Latin countries usually require an interstitial period between the 32nd and 33rd degrees, allowing all members of the

32nd degree who are interested, to be invested in the 33rd. This may seem easy compared to the realities of other countries, including the two US Supreme Councils. Further analysis indicates that this is not the case.

Taking Brazil for example, which is the second-largest Masonic nation in the world, behind the only the USA, statutorily members can only be admitted to each degree by initiation if they present a written work. Besides, the twelve minimum interstices between the 3rd and the 33rd degrees add up to 69 months, which, in practice, reflects between six to nine years of the course. During this period, the Brazilian Scottish Rite Mason will attend more than 300 meetings, between his blue lodge and the bodies of the high degrees, because all the bodies require a minimum of presence. In contrast, a North American freemason can arrive, from Apprentice to the 32nd degree, in less than 20 meetings and in an interval of time that can be less than six months. In other words, the difficulty, the filter, in the USA case, is restricted to the end; while in the Brazilian case it occurs day by day, for years. It is no accident that many brothers call the high degrees of Scottish Rite in Brazil as "College of Freemasonry".

The 33rd degree is granted by the Supreme Council, under the presidency of the Sovereign Grand Commander or by someone determined by him to conduct the work. In it, those two Grand Masters killed during the allegorical life of the Scottish Rite Mason are remembered with the deserved prominence. Still, much of the ceremony revolves around number 5312, which was the year that the Order of the Temple was destroyed.

MORAL:

Similar to what happened in the preceding degree, in the 33rd degree the member does not learn a new moral lesson but takes on new commitments. In this case, to devote himself to God, to the Fatherland, and Humanity; and preserve the Masonic Order in general, and the Scottish Rite in particular. This commitment is sealed solemnly and symbolically, with the cross of a sword as a symbol of devotion to God, with its blade wrapped around the nation's flag as a symbol of devotion to the country, and the Scottish Rite standard as a symbol of it.

SYMBOLOGY:

The double-headed black eagle, the greatest symbol of the Scottish Rite and which bears its standard, having in its claws a sword from which hangs a belt with the motto DEUS MEUNQUE JUS (God and my Right) and a crown over their heads. Above, you can see other motto, ORDO AB CHAO (Order out of Chaos).

BIBLICAL PASSAGE:

Behold, bless ye the Lord, all ye servants of the Lord, which by night stand in the house of the Lord.

Lift up your hands in the sanctuary, and bless the Lord.

The Lord that made heaven and earth bless thee out of Zion.

Psalms, 134: 1-3.

33rd degree considerations

Considering the common understanding among scholars of the rite, that the 33rd degree, the last and only honorary, was created by the eleven Gentlemen of Charleston, and not borrowed from the Rite of Heredom or other rites like the other degrees, it is suggested that the Templar symbolism contained in this may have been due to the coherence, influence, and inspiration of the preceding three degrees, allegorically Templar: 30th, 31st, and 32nd degrees.

Despite this, the 33rd degree is not understood as a "Templar" degree like its predecessors, not only for its originally meritocratic character but for its allegorical position. Having the symbolic connection between the Order of the Temple and the Masonic Order so widely explored by the high degrees, we see an evolution from the Templar to the Freemason, similar to what happened earlier, between the mason and the warrior. The 29th degree inaugurates a first moment after the end of the Order of the Temple (Templar in exile); then, the 30th degree provides an initiation to something similar to a "new Templar" or "modern Templar" (which is not yet Freemasonry); the 31st and 32nd degrees symbolize the symbolic death of that new Templar and his reflection on life and its real meaning; to finally be born again, now as a Freemason, in the investiture to the 33rd degree.

This allegorical sense can be observed by the fact that the candidate for the 33rd degree enters the ceremony stripped of his insignia, exactly to remember when, after dying for the "profane" life, he was born for Freemasonry, when he was initiated. Also because the ceremony is called in many versions as "regeneration" which, theologically, means "rebirth". Yet, for the reappearance of the proof of the sacred chalice, before present in the initiation to the degree of Apprentice in the versions of the Scottish Rite Symbolic Degrees.

Once again, there is no escaping the remembrance of Ouroboros' symbology. That mason, after so many trips, so many experiences, has become a warrior, then a warrior-monk (Templar), dies and he is reborn ... A Freemason: a speculative mason. What a lesson! **ORDO AB CHAO**.

5. FINAL CONSIDERATIONS

Unfortunately, this wonderful adventure comes to an end.

Philosopher Walter Benjamin argued that history should give more value to the small, the vanquished, and the forgotten details.[147] In the chapter dedicated to the history of the Rite, this theory, so consistent with Masonic narratives,[148] was not ignored and it sought to do justice to those characters and facts forgotten or ignored by a good portion of the Masonic literature.

We traveled through the evolution of the so-called Scottish Freemasonry in France, the development of the Rite of Heredom, its crossing to the New World, and the development of the Ancient and Accepted Scottish Rite. With that, we honor the memory of characters like Radclyffe, unknown to almost all current Scottish Rite Masons.

Then, we understand the process of exporting Scottish Rite to France and its expansion throughout the world thanks, mainly, to one of the parents of the rite, the Count of Grasse-Tilly. He, the main responsible directly or indirectly for the arrival of the Scottish Rite in so many countries is scorned by a large part of those who dedicated themselves to writing something about the rite.

So, we were aware that, with the worldwide expansion, in a few decades, that original concern of the parents of the rite, the eleven Gentlemen of Charleston, of the chaos over the Order, returned to plague new leaders, like Albert Pike. From such concern, the Lausanne Congress was born, and what was to be the point of unity, became the divider of Freemasonry in the world, taking the most basic principle of Freemasonry, of belief in a Higher Being, as the pivot of discord. Another illustrious stranger was introduced to us, the Scottish Mackersey. With the unfolding of his initiative, the Grand Orient of France and its closest followers fell from grace, while England changed the name from the Ancient and Accepted Scottish Rite to the Ancient and Accepted Rite in its jurisdiction.

All these forgotten personalities and facts were not small or vanquished, but, perhaps due to carelessness or lack of commitment to the most basic principles of research (such as impartiality, depth, and transparency), some authors despised them in their fanciful and narrative historical narratives. shallow about the Scottish Rite, to the detriment of its incredible true history, involving centuries, cultures, beliefs, and different countries.

Then, we set out for what matters in a "beautiful system of morality". Each Scottish Rite degree has been decoded. In the inauguration of the study of each degree, there is a direct quote, mostly by Albert Pike, originally published in Morals and Dogma. We sought to identify the chronological position of each legend, which was unraveled and accompanied by curiosities regarding its different versions. Relationships with narratives of other degrees have also been explored. Thereafter, the moral lessons of each degree were deciphered and commented on, as well as the main symbol or symbols highlighted and interpreted. Finally, the biblical passage that consecrates the degree is brought to light for reflection.

Still, an analysis of each group of degrees was made, showing the invisible weft that exists between them and how they complement each other, not only the degrees but also their groups, forming an evolutionary scale very well structured in the science of Masonic morality. The available appendices collaborate for its consultation, vision, and systematic study.

As can be seen, the Freemason who decides to attend this "college of Freemasonry", which is the Scottish Rite, has access to wonderful historical, philosophical, moral, esoteric, and theological content. As in any higher education course, knowledge is at your fingertips and it only depends on it to absorb it or not, as well as to define the quantity and intensity in which you will do it. Also, as in any course, some students putting it off and end up being able to graduate, as well as those who dedicate themselves hard to become true masters in what they do. If you have reached the end of this work, I imagine you are of this second type.

Considering that Masonic knowledge is veiled in allegories, only those like you, who study and research, really are in a position to learn and fully understand it. So, when experiencing all the allegorical and real evolution offered by the degrees, reaching investiture at 33rd degree, understanding oneself is returning to a position similar to that of an Apprentice, being a relief and consolation to whom something has learned, and an unacceptable offense to whom learned nothing. This is because moral knowledge, when properly applied, provides wisdom, which is Solomon's true key. Wisdom goes hand in hand with the humility and recognition common to every wise man: that the more you learn, the more you realize how little you know.

This evolution took place in a coherent, gradual, and, above all, balanced manner. There are 32 degrees of course and, by dividing them dually, two groups of 16 degrees are formed. It is not by chance that the allegories of the first group, from the 1st to the 16th degrees, take place in the Old Era. While those of the second group, from the 17th to the 32nd degrees, are set in the Vulgar Era. In the first group, masons build exterior temples. In the second, knights build interior temples. Each group is marked with the tragic loss of a Grand Master.

Thus, the 32 degrees are, in some way, connected to the temple. Under that temple, directly or indirectly, there were these two Grand Masters, who were heroes and martyrs. Hiram Abiff commanded the construction of the first Temple, while Jacques de Molay commanded the Order of the Temple; among them, almost two thousand years. Their deaths were avenged, but each in a different way. That is because moral evolution occurred. The desire for persecution and bloodshed has been replaced by faith in divine justice. The selfish feeling of revenge has given way to the selfless concern that this injustice does not happen to other people. Then, the 33rd degree, of an honorary character, comes to honor both.

Much is taught in these thirty-three degrees. Perseverance, righteousness, secrecy, fidelity, fervor, zeal, justice, impartiality, equity, benevolence, generosity, combating ignorance and fanaticism, service to others, search for the truth, mood, trust, discretion, sincerity, moderation, tolerance, veneration for God, patriotism, faith, hope, charity, bravery, altruism, humility, patience, renounce, forgiveness. These are just the most evident ethical and moral principles taught by the Scottish Rite degrees and which, together with other more latent ones, form the morality of a member of the rite.

Any man who dedicates himself to learning, understanding, and practicing these principles will be morally equal to the best men who have ever walked the surface of this planet. It must be for this that you dedicate so much time, money, and efforts with Freemasonry: you are investing in the construction and renovation of your inner temple, in search of being able to collaborate for the happiness and well-being of society. It definitely cannot be for medals and titles. It would be a huge waste of time and resources.

While teaching is collective; the process of learning, understanding, interior transformation (polishing the rough stone), and practicing such teachings is individual. As already mentioned, many are not keen on learning. Others learn, but do not understand. Yet, among those who understand, there are those with difficulties in putting the teachings into practice, especially in times of ordeals. Thus, the Scottish Rite by itself does not make any man better, being, in fact, a path for this, which each brother must seek to follow according to his limitations and aspirations.

I am not ashamed to serve as an example to illustrate this truth: On one occasion, upon reaching another Scottish Rite degree, I was able to easily identify the veiled moral lesson in the allegory presented. I just didn't agree with that lesson. When I lay in bed that night after the meeting, I still spent a few minutes reflecting on that lesson before I went to sleep. In vain. I traveled to the kingdoms of Morpheus without any remorse for disagreeing with the teaching of such degree and woke up with the same opinion. Some time has passed, years in fact, in which I have had the opportunity to review, for a few times, the initiation of that degree. The disagreement persisted and the feeling of witnessing that dissonant narrative was almost embarrassing. Then, on a beautiful day when the degree would once again be awarded to others, and there was no hope in me of leaving that meeting happy and satisfied, I attended that initiation and ... I had an insight. It all made perfect sense. For a moment, I was astonished. Perhaps the experiences that I had in the years between my initiation in that degree and that review, new things that I learned in the meantime, or some inspiration that I gained, something contributed to making that enlightenment possible.

The truth is that, although I learned the lesson of the degree at the time of my initiation, I did not understand it. This is relatively common. It is like learning to read, but not understanding what is written, a phenomenon known as functional illiteracy. Or learning formulas at school, but not understanding why they exist and how they can be useful. The famous work "A Dog's Will", by Ariano Suassuna, immortalized an expression copiously spoken by the character Chicó, who said: "I don't know. I just know it was like that". This expression illustrates well the situation of learning something, like a story, being able to pass it on, without understanding it. Masonic lessons are not immune to this.

Now, the most important: this science of morality is an applied science. In addition to learning and understanding the lessons, you must practice them. There is no other reason to even learn them if not to practice them. Otherwise, it would be like empty formulas, the kind that you learned in school in adolescence and wondered when you would use it in life. And then, I conclude my example (or confession): I learned the lesson, it took me a long time to understand it and, since then, I try to practice it. But it is a daily exercise. In the beginning, it is more difficult and, over time, it becomes almost automatic, with errors increasingly rare. Thus, there are so many lessons yet to be better understood and exhaustively practiced in pursuit of their excellence, that feeling at the beginning when reaching the end, an apprentice when becoming an inspector general honorary, is something natural.

This work is here to assist you in this process of learning and understanding, serving as kind of textbook for the student who does not care to study beyond that content seen in the classroom with his colleagues; that student who is not content with just learning the formulas, wishing to understand them and, finally, use them. Albert Pike noted that "What we do for ourselves dies with us. What we do for others and the world remains and is immortal". For it is by using, applying, practicing this science of morality that humanity can be made happy.

THE END.

6. BIBLIOGRAPHY

Actas de la XIX Conferencia Mundial de Supremos Consejos 33°. Lisboa: 13 a 17 de Mayo, 2015. *Supremo Conselho para Portugal dos Soberanos Grandes Inspectores Gerais do 33° e Último Grau do R.E.A.A.*

Ames, Kenneth L. 1996. *Theatre of the Fraternity: Staging the Ritual Space of the Scottish Rite of Freemasonry*. Jackson, Mississippi: University Press of Mississippi.

Anderson, James. 1997. *As Constituições dos Franco-Maçons*. Trad. João Nery Guimarães. Brasília: Editora do Grande Oriente do Brasil.

Astréa: Journal of Masonic Studies. 2000. Ano: LXXIII, Número 06. Rio de Janeiro.

Barr, J. 1985. *Why the World Was Created in 4004 BC: Archbishop Ussher and Biblical Chronology*. vol. 67, n.2, pp. 575-608. Bulletin of the John Rylands University

Batalla, J. M. B. *A sobrevivência extraordinária das ordens da Sabedoria do Rito Moderno Francês no Brasil*. Trad. José Antônio Filardo. Revista Bibliot3ca. Available in: https://bibliot3ca.com/a-sobrevivencia-extraordinaria-das-ordens-da-sabedoria-do-rito-moderno-frances-no-brasil/ Access in: August, 21, 2019.

Bauer, A.; Meyer, G. 2012. *Le Rite Français*. Paris: Presses Universitaires de France.

Behring, Mário. 1928. *Ritual do Gráo de Aprendiz-Maçon*. Rio de Janeiro: Typographia "DELTA".

Benimeli, José Antonio Ferrer. 2015. *Masonería, Iglesia, Revolución e Independencia*. Bogotá: Editorial Pontificia Universidad Javeriana.

Benjamin, Walter. 1994. *Obras Escolhidas Vol. I - Magia e técnica, arte e política: ensaios sobre literatura e história da cultura.* 7a. ed. São Paulo: Brasiliense, 1994.

Bernheim, Alain. *Le Convent des Suprêmes Conseils du Rite Écossais Ancienet Accepté. Parte 1.* Pietre-Stones Review of Freemasonry. Disponível em: http://www.freemasons-freemasonry.com/bernheim_convent01.html

Bernheim, Alain. *Le Convent des Suprêmes Conseils du Rite Écossais Ancien et Accepté. Parte 2.* Pietre-Stones Review of Freemasonry. Disponível em: http://www.freemasons-freemasonry.com/bernheim_convent02.html

Bernheim, Alain. *Le Convent des Suprêmes Conseils du Rite Écossais Ancien et Accepté. Parte 3.* Pietre-Stones Review of Freemasonry. Disponível em: http://www.freemasons-freemasonry.com/bernheim_convent03.html

Bullock, Steven C. 1996. *Revolutionary Brotherhood: Freemasonry and the Transformation of the American Social Order, 1730–1840.* Chapel Hill: University of North Carolina Press, pp. 239–273.

Campbell, Joseph. 2008. *Mito e Transformação*. São Paulo: Editora Ágora.

Carvalho, João Alexandre Rangel. 2005. *Sucesso em Sydney*. Ano LXXVIII, Edição 16. Astréa: Journal of Masonic Studies. LXXVIII, Number 16.

Carvalho, W. A. 2010. *Uma pequena história da Maçonaria no Brasil.* REHMLAC, V.2, N.1, p. 30-58.

Casado, Galo Sánchez. 2009. *Los altos grados de la masonería.* Madrid: Ediciones Akal.

Cassard, Andres. 1867. *Manual de la Masonería, el tejador de los Ritos Antiguo Escoces, Frances y de Adopcion*. New York: George R. Lockwood, p. 361.

Castellani, José 2001. *Fragmentos da Pedra Bruta*. Londrina: Editora Maçônica "A Trolha".

Clavel, F. T. B. 1843. *Histoire pittoresque de la Franc-Maçonnerie et des Sociétés Secrètes Anciennes et Modernes.* Paris: Deuxième Édition.

Clawson, Mary Ann. 2007. *Masculinity, Consumption and the Transformation of Scottish Rite Freemasonry in the Turn-of-the-Century United States*. Vol.19 No.1, 2007, pp. 101–121. Gender & History.

Coil, Henry Wilson; BROWN, William M. 1961. *Coil's Masonic Encyclopedia.* New York: Ed. Macoy.

Cuccia, Andrea. 2004. *Dieci tavole architettoniche sulla massoneria.* Soveria Mannelli: Rubbettino.

Daruty, Jean Émile. 1879. *Recherches sur le Rite Écossais Ancien et Accepté.* Paris: Chez le F. Panisset.

De Hoyos, Arturo. 2016. *Scottish Rite Ritual, Monitor & Guide*. 2016. 3rd. edition, Corrected. Washington, D.C.: Supreme Council, 33°, S. J.

De Hoyos, Arturo; Morris, Brent. 2004. *Freemasonry in Context: History, Ritual, Controversy.* Lanham, MD: Lexington Books.

Delaunay, F. H. S. 1820, p.145. *Manuel Maçonnique ou Tuileur de tousles Rites de Maçonnerie pratiqués en France par un Vétéran de la Maçonnerie.* Paris: Hubert &Brun.

Dermott, Laurence. 1778. *AHIMAN REZON or a help to all that are, or would be Free and Accepted Masons*. 3rd Edition. London: James Jones.

Dumenil, Lynn. 1984. *Freemasonry and American Culture, 1880–1930*. Princeton, NJ: Princeton University Press.

Flandreu, Marc. 2016. *Anthropologists in the Stock Exchange: A Financial History of Victorian Science*. Chicago and London: The University of Chicago Press.

Foucault, Michel. 2004. *Vigiar e Punir*. Petrópolis: Editora Vozes.

Fox, William L. 1997. *Lodge of the Double-Headed Eagle: Two Centuries of Scottish Rite Freemasonry in America's Southern Jurisdiction*. pp. 146–1477. Fayetteville: University of Arkansas Press.

Freitas Neto, Edgard da Costa. 2019. *REDES DE SOCIABILIDADE, REDES DE PODER: Maçonaria e Diplomacia Track 2 na África Francófona*. 197 p. Dissertation (MSc in International Relations). Universidade Federal da Bahia. Salvador.

Garcia, Aquiles. 2012. *Maçonaria: da gênese dos Supremos Conselhos de Charleston e do Brasil ao Cisma de 1927*. p. 103. São Paulo: Livronovo.

Gould, Robert Freke. 2007. *The Concise History of Freemasonry*. Mineola, NY: Dover Publications.

Grande Oriente Unido & Supremo Conselho do Brasil. Outubro a Dezembro de 1873. *BOLETIM e Jornal Official da Maçonaria Brazileira*. Ano 02, N. 10 a 12. Rio de Janeiro: Typographia do GOUSCB.

Guarner, Vivanco. 1961. *Historia del Supremo Consejo del Grado 33 para Espana y sus Dependencias y de la Masoneria Espanola*. Mexico, DF: publicação própria.

Guia dos maçons escocezes ou reguladores dos tres graos symbolicos do rito antigo e acceito. 1834. Primeira Parte. Venerável Mestre. Rio de Janeiro: Typ. Imp. e Const. de Seignot-Plancher e Cia.

Harland-Jacobs, Jessica.2007. *Builders of Empire: Freemasons and British Imperialism, 1717-1927*. Chapel Hill: The University of North Carolina Press.

Harland-Jacobs, Jessica. 1999. *"Hands Across the Sea": The Masonic Network, British Imperialism, and North Atlantic World*. Vol. 89, Issue 2, p. 237–253. Geographical Review.

Hodapp, C. 2015. *Maçonaria para Leigos*. Tradução da 2a. edição, p13. Rio de Janeiro, RJ: Alta Books.

Hodapp, Christopher. 2013. *Freemasons for Dummies*. Hoboken, NJ: Wiley Publishing Inc.

Holy Bible. 1991. *King James Version*. Wichita, Kansas: Heirloom Bible Publishers.

Horne, Alex. 1978. *King Solomon's Temple in the Masonic tradition*. Chatsworth, CA: Wilshire Book.

Ismail, Kennyo. 2015. *A Origem e o Desenvolvimento do Rito Escocês Antigo e Aceito*. n.37, jul-dez, 2015, p.11-14. Revista Astréa.

Ismail, Kennyo. 2016. *Ahiman Rezon: A Constituição dos Maçons Antigos*. Londrina: A Trolha.

Ismail, Kennyo .2012. *Desmistificando a Maçonaria*. São Paulo: Universo dos Livros.

Ismail, Kennyo. 2014. *O Líder Maçom: Como a Maçonaria tem formado líderes nos últimos séculos e colaborado para a felicidade da humanidade*. Londrina: A Trolha.

Ismail, Kennyo. Autumn, 2013. *The Rosicrucian Tradition and its Orders*. N. 22, p. 23-27. The Journal of the Masonic Society.

Jenkyns, Michael. M. W. Bro. Thomas Douglas Harington. 2002. *The Newsletter of the Committee on Masonic Education - The Grand Lodge of Canada in the Province of Ontario*. Vol. 18, No. 1.

Kinney, Jay. 2009. *The Masonic Myth: Unlocking the Truth About the Symbols, the Secret Rites, and the History of Freemasonry*. San Francisco, CA: Harper One.

Knox, William. 1907. *What Excuse?*. N.7, 1907, p. 253-254. *The New Age Magazine*.

Lindsay, R. S. 1958. *The Scottish Rite for Scotland*. Edinburgh: W & R Chambers.

Lomas, Robert. 2006. *The Early History of Freemasonry, in: Olsen, Oddvar. The Templar Papers*. Franklin Lakes, NJ: The Career Press.

Lopez-Penha, H. 1952. *Resena Histórica del Supremo Consejo del Grado 33 y Ultimo del Rito Escocés Antiguo y Aceptado para la República Dominicana*. Trujillo: Editora Montalvo.

Mackey, A. G. 1914. *An Encyclopedia of Freemasonry and its Kindred Sciences*. New York e Londres: The Masonic History Company.

Mandleberg, J. 1997. *The Lausanne Congress of 1875*. Vol. 6, 1997, p. 83-112. Heredom.

McClenachan, Charles T. 1914. *The Book of the Ancient and Accepted Scottish Rite of Freemasonry*. New York: Macoy Publishing & Masonic Supply Co.

Morris, Brent. 2006. *The Complete Idiot's Guide to Freemasonry*. New York: Alpha Books/Penguin.

Mosca, Gaetano. 1975. *História das Doutrinas Políticas – desde a Antiguidade*. 4ª Edição. Rio de Janeiro: Zahar.

Naudon, Paul. 1993. *Histoire, Rituels et Tuileur des Hauts Grades Maçonniques*. 5th edition. Paris: Éditions Dervy.

Nicholson, Daniel Norris. 1893. *Text-Book of the Ancient and Accepted Scottish Rite of Freemasonry of Vermont*. Burlington: Vermont Consistory.

O'Donnell, Francis H. E. 1906. *Philosophy and the Drama in Freemasonry*. N.4(5), p. 475-476. The New Age Magazine.

Orval, José. 2006. *Une histoire humaine de la Franc-Maçonnerie spéculative*. Liege: Céfal.

Pareto, Vilfredo. 1987. *Manual de Economia Política*. Tradução de João Guilherme Vargas Netto. 2ª ed. São Paulo: Nova Cultural.

Perramón, Edgar. 2010. *Breve história del Supremo Consejo de la Masonería Venezolana*. Caracas: edição do autor.

Pike, Albert. 1905. *Morals and Dogma of the Ancient and Accepted Scottish Rite of Freemasonry*. Charleston: Supreme Council of the Southern Jurisdiction.

Pike, Albert. 1993. *The Porch and the Middle Chamber - The Book of the Lodge*. Whitefish, MT: Kessinger Publishing.

Pike, Albert. 1887. *Liturgy of the Ancient and Accepted Scottish Rite of Freemasonry for the Southern Jurisdiction of the United States*. IV Volumes. New York: Macoy.

Pires, Joaquim da Silva. 2015. *A Cisão Maçônica Brasileira de 1927*. Londrina: Editora Maçônica "A Trolha".

Planas, J. A. 2016. *Masones en la nobleza de España: Una hermandad de iluminados*. Madrid: La Esfera de los Libros.

Preston, William. 1867. *Illustrations of Masonry*. p.37. New York: Masonic Publishing and Manufacturing Co.

Prober, Kurt. 1981. *História do Supremo Conselho do Grau 33 do Brasil*. Rio de Janeiro: Editora Livraria Kosmos.

Proceedings of the *Supreme Council of Sovereign Grand Inspectors General of the Thirty-third and Last Degree of the Ancient Accepted Scottish Rite of Freemasonry for the Northern Masonic Jurisdiction of the United States of America.* 1881. 20th of September. Own Publication.

Proceedings of the *Supreme Council of the Thirty-Third Degree of the Ancient and Accepted Scottish Rite of Freemasonry of Canada.* 16th to 18th of September 2010. 136th Annual Session: Moncton, New Brunswick.

Ribeiro, J. G. C. 2017. *+ Fios da Meada. Vol. 1.* Rio de Janeiro: Infinity.

Ribeiro, J. G. C. 2018. *+ Fios da Meada. Vol. 2.* Rio de Janeiro: Infinity.

Ribeiro, João Guilherme da Cruz. 2007. *Os fios da meada: origens, evolução e imagens do Rito Escocês Antigo e Aceito.* Rio de Janeiro: Infyarte.

Rousseau, J. J. 1999. *O Contrato Social.* São Paulo: Martins Fontes.

Sánchez, Manuel Romo. 1º julio 2009. *Antecedentes para la historia de la masonería capitular en Chile entre 1895 y 1903.* Nº 18. ARCHIVO MASÓNICO, Revista Cuatrimestral. Santiago, Chile, 1º julio 2009.

Sargent, Epes W. 1907. *Detail and the Drama of the Degree.* N.7, pp. 175–177. The New Age Magazine.

SCF. 1994. *Ordo ab Chao.* Número 30 (p. 147) e Número 39-40 (p. 151).

SCG33REAAMRFB. 2002. *Estatuto.* Rio de Janeiro: editado pelo autor.

SCG33REAAMRFB. 2009. *Ritual do Gr.'.14 - G.'. Eleito ou Perf.'. e Sub.'. Maçom e GGr.'.* Intermediários 10, 11, 12 e 13. Rio de Janeiro: publicado pelo autor.

SCG33REAAMRFB. 2010. *Ritual do Gr.'.15 - CCav.'. do Or.'., da Esp.'. e da Águia.* Rio de Janeiro: publicado pelo autor.

SCG33REAAMRFB. 2011. *Ritual do Gr.'.18 -C.'. Rosa Cruz ou C.'. da Águia Branca e do Pelicano.* Rio de Janeiro: publicado pelo autor.

SCG33REAAMRFB. 2011. *Ritual do Gr.'.28 - Cav.'. do Sol ou Princ.'. Adepto e GGr.'.* Intermediários 23, 24, 25, 26 e 27. Rio de Janeiro: publicado pelo autor.

Schuchard, Marsha Keith. 2002. *Restoring the Temple of Vision: Cabalistic Freemasonry and Stuart Culture.* Leiden: E. J. Brill.

Simon, J. 2013. *Rituel des trois premiers degrés selon les anciens cahiers - 5829.* Bonneuil-en-Valois: Éditions de la Hutte.

Sommers, Susan Mitchell. Autumn 2013. *Robert Thomas Crucefix, Redux.* p.73-97. Journal for Research into Freemasonry and Fraternalism.

Southern Jurisdiction. August, 2011. *Supreme Council of the Thirty-third Degree Ancient & Accepted Scottish Rite of Freemasonry*. Statutes.

Stevenson, David. 2002. *James Anderson: Man and Mason*. Volume 10, p. 93-138. Heredom.

Studart, H.; Ismail, K. 2014. *O Encontro de Hiram Abiff com Benjamin na casa de Ricoeur*. Vol. 2, n.1, p. 21-36. C&M. Brasília.

Supremo Conselho do Brasil. *Decreto No. 07*, de 03 de agosto de 1927.

Supremo Conselho do Brasil. 1927. *Astréa: Journal of Masonic Studies*. Year I, Number 7. Rio de Janeiro.

Supremo Conselho dos SSS GGG III GGG 33 e Ult. Gr. REAA para o Imp. do Braz. *Decretos*. 1837. Rio de Janeiro: Typographia Imparcial do Ir. Francisco de Paula Brito.

Tabbert, Mark A. 2005. *American Freemasons: Three Centuries of Building Communities*. New York and London: New York University Press.

Torres-Cuevas, Eduardo. 2013. *Historia de la masonería cubana: seis ensayos*. La Habana: Imagen Contemporanea.

Tresner, Jim. 2000. *Vested in Glory*. Washington, DC: Scottish Rite Research Society.

Valdés, Roberto. 2009. *Origen, miembros y primeras acciones de la masonería en El Salvador (1871-1872)*. Vol. 1, N.1. REHMLAC.

Xavier, Francisco Cândido. 2002. *Nosso Lar (pelo espírito André Luiz)*. Rio de Janeiro: Federação Espírita Brasileira.

Waite, Arthur Edward. 2007. *A New Encyclopedia of Freemasonry. Volume II*. New York: Cosimo.

Zeldis, Leon. 2011. *Illustrated by Symbols*. Vol. 64, n. 02, p. 72-73. New York, NY: Philalethes, The Journal of Masonic Research & Letters.

APPENDICES

ABOUT THE AUTHOR

Kennyo Ismail is a writer, technical reviewer, speaker, university professor, and researcher. As an administrator, he worked in large Brazilian companies, such as Brasil Telecom, Oi Telecom, and Diários Associados, as well as in organs of the district and federal public administration in Brazil. And as an academic, he maintained a teaching or research link with institutions such as UnB, FGV, Ibmec, IDP, Anhanguera, and Uninter.

His first contact with Freemasonry was thanks to the Order of DeMolay. He was, as an active member, Master Councilor, Illustrious Knight Commander, Regional Master Councilor, Deputy State Master Councilor, and State Master Councilor. As a Freemason, he was able to repay the Order of DeMolay by serving as President of the Advisory Council, member of the National Commission for Fraternal Relations, and President of the National Commissions on International Relations and Education. He is a Chevalier and Active Legionnaire of Honor.

In Freemasonry, he is a Past Master, having been Worshipful Master of "Flor de Lótus" Lodge # 38 and "Dom Bosco" Lodge of Research # 33, both affiliated with the Grand Lodge of the Federal District of Brazil. He is an honorary member of the Blue Lodges "Construtores do Adro # 225 ", Construtores da Esperança # 226" and "Ahiman Rezon # 256", affiliated with the Grand Lodge of the State of Bahia; the "Arautos dos Ritos Maçônicos # 747" lodge, affiliated to the Grand Lodge of the State of São Paulo; "Tiradentes" Lodge, affiliated to the Grand Lodge of the State of Espírito Santo; and "Deus, Amor e Liberdade" Lodge, affiliated to the Grand Orient of Goiás. He was also Grand Librarian of the Grand Lodge of the Federal District of Brazil.

In the York Rite, he is Past High Priest of the "Fredericksburg # 16" Chapter of Royal Arch Masons; Past Illustrious Master of the "União e Harmonia # 31" Council of Cryptic Masons and Past Grand Master of the Grand Council of Cryptic Masons of Brazil; as well a Knight Templar.

He is 33rd degree of the Ancient and Accepted Scottish Rite, Inspector General Honorary of the Supreme Council of Degree 33 of the Ancient and Accepted Scottish Rite of Freemasonry for the Federative Republic of Brazil; and at Shriners, he was President of the Almas Brasília Shriners Club (2014), and member of the Membership Committee of the Almas Temple (2015), of Washington, DC.

In the Grand College of The Holy Royal Arch Knight Templar Priest and Order of Holy Wisdom, he is a member of the Order of Sacred Wisdom, and Past High Priest of the Villas-Boas Tabernacle.

He is Editor-in-Chief of the "Ciência & Maçonaria" (Science & Freemasonry) Journal, the first academic-scientific journal dedicated to the study of Freemasonry in South America, linked to UnB; professor of Continued Education Courses in "History of Freemasonry" by UnyLeya and in "Masonology" by Uninter; and manager of UniCMSB, an online Masonic education platform of the Confederation of Symbolic Masonry of Brazil, which brings together the 27 Brazilian Grand Lodges.

A well-known Masonic speaker in Brazil, he is the author of several articles published in various Masonic magazines and websites in Brazil and other countries, such as in the journals of The Masonic Society and The Philalethes Society. He was a technical reviewer and prefaced the Brazilian edition of the book "Freemasons for Dummies", published by AltaBooks (2015); translated and commented on the book "Ahiman Rezon", published by A Trolha (2016); and is the author of the books: "Desmistificando a Maçonaria" (2012), "O Líder Maçom" (2014), "Debatendo Tabus Maçônicos" (2016), "História da Maçonaria Brasileira para Adultos" (2017), "Um Clone para Deus"(2017),"O Livro do Venerável Mestre"(2018), "Ordem sobre o Caos"(2020), and "Maçonaria Brasileira: uma história ocultada" Volumes 1 and 2 (2021).

LATIN TERMS IN FREEMASONRY

Anno Caedio - "Year of the Fall". It refers to 1314 and the end of the Templar Order.

Anno Domini - "Year of the Lord". It is the same as "A.D.".

Ad Majorem Dei Gloriam - "To the Lord's Greatest Glory". It is the motto of the Jesuits.

Anno Lucis - "Year of the Light". Masonic calendar for the symbolic degrees, inspired by the Anno Mundi, and which adds four thousand years to the current year.

Anno Laotomorum - "Year of Freemasonry". It is the same as Anno Lucis.

Anno Mundi - "Year of the World". It refers to calculations that sought to determine the age of the world based on the Bible. Among them, we highlight the calculations of Pastor James Ussher, who determined the creation of the world as having occurred on October 23, 4,004 BC, and this calculation served as the basis for the creation of *Anno Lucis* (or *Laotomorum*), adopted in Symbolic Freemasonry.

Anno Ordinis - "Year of the Order". Known as the Templar calendar, it is calculated by subtracting 1,118, the year in which the Order appeared, from the current year.

Ars Quatuor Coronatorum - "Art of Quatuor Coronati". Refers to the journal of the premier lodge of research in the world.

Ad Universi Terrarum Orbis Summi Architecti Gloriam - To the Glory of the Great Architect of the Universe. This term is widely used in Masonic certificates.

Audi, Vide, Tace - "Listen, see, be silent" is the motto on the coat of arms of the United Grand Lodge of England.

Deo, regi, et fratribus, honor fidelitas, benevolentia - "By God, king and brothers, honor, fidelity and benevolence". It is one of the mottos of the Royal Arch.

Deus Meumque Jus - "God and my Right". Originally adopted by King Richard "Lion Heart", in the 12th century, was later adopted by the Stuartist dynasty, already in the 17th century.

Deus Vult - "God wants". Term credited to Pope Urban II when summoning the First Crusade.

Dixitque Deus fiat lux et facta est lux - "And God said, let there be light, and there was light ". Latin passage from Genesis, 1: 3.

Ex Oriente Lux - "The Light that comes from the East". The term is believed to have Roman origins and referred exclusively to sunrise orientation. Subsequently, it became a Christian proverb when referring that the light (Christianity) would have come from the East.

Fortitudine Ejus Rhodum Tenuit - "For his courage, he kept Rhodes". This motto originated in the Order of Hospitallers pays homage to its Grand Master, Philippe Villiers de L'Isle-Adam, who commanded the Order during the siege of Rhodes by the Ottomans. Disadvantaged by at least 1 x 40 men, he managed to keep Rhodes for six months, in 1522, finally negotiating an honorable surrender from the island, with the safe withdrawal of his knights and civilians eager to accompany them to Crete.

Gloria Dei est Celare Verbum - "The glory of God is to hide the word". It is the first excerpt from a biblical proverb, Proverbs, 25: 2.

Iesus Nazareuns, Rex Iudaeorum - "Jesus of Nazareth, King of the Jews". Acronym: INRI. Present in the 18th degree of the Scottish Rite.

Igne Natura Renovatur Integra - "Through fire nature is entirely renewed". Acronym: INRI. Present in the 18th degree of the Scottish Rite.

In Hoc Signo Vinces - "By this sign, you will win". Constantine I's motto and later adopted by the Knights Templar of the York Rite.

Invenimus cultor dei civil mundi - "We find the worship of God, Oh citizen of the world". This sentence is present in the Royal Arch.

Laborate Est Orare - "To work is to pray". Benedictine motto. This motto was later adopted by the Ramsay Clan, to which Chevalier Ramsay, author of the famous Masonic speech, belonged.

Laus Deo - "Praise be to God". It is in the 32nd degree of the Scottish Rite.

Lux in tenebris - "Light in the darkness". Excerpt from the Gospel of John, 1: 5.

Lux Inens agitates us - "The inner light guides us". It is in the 32nd degree of the Scottish Rite.

Magna est Veritas et Praevalabit - "The truth is powerful and will prevail". Motto of the Order of the Red Cross.

Nec Proditor, nec Proditus, Innocens foret - "Neither traitor nor betrayed, consider him innocent". It appears in the 30th degree of the Scottish Rite.

Ne Plus Ultra - "Nothing more". It appears in the 30th degree of the Scottish Rite.

Ne Varietur - Latin term that can be translated as "It does not vary". Refers to the signature.

Nil nisi clavis deest - "Nothing is missing but the key". It is one of the mottos of the Royal Arch.

Ordo ab Chao - Order out of Chaos. This is the motto of the Scottish Rite and its 33rd degree.

Paternus Deus, Humana Fraternitas - Fatherhood of God, the brotherhood of men.

Pax Vobiscum - "May peace be with you". This expression is related to the 18th degree of the Scottish Rite.

Pro Patria et Populo - "For the country and the people". It is the motto of the 9th degree of the Scottish Rite.

Rose Croix - Rose Cross, 18th degree of the Scottish Rite.

Ritûs Scotici Antiqui Accepti - Ancient and Accepted Scottish Rite.

Sic Transit Gloria Mundi - "The glory of the world is transitory". Term adopted in versions of initiation to the degree of Apprentice of the Scottish Rite.

Si talia jungere possis sit tibi scire satis - "If you can understand these things, you know enough". It is one of the mottos of the Royal Arch.

Sit lux, et lux fuit - "Let there be light, and there was light ". Taken from Genesis, 1: 3, and widely used in rituals of initiation to the degree of Apprentice.

Spes Mea in Deo Est - "My hope is in God". It is the chapter of the 32nd degree of the Scottish Rite.

Sanctum Sanctorum - "Holy of Holies". Most sacred site of the Temple of Solomon.

Veut Dieu Saint Amour - "Desire for the Holy Spirit of God". The French term is credited with the use of the Knights Templar, as if it were a kind of evolution of the term of the First Crusade, *Deus Vult*.

Virtus Junxit Mors Non Separabit - "What virtue has united, death will not separate". It is the motto of the 14th degree of the Scottish Rite.

SCOTTISH RITE – DEGREE DIVISIONS

#	DEGREE	BY CONTENT	BY BODY
1°	Apprentice	Introductory Degrees	Symbolic Degrees
2°	Fellow Craft		
3°	Master Mason	Dramatic Degree	
4°	Secret Master	Inventory Degrees	Ineffable Degrees
5°	Perfect Master		
6°	Intimate Secretary		
7°	Provost and Judge		
8°	Intendant of the Building		
9°	Elu of the Nine	Elected or Elus Degrees	
10°	Elu of the Fifteen		
11°	Elu of the Twelve		
12°	Grand Master Architect	Triumphant Degrees	
13°	Royal Arch of Solomon		
14°	Perfect Elu		
15°	Knight of the East, of the Sword, or the Eagle	Historical Degrees	Chapter Degrees
16°	Prince of Jerusalem		
17°	Knight of the East and West	Doctrinal Degrees	
18°	Knight of the Rose Croix		
19°	Grand Pontiff		Philosophical Degrees
20°	Master of the Symbolic Lodge	Social Degrees	
21°	Noachite, or Prussian Knight		

<table>
<tr><td>22°</td><td>Knight of the Royal Axe</td><td></td><td rowspan="9"></td></tr>
<tr><td>23°</td><td>Chief of the Tabernacle</td><td rowspan="5">Esoteric or Theological Degrees</td></tr>
<tr><td>24°</td><td>Prince of the Tabernacle</td></tr>
<tr><td>25°</td><td>Knight of the Brazen Serpent</td></tr>
<tr><td>26°</td><td>Prince of Mercy</td></tr>
<tr><td>28°↓</td><td>Knight of the Sun</td></tr>
<tr><td>27°↑</td><td>Knight Commander of the Temple</td><td rowspan="6">Templar Degrees</td></tr>
<tr><td>29°</td><td>Scottish Knight of St. Andrew</td></tr>
<tr><td>30°</td><td>Knight Kadosh</td></tr>
<tr><td>31°</td><td>Inspector Inquisitor</td><td rowspan="2">Administrative Degrees</td></tr>
<tr><td>32°</td><td>Master of the Royal Secret</td></tr>
<tr><td>33°</td><td>Inspector General</td><td>Honorary Degree</td></tr>
</table>

SCOTTISH RITE – LESSONS AND SYMBOLS

#	DEGREE	SYMBOL(S)	LESSON(S)
1°	Apprentice	24 inch gauge	Belief in a Supreme Being
2°	Fellow Craft	Flaming Star	Persistence
3°	Master Mason	Acacia	Soul Balance and Immortality
4°	Secret Master	Ivory Key	Secrecy and Loyalty
5°	Perfect Master	Cinerary urn	Death and Family
6°	Intimate Secretary	Delta Triple	Fervor and Zeal
7°	Provost and Judge	Golden Key	Justice, Impartiality and Equity
8°	Intendant of the Building	Scales	Benevolence and Charity
9°	Elu of the Nine	Dagger	Combating Ignorance
10°	Elu of the Fifteen	Three severed heads over the city gates	Fighting Intolerance and Fanaticism
11°	Elu of the Twelve	Flaming Heart and Sword	Service and Truth
12°	Grand Master Architect	Five Columns of Architecture Orders	Work and Trust
13°	Royal Arch of Solomon (Knight of the Ninth Arch)	Agate cube with gold plate	Truth and Retribution
14°	Perfect Elu (Grand Elect, Perfect and Sublime Mason)	Golden triangle engraved with Ineffable Name	Justice, Law and Truth
15°	Knight of the East, of the Sword, or the Eagle	Bridge	Faithfulness and Perseverance
16°	Prince of Jerusalem	Scale with dagger between plates	Justice and Equity
17°	Knight of the East and West	Book with the Seven Seals	Virtue and Truth
18°	Knight of the Rose Croix	Rose Croix and Pelican	Charity

19°	Grand Pontiff	New Jerusalem	Virtue, Sincerity, Moderation, Truth, Justice and Tolerance
20°	Master of the Symbolic Lodge	Octagon formed by the base of 5 squares and 3 triangles	Veneration to God, Charity, Generosity, Heroism, Honor, Patriotism, Justice, Tolerance and Truth
21°	Noachite, or Prussian Knight	Downward arrow overlapping a triangle	Justice and Charity
22°	Knight of the Royal Axe (Prince of Libanus)	Axe	Work
23°	Chief of the Tabernacle	Hyssop Branch	Faith, Hope and Charity; Strength, Prudence, Temperance and Justice
24°	Prince of the Tabernacle	The lamp of Trismegistus, the cloak of Apollonius and the rod of the Patriarchs	Search for Truth
25°	Knight of the Brazen Serpent	Snake wrapped around a rod	Don't idolize
26°	Prince of Mercy	Flaming Heart with the initials IHS	Religious Tolerance
27°	Knight Commander of the Temple	Lorena Cross	Bravery and Altruism
28°	Knight of the Sun	Pentagram	Natural Theology
29°	Scottish Knight of St. Andrew	Cross of Saint Andrew	Humility, Patience and Renunciation
30°	Knight Kadosh	Templar Banner	Justice and Truth
31°	Inspector Inquisitor	Maat scale	Forgiveness
32°	Master of the Royal Secret	Camp	Review of previous lessons
33°	Inspector General	Double-headed eagle	God, Fatherland and Humanity

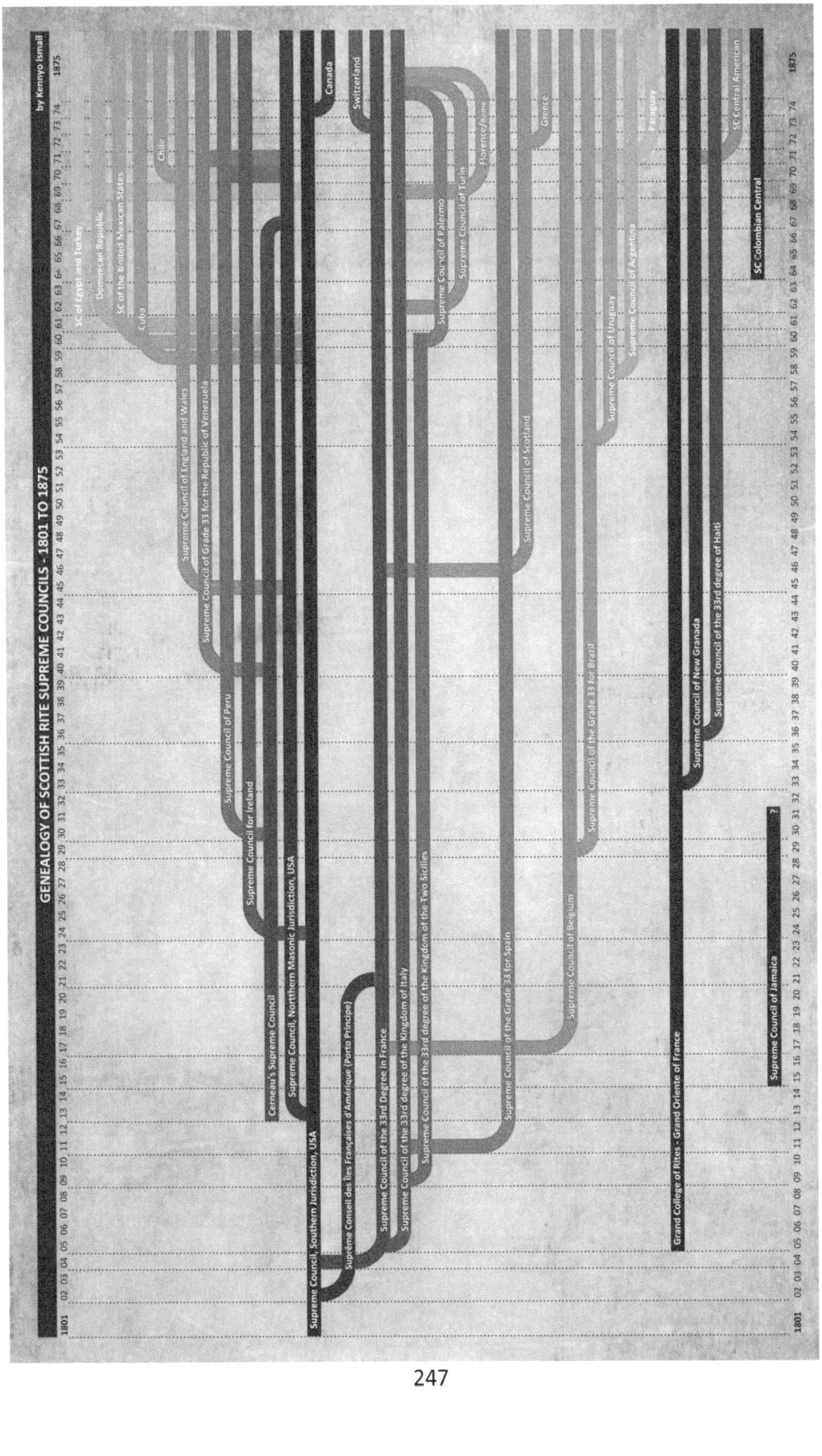

GENEALOGY OF SCOTTISH RITE SUPREME COUNCILS - 1801 TO 1875
by Kennyo Ismail
1801 02 03 04 05 06 07 08 09 10 11 12 13 14 15 16 17 18 19 20 21 22 23 24 25 26 27 28 29 30 31 32 33 34 35 36 37 38 39 40 41 42 43 44 45 46 47 48 49 50 51 52 53 54 55 56 57 58 59 60 61 62 63 64 65 66 67 68 69 70 71 72 73 74 1875
SC of Egypt and Turkey
Dominican Republic
SC of the United Mexican States
Cuba
Chile
Supreme Council of England and Wales
Supreme Council of Grade 33 for the Republic of Venezuela
Supreme Council of Peru
Supreme Council for Ireland
Cerneau's Supreme Council
Supreme Council, Northern Masonic Jurisdiction, USA
Supreme Council, Southern Jurisdiction, USA
Canada
Suprême Conseil des Îles Françaises d'Amérique (Porto Principe)
Switzerland
Supreme Council of the 33rd Degree in France
Supreme Council of the 33rd degree of the Kingdom of Italy
Supreme Council of the 33rd degree of the Kingdom of the Two Sicilies
Supreme Council of Palermo
Supreme Council of Turin
Florence/Rome
Supreme Council of the Grade 33 for Spain
Supreme Council of Scotland
Greece
Supreme Council of Belgium
Supreme Council of the Grade 33 for Brazil
Supreme Council of Uruguay
Supreme Council of Argentina
Paraguay
Grand College of Rites - Grand Oriente of France
Supreme Council of New Granada
Supreme Council of the 33rd degree of Haiti
SC Central American
Supreme Council of Jamaica
?
SC Colombian Central

NOTES

[1] Zeldis, Leon. 2011. Illustrated by Symbols. New York, NY: Philalethes, The Journal of Masonic Research & Letters, Vol. 64, n. 02, p. 72-73.

[2] Preston, William. 1867. Illustrations of Masonry. New York: Masonic Publishing and Manufacturing Co., p.37.

[3] Coil, Henry Wilson; Brown, William Moseley. 1961. Coil's Masonic Encyclopedia. New York: Ed. Macoy, p. 159.

[4] Hodapp, Christopher. 2013. Freemasons for Dummies. 2nd edition. Hoboken, NJ: John Wiley & sons, Inc., p.13.

[5] Kinney, Jay. 2009. The Masonic Myth: Unlocking the Truth About the Symbols, the Secret Rites, and the History of Freemasonry. San Francisco, CA: Harper One, p. 23.

[6]Behring, Mário. 1928. Ritual do Gráo de Aprendiz-Maçon. Rio de Janeiro: Typographia DELTA, p. 9.

[7] Dermott, Laurence. 1778. AHIMAN REZON or a help to all that are, or would be Free and Accepted Masons. 3rd Edition. London: James Jones, p. XXVII.

[8] Tresner, J. 2000. Vested in Glory. Washington, DC: Scottish Rite Research Society.

[9] Kleinknecht, C. F. 2000. Forms and Traditions of the Scottish Rite. Washington, DC: Scottish Rite Research Society.

[10] Schuchard, Marsha Keith. 2002. Restoring the Temple of Vision: Cabalistic Freemasonry and Stuart Culture. Leiden: E. J. Brill.

[11] Lomas, Robert. 2006. The Early History of Freemasonry, in: Olsen, Oddvar. 2006. The Templar Papers. Franklin Lakes, NJ: The Career Press.

[12] Simon, J. 20--. Rituel des trois premiers degrés selon les anciens cahiers - 5829. Bonneuil-en-Valois: Éditions de la Hutte.

[13] Ismail, K. 2016. Debatendo Tabus Maçônicos. Londrina: A Trolha, p. 158.

[14] Clavel, F. T. B. 1843. Histoire pittoresque de la Franc-Maçonnerie et des Sociétés Secrètes Anciennes et Modernes. Paris: Deuxième Édition, p. 228-229.

[15] Mackey, A. G. 1914. An Encyclopedia of Freemasonry and tis Kindred Sciences. New York and London: The Masonic History Company, p. 54-55.

[16] Mackey, A. G. 1914. An Encyclopedia of Freemasonry and tis Kindred Sciences. New York and London: The Masonic History Company, p. 311-312.

[17] Morris, Brent. 2006. The Complete Idiot's Guide to Freemasonry. New York: Alpha Books/Penguin.

[18] Coil, Henry Wilson; Brown, William Moseley. 1961. Coil's Masonic Encyclopedia. New York: Ed. Macoy.

[19] Mackey, A. G. 1914. An Encyclopedia of Freemasonry and tis Kindred Sciences. New York e Londres: The Masonic History Company.

[20] Mackey, A. G. 1914. *An Encyclopedia of Freemasonry and tis Kindred Sciences*. New York e Londres: The Masonic History Company, p. 555.

[21] Mackey, A. G. 1914. An Encyclopedia of Freemasonry and tis Kindred Sciences. New York e Londres: The Masonic History Company, p. 672.

[22] Pike, Albert. 1887. Liturgy of the Ancient and Accepted Scottish Rite of Freemasonry for the Southern Jurisdiction of the United States. Part. IV. New York: Macoy.

[23] Coil, Henry Wilson; Brown, William Moseley. 1961. Coil's Masonic Encyclopedia. New York: Ed. Macoy.

[24] Lindsay, R. S. 1958. The Scottish Rite for Scotland. Edinburgh: W & R Chambers.

[25] De Hoyos, Arturo. 2016. "A Brief History of Freemasonry and the Origins of the Scottish Rite". In: Scottish Rite Ritual Monitor & Guide. 3rd edition, corrected. Washington, D.C.: Supreme Council, 33°, S.J..

[26] Stevenson, David. 2002. James Anderson: Man and Mason. *Heredom*. Vol. 10, p. 93-138.

[27] Mackey, A. G. *An Encyclopedia of Freemasonry and its Kindred Sciences*. New York and London: The Masonic History Company, 1914.

[28] Daruty, Jean Émile. 1879. *Recherchessur le Rite Écossais Ancien et Accepté*. Paris: Chez le F. Panisset.

[29] Coil, Henry Wilson; Brown, William M. 1961. *Coil's Masonic Encyclopedia*. New York: Ed. Macoy.

[30] Simon, Jacques. 2013. REAA: Rituel des trois premiers degrés selon les anciens cahiers – 5829. Bonneuil-en-Valois: Éditions de La Hutte.

[31] Waite, Arthur Edward. 2007. *A New Encyclopedia of Freemasonry*. Vol. II. New York: Cosimo, 2007.

[32] Gould, Robert Freke. 2007. *The Concise History of Freemasonry*. Mineola, NY: Dover Publications.

[33] Tabbert, Mark A. 2005. American Freemasons: Three Centuries of Building Communities. New York and London: New York University Press.

[34] Simon, Jacques. 2013. REAA: Rituel des trois premiers degrés selon les anciens cahiers – 5829. Bonneuil-en-Valois: Éditions de La Hutte.

[35] Ribeiro, João Guilherme da Cruz. 2007. Os fios da meada: origens, evolução e imagens do Rito Escocês Antigo e Aceito. Rio de Janeiro: Infyarte, p.47-48.

[36] De Hoyos, Arturo. 2016. *Scottish Rite Ritual, Monitor & Guide*. 3rd. edition, Corrected. Washington, D.C.: Supreme Council, 33°, S. J.

[37] Supreme Conseil de France. 1994. Ordo ab Chao. Number 30 (p. 147) and Number 39-40 (p. 151).

[38] Bernheim, Alain. Le Convent des Suprêmes Conseils du Rite Écossais Ancien et Accepté. Part 1. Pietre-Stones Review of Freemasonry. Available in: http://www.freemasons-freemasonry.com/bernheim_convent01.html

[39]Mandleberg, J. 1997. The Lausanne Congress of 1875. Heredom, Vol. 6, p. 83-112.

[40] Bernheim, Alain. Le Convent des Suprêmes Conseils du Rite Écossais Ancien et Accepté. Part 2. Pietre-Stones Review of Freemasonry. Available in:http://www.freemasons-freemasonry.com/bernheim_convent02.html

[41] HODAPP, Christopher. 2005. *Freemasons for Dummies*. Hoboken, NJ: Wiley Publishing Inc..

[42] De Hoyos, Arturo. 2016. *Scottish Rite Ritual, Monitor & Guide*. 3rd. edition, Corrected. Washington, D.C.: Supreme Council, 33°, S. J.

[43] Dumenil, Lynn. 1984. *Freemasonry and American Culture, 1880–1930*. Princeton, NJ: Princeton University Press.

[44]Bullock, Steven C. 1996. Revolutionary Brotherhood: Freemasonry and the Transformation of the American Social Order, 1730–1840. Chapel Hill: University of North Carolina Press, pp. 239–273.

[45] Clawson, Mary Ann. 2007. Masculinity, Consumption and the Transformation of Scottish Rite Freemasonry in the Turn-of-the-Century United States. Gender & History, Vol.19 N.1, pp. 101–121.

[46] Fox, William L. 1997. *Lodge of the Double-Headed Eagle: Two Centuries of Scottish Rite Freemasonry in America's Southern Jurisdiction*. Fayetteville: University of Arkansas Press, pp. 146–1477.

[47] O'Donnell, Francis H. E. 1906. Philosophy and the Drama in Freemasonry. The New Age Magazine, N.4(5), p. 475-476.

[48] Knox, William. 1907. What Excuse? The New Age Magazine, N.7, p. 253-254.

[49] Sargent, Epes W. 1907. Detail and the Drama of the Degree. The New Age Magazine, N.7, pp. 175–177.

[50] Ames, Kenneth L. 1996. *Theatre of the Fraternity: Staging the Ritual Space of the Scottish Rite of Freemasonry*. Jackson, Mississippi: University Press of Mississippi.

[51] De Hoyos, Arturo. 2016. *Scottish Rite Ritual, Monitor & Guide*. 3rd. edition, Corrected. Washington, D.C.: Supreme Council, 33°, S. J.

[52] Clavel, François-Timoléon Bègue. 1843. Histoire pittoresque de la franc-maçonnerie et des sociétés secrètes. Paris: Pagnerre éditeur.

[53] Proceedings of the Supreme Council of Sovereign Grand Inspectors General of the Thirty-third and Last Degree of the Ancient Accepted Scottish Rite of Freemasonry for the Northern Masonic Jurisdiction of the United States of America. 20th of September, 1881.

[54] Guarner, Vivanco. 1961. Historia del Supremo Consejo del Grado 33 para Espana y sus Dependencias y de la Masoneria Espanola. Mexico, DF: own publication.

[55] Based on: https://scottishritenmj.org/about/history

[56] De Hoyos, Arturo; Morris, Brent. 2004. Freemasonry in Context: History, Ritual, Controversy. Lanham, MD: Lexington Books.

[57] Bulletin of the Grand Orient of Brazil. 1882. N. 2, Year 11. Rio de Janeiro: J. P. Hildebrandt.

[58] Benimeli, José Antonio Ferrer. 2015. *Masonería, Iglesia, Revolución e Independencia*. Bogotá: Editorial Pontificia Universidad Javeriana.

[59] Perramón, Edgar. 2010. Breve história del Supremo Consejo de la Masonería Venezolana. Caracas: own edition.

[60] Sommers, Susan Mitchell. Robert Thomas Crucefix, Redux. Journal for Research into Freemasonry and Fraternalism, (Autumn 2013), 73-97.

[61] Torres-Cuevas, Eduardo. 2013. *Historia de la masonería cubana: seis ensayos*. La Habana: Imagen Contemporanea.

[62] Cuccia, Andrea. 2004. Dieci tavole architettoniche sulla massoneria. Soveria Mannelli: Rubbettino.

[63] Lopez-Penha, H. H. 1952. *Resena Histórica del Supremo Consejo del Grado 33 y Ultimo del Rito Escocés Antiguo y Aceptado para la República Dominicana*. Trujillo: Editora Montalvo.

[64] Flandreau, Marc. 2016. *Anthropologists in the Stock Exchange: A Financial History of Victorian Science*. Chicago and London: The University of Chicago Press.

[65] Proceedings of the Supreme Council of Sovereign Grand Inspectors General of the Thirty-third and Last Degree of the Ancient Accepted Scottish Rite of Freemasonry for the Northern Masonic Jurisdiction of the United States of America. 20th of September, 1881.

[66] Sánchez, Manuel Romo. Antecedentes para la historia de la masonería capitular en Chile entre 1895 y 1903. ARCHIVO MASÓNICO, Revista Cuatrimestral. Nº 18. Santiago, Chile, 1º julio 2009.

[67] Valdés, Roberto. Origen, miembros y primeras acciones de la masonería en El Salvador (1871-1872). REHMLAC, Vol. 1, N. 1, May-Nov 2009, p. 157-171.

[68] Source: http://www.scg33.org.py/

[69] Bulletin of the United Grand Orient and Supreme Council of Brazil. Year 02, N. 10 to 12. Rio de Janeiro: Typography of the GOUSCB, October to December 1873.

[70] Jenkyns, Michael. M. W. 2002. Bro. Thomas Douglas Harington. The Newsletter of the Committee on Masonic Education - The Grand Lodge of Canada in the Province of Ontario. Vol. 18, No. 1.

[71] Vide: Harland-Jacobs, Jessica. 1999. “Hands Across the Sea”: The Masonic Network, British Imperialism, and North Atlantic World. *Geographical Review*, Vol. 89, Issue 2, p. 237–253.

[72] Harland-Jacobs, Jessica. 2007. *Builders of Empire: Freemasons and British Imperialism, 1717-1927*. Chapel Hill: The University of North Carolina Press.

[73] Foucault, Michel. 2004. *Vigiar e Punir*. Petrópolis: Editora Vozes.

[74] Freitas Neto, Edgard da Costa. 2019. REDES DE SOCIABILIDADE, REDES DE PODER: Maçonaria e Diplomacia Track 2 na África Francófona. Dissertation (MSc in International Relations). Universidade Federal da Bahia. Salvador, 197 p..

[75] Fox, William. 1997. *Lodge of the Double-Headed Eagle: two centuries of Scottish Rite Freemasonry in America's Southern Jurisdiction*. Fayetteville: The University of Arkansas Press.

[76] Casado, Galo Sánchez. 2009. *Los altos grados de la masonería*. Madrid: Ediciones Akal.

[77] Naudon, Paul. 1993. *Histoire, Rituels et Tuileur des Hauts Grades Maçonniques*. 5th edition. Paris: Éditions Dervy.

[78] Fox, William. 1997. *Lodge of the Double-Headed Eagle: two centuries of Scottish Rite Freemasonry in America's Southern Jurisdiction*. Fayetteville: The University of Arkansas Press.

[79] Suprême Conseil de France. Chronologie de Deux Siecles d'histoire: 1804 -2004. Link: https://www.scdf.net/manager/uploads/Deux%20siecles%20d'histoire.pdf

[80] The Northern Light. Editorial. Vol. 1, N. 02, April, 1970.

[81] The White House. The Daily Diary of President Ronald Reagan. Link: https://www.reaganfoundation.org/media/103803/052285.pdf

[82] The Northern Light. Vol. 19, N. 02, May, 1988.

[83] Astréa, Journal of Masonic Studies. 2000. Year: LXXIII, Number 06. Rio de Janeiro.

[84] Carvalho, João Alexandre Rangel. Sucesso em Sydney. Astréa: Journal of Masonic Studies. Year LXXVIII, Number 16. March to July, 2005.

[85] Proceedings of the Supreme Council of the Thirty-Third Degree of the Ancient and Accepted Scottish Rite of Freemasonry of Canada. 136th Annual Session. Moncton, New Brunswick: 16th to 18th of September 2010.

[86] Actas de la XIX Conferencia Mundial de Supremos Consejos 33º. Supremo Conselho para Portugal dos Soberanos Grandes Inspectores Gerais do 33º e Último Grau do R.E.A.A. Lisboa: 13 a 17 de Maio, 2015.

[87] Pike, Albert. 1905. Morals and Dogma of the Ancient and Accepted Scottish Rite of Freemasonry. Charleston: Supreme Council of the Southern Jurisdiction, p. 06.

[88] Behring, Mário. 1928. Ritual do Gráo de Aprendiz-Maçon. Rio de Janeiro: Typographia DELTA, p. 67.

[89] Behring, Mário. 1928. Ritual do Gráo de Aprendiz-Maçon. Rio de Janeiro: Typographia DELTA, p. 53.

[90] Behring, Mário. 1928. Ritual do Gráo de Aprendiz-Maçon. Rio de Janeiro: Typographia DELTA, p. 81.

[91] Behring, Mário. 1928. Ritual do Gráo de Aprendiz-Maçon. Rio de Janeiro: Typographia DELTA, p. 53.

[92] Pike, Albert. 1905. Morals and Dogma of the Ancient and Accepted Scottish Rite of Freemasonry. Charleston: Supreme Council of the Southern Jurisdiction, p. 26.

[93] Pike, Albert. 1905. Morals and Dogma of the Ancient and Accepted Scottish Rite of Freemasonry. Charleston: Supreme Council of the Southern Jurisdiction, p. 89.

[94] Rousseau, J. J. 1999. *O Contrato Social*. São Paulo: Martins Fontes.

[95] Pike, Albert. 1905. Morals and Dogma of the Ancient and Accepted Scottish Rite of Freemasonry. Charleston: Supreme Council of the Southern Jurisdiction, p. 109.

[96] Pike, Albert. 1905. Morals and Dogma of the Ancient and Accepted Scottish Rite of Freemasonry. Charleston: Supreme Council of the Southern Jurisdiction, p. 115.

[97] Pike, Albert. 1905. Morals and Dogma of the Ancient and Accepted Scottish Rite of Freemasonry. Charleston: Supreme Council of the Southern Jurisdiction, p. 124.

[98] Pike, Albert. 1905. Morals and Dogma of the Ancient and Accepted Scottish Rite of Freemasonry. Charleston: Supreme Council of the Southern Jurisdiction, p. 127.

[99] Pike, Albert. 1905. Morals and Dogma of the Ancient and Accepted Scottish Rite of Freemasonry. Charleston: Supreme Council of the Southern Jurisdiction, p. 147.

[100] Pike, Albert. 1905. Morals and Dogma of the Ancient and Accepted Scottish Rite of Freemasonry. Charleston: Supreme Council of the Southern Jurisdiction, p. 159.

[101] Pike, Albert. 1905. Morals and Dogma of the Ancient and Accepted Scottish Rite of Freemasonry. Charleston: Supreme Council of the Southern Jurisdiction, p. 325-326.

[102] Pike, Albert. 1905. Morals and Dogma of the Ancient and Accepted Scottish Rite of Freemasonry. Charleston: Supreme Council of the Southern Jurisdiction, p. 170.

[103] Pike, Albert. 1905. Morals and Dogma of the Ancient and Accepted Scottish Rite of Freemasonry. Charleston: Supreme Council of the Southern Jurisdiction, p. 178.

[104] De Hoyos, Arturo. 2016. *Scottish Rite Ritual, Monitor & Guide*. 3rd. edition, Corrected. Washington, D.C.: Supreme Council, 33°, S. J., p. 275-276.

[105] André Luiz. 2000. *The Astral City*. Ellon College, N.C.: Christian Spirit Center, p. 117.

[106] Pike, Albert. 1905. Morals and Dogma of the Ancient and Accepted Scottish Rite of Freemasonry. Charleston: Supreme Council of the Southern Jurisdiction, p. 195.

[107] Dermott, Laurence. 1778. *AHIMAN REZON or a help to all that are, or would be Free and Accepted Masons*. 3rd Edition. London: James Jones, p. 23.

[108] Pike, Albert. 1905. Morals and Dogma of the Ancient and Accepted Scottish Rite of Freemasonry. Charleston: Supreme Council of the Southern Jurisdiction, p. 216.

[109] Pike, Albert. 1905. Morals and Dogma of the Ancient and Accepted Scottish Rite of Freemasonry. Charleston: Supreme Council of the Southern Jurisdiction, p. 229.

[110] Campbell, Joseph. 2008. *Mito e Transformação*. São Paulo: Editora Ágora.

[111] Ismail, Kennyo. The Rosicrucian Tradition and its Orders. *The Journal of the Masonic Society*, N. 22, Autumn 2013, p. 23-27.

[112] Pike, Albert. 1905. Morals and Dogma of the Ancient and Accepted Scottish Rite of Freemasonry. Charleston: Supreme Council of the Southern Jurisdiction, p. 238.

[113] Pike, Albert. 1905. Morals and Dogma of the Ancient and Accepted Scottish Rite of Freemasonry. Charleston: Supreme Council of the Southern Jurisdiction, p. 245.

[114] Pike, Albert. 1905. Morals and Dogma of the Ancient and Accepted Scottish Rite of Freemasonry. Charleston: Supreme Council of the Southern Jurisdiction, p. 275.

[115] McClenachan, Charles T. 1914. *The Book of the Ancient and Accepted Scottish Rite of Freemasonry*. New York: Macoy Publishing & Masonic Supply Co..

[116] McClenachan, Charles T. 1914. The Book of the Ancient and Accepted Scottish Rite of Freemasonry. New York: Macoy Publishing & Masonic Supply Co., p. 239.

[117] Pike, Albert. 1905. Morals and Dogma of the Ancient and Accepted Scottish Rite of Freemasonry. Charleston: Supreme Council of the Southern Jurisdiction, p. 309.

[118] Pike, Albert. 1905. Morals and Dogma of the Ancient and Accepted Scottish Rite of Freemasonry. Charleston: Supreme Council of the Southern Jurisdiction, p. 320.

[119] Pike, Albert. 1905. Morals and Dogma of the Ancient and Accepted Scottish Rite of Freemasonry. Charleston: Supreme Council of the Southern Jurisdiction, p. 328-330.

[120] Delaunay, F. H. S. 1820. *Manuel Maçonnique ou Tuileur de tousIesRites de Maçonnerie pratiqués en France par un Vétéran de la Maçonnerie*. Paris: Hubert & Brun, p. 145.

[121] Cassard, Andres. 1867. *Manual de la Masonería, el tejador de los Ritos Antiguo Escoces, Frances y de Adopcion*. New York: George R. Lockwood, p. 361.

[122] Pike, Albert. 1905. Morals and Dogma of the Ancient and Accepted Scottish Rite of Freemasonry. Charleston: Supreme Council of the Southern Jurisdiction, p. 326.

[123] Pike, Albert. 1905. Morals and Dogma of the Ancient and Accepted Scottish Rite of Freemasonry. Charleston: Supreme Council of the Southern Jurisdiction, p. 337.

[124] Dermott, Laurence. 1778. *AHIMAN REZON or a help to all that are, or would be Free and Accepted Masons*. 3rd Edition. London: James Jones, p. 27.

[125] Horne, Alex. 1978. *King Solomon's Temple in the Masonic tradition*. Chatsworth, CA: Wilshire Book.

[126] Pike, Albert. 1905. Morals and Dogma of the Ancient and Accepted Scottish Rite of Freemasonry. Charleston: Supreme Council of the Southern Jurisdiction, p. 340.

[127] Pike, Albert. 1905. *Morals and Dogma of the Ancient and Accepted Scottish Rite of Freemasonry*. Charleston: Supreme Council of the Southern Jurisdiction, p. 327.

[128] Pike, Albert. 1905. Morals and Dogma of the Ancient and Accepted Scottish Rite of Freemasonry. Charleston: Supreme Council of the Southern Jurisdiction, p. 355.

[129] Pike, Albert. 1905. Morals and Dogma of the Ancient and Accepted Scottish Rite of Freemasonry. Charleston: Supreme Council of the Southern Jurisdiction, p. 384.

[130] Coil, Henry Wilson; Brown, William M. 1961. *Coil's Masonic Encyclopedia*. New York: Ed. Macoy, p.159.

[131] Pike, Albert. 1905. Morals and Dogma of the Ancient and Accepted Scottish Rite of Freemasonry. Charleston: Supreme Council of the Southern Jurisdiction, p. 515-516.

[132] Pike, Albert. 1905. Morals and Dogma of the Ancient and Accepted Scottish Rite of Freemasonry. Charleston: Supreme Council of the Southern Jurisdiction, p. 524.

[133] De Hoyos, Arturo. 2016. *Scottish Rite Ritual, Monitor & Guide*. 3rd. edition, Corrected. Washington, D.C.: Supreme Council, 33°, S. J., p. 625.

[134] Pike, Albert. 1905. Morals and Dogma of the Ancient and Accepted Scottish Rite of Freemasonry. Charleston: Supreme Council of the Southern Jurisdiction, p. 165-166.

[135] Pike, Albert. 1905. Morals and Dogma of the Ancient and Accepted Scottish Rite of Freemasonry. Charleston: Supreme Council of the Southern Jurisdiction, p. 578.

[136] Pike, Albert. 1905. Morals and Dogma of the Ancient and Accepted Scottish Rite of Freemasonry. Charleston: Supreme Council of the Southern Jurisdiction, p. 708.

[137] Pike, Albert. 1905. Morals and Dogma of the Ancient and Accepted Scottish Rite of Freemasonry. Charleston: Supreme Council of the Southern Jurisdiction, p. 710-715.

[138] Pike, Albert. 1905. Morals and Dogma of the Ancient and Accepted Scottish Rite of Freemasonry. Charleston: Supreme Council of the Southern Jurisdiction, p. 807-808.

[139] Pike, Albert. 1905. Morals and Dogma of the Ancient and Accepted Scottish Rite of Freemasonry. Charleston: Supreme Council of the Southern Jurisdiction, p. 819.

[140] De Hoyos, Arturo. 2016. *Scottish Rite Ritual, Monitor & Guide*. 3rd. edition, Corrected. Washington, D.C.: Supreme Council, 33°, S. J., p. 739.

[141] De Hoyos, Arturo. 2016. *Scottish Rite Ritual, Monitor & Guide*. 3rd. edition, Corrected. Washington, D.C.: Supreme Council, 33°, S. J., p. 751.

[142] Pike, Albert. 1905. Morals and Dogma of the Ancient and Accepted Scottish Rite of Freemasonry. Charleston: Supreme Council of the Southern Jurisdiction, p. 829-830.

[143] Tresner, Jim. 2000. Vested in Glory. Washington, DC: Scottish Rite Research Society, p. 171.

[144] Pike, Albert. 1905. Morals and Dogma of the Ancient and Accepted Scottish Rite of Freemasonry. Charleston: Supreme Council of the Southern Jurisdiction, p. 852-853.

[145]McClenachan, Charles T. 1914. The Book of the Ancient and Accepted Scottish Rite of Freemasonry. New York: Macoy Publishing & Masonic Supply Co., p. 489.

[146] Southern Jurisdiction, Supreme Council of the Thirty-third Degree Ancient & Accepted Scottish Rite of Freemasonry. *Statutes*. August, 2011.

[147] Benjamin, Walter. 1994. Obras Escolhidas Vol. I - Magia e técnica, arte e política: ensaios sobre literatura e história da cultura. 7a. ed. São Paulo: Brasiliense.

[148] Studart, H.; Ismail, K. O Encontro de Hiram Abiff com Benjamin na casa de Ricoeur. *C&M*. Brasília, Vol. 2, n.1, p. 21-36, jan/jun, 2014.

Printed in France by Amazon
Brétigny-sur-Orge, FR

13381877R00147